HER FACE IN THE MIRROR

HER FACE IN THE MIRROR

JEWISH WOMEN ON
MOTHERS AND DAUGHTERS

෯

EDITED BY

FAYE MOSKOWITZ

BEACON PRESS
Boston

Beacon Press
25 Beacon Street
Boston, Massachusetts 02108-2892

Beacon Press books
are published under the auspices of
the Unitarian Universalist Association of Congregations.

99 98 97 96 95 94   8 7 6 5 4 3 2 1

Text design by Janis Owens
Composition by Wilsted & Taylor

Library of Congress Cataloging-in-Publication Data

Her face in the mirror: Jewish women on mothers and daughters /
  edited by Faye Moskowitz.
    p.   cm.
  ISBN 0-8070-3614-5
  1. Jewish women—United States.   2. Mothers and daughters—United States.
I. Moskowitz, Faye.
HQ1172.H4   1994
306.874'3—dc20   94-8426
                                                                CIP

In loving memory of
SOPHIE EISENBERG STOLLMAN
(may she rest in peace)
for all she was and all she might have been

and in celebration of
Shoshana, Elizabeth, Julie, Heidi, and Helen—
daughters all.

CONTENTS

CONTENTS

PART THREE:
SURVIVING, PRESERVING,
BELONGING

CONTENTS

PART FOUR:
TALKING BACK

CONTENTS

PART FIVE:
LEAVING HOME

CONTENTS

PART SIX:
WHEN HER MOTHER DIES,
HER MOTHER'S DAUGHTER . . .

CONTENTS

ACKNOWLEDGMENTS

To all the Jewish women whose reflections on the singular relationship between mothers and daughters have filled this book with grace.

And with special thanks to Deb Chasman, my editor, for her intelligence, her patience, and her serenity.

INTRODUCTION

$\mathcal{M}$any months ago I set out to put together a collection of writings about mothers and daughters by Jewish American women. "Set out" seems an appropriate way to describe the process, for in a sense, though I didn't realize it at the time, I had embarked on a quest, not only for the makings of a book, but for an ineluctable something I thought I had long ago lost.

These months of reading about mothers and daughters have not always been easy ones. My own mother has been dead for almost fifty years. In my anger or sorrow or sense of abandonment—who knows why?—I had long ago cut much of her from my memory; she was an exposed nerve I needed to keep from air. So systematic was my surgery, I retained only one vision of what she looked like and that from a photo I found years after her death. I had few memories of the simplest acts of motherhood—of her dressing me as a child, combing my hair, giving me food. I could scarcely recollect her voice, her laughter, the sound of her tears. And this from one whose recall is so unrelenting I can remember the mothball and furniture polish scent of my Aunt Bessie's home when I was five, can evoke an early school-room complete with pupils and my teacher holding the long pole with which she raises and lowers the dark green shades at the tall windows.

Within days after I began calling writer friends, asking them for work and consulting with them about Jewish women they knew who might be writing about mothers and daughters, my letter carrier was dropping bundles of manila envelopes, fat with manuscripts, inside my front door. My mouth began to water. I felt exhilarated by the quality of the work; it was passionate, unsentimental, and resonant.

I hunted up my 1946 edition of Oscar Williams's *A Little Treasury of Modern Poetry*, its blue binding faded from being left out in the rain by my younger daughter one year. (I was sixteen when I memorized half its contents and first saw in the photograph of Muriel Ruykeyser at the end that a poet could not only be a woman, but a Jewish one like me.) I haunted Gelman Library at George Washington University, where I teach, going back and sifting through fifty years of work that had held up for me a mirror to my own reflection, writing that had validated my own experiences and ultimately had become part of my consciousness as a writer.

There was the abortionist chapter in Kate Simon's *Bronx Primitive*, for instance, a description of an incident whose reading scarred me as it had so clearly permanently marked the author. I wanted that chapter for the book. And Kim Chernin—what of *In My Mother's House*, her struggle to understand her Communist mother and the effects of her mother's activism on Chernin's own life? Surely the sublime epilogue had to be included for every Jewish "red diaper baby," now grown, and for the rest of us, too. And Tillie Olsen, my personal mentor, inspiration to the silenced—how could I not include her? On and on I went, rereading, selecting, remembering. And the mail kept coming.

Early on I understood I would have to limit the work included to that of Jewish American women writing in English in the postwar years. Such narrowing of focus, vivid though the view might be, meant forgoing the writings of our Jewish American foremothers—Mary Antin, Anna Yezierska, Edna Ferber, Fannie Hurst, Tess Slesinger, Jo Sinclair, the list goes on and on—but I did so, confident in the belief that the literary foundations they constructed for us are firm enough to allow their daughters and granddaughters to stand alone. Our predecessors have accomplished what any good mother might strive for: ultimate independence for her daughter, but with the memory, always, of her mother's voice in her ear.

As I envisioned it, the book's outermost reach would encompass writings about the immigrant experience of the twenties and the lingering chill of the Great Depression. Even more significantly, the establishment of the State of Israel, the civil rights movement, the Kennedy and King assassinations, Viet Nam, the antiwar protests, the sexual revolution, the feminist movement, the Cold War and its aftermath, the AIDS epidemic—all would serve as stage and backdrop for the personal dramas played out in the anthology's sections.

I say "stage and backdrop" because in the past, expectations of Jewish women in the Jewish community have been essentially conservative. Until recently there have been few avenues for self-expression within the tradition. A Jewish woman's canvas, if she had one at all, would depict the details of domesticity, the food and furnishings and the ritual celebrations both religious and secular that have traditionally been both a woman's purview and her purdah, the means by which she was at once empowered and, some would say, kept powerless.

Over it all, in the foreground and background like a merciless spotlight would hover the single blinding inexplicable event that shaped the consciousness of every Jew in the latter part of the twentieth century: the experience of the Holocaust.

I realized, with no little frustration, that no single book could pretend to be anything more than a representation of the wealth of Jewish women's writings unfurling like banners in the second half of the century. I would have to settle for a sampling, and I ask forgiveness now of both authors and readers for the omissions that could fill any number of volumes like this one.

I also wanted a mixture of genres—short stories, poems, essays, and novel excerpts—so that one form might play off against another, one exploration of a particular theme might be enriched by its proximity to a similar theme presented in a different form. By the artful juxtapositioning of pieces I hoped to dramatize the blurring of lines between genres (a process that has been evolving steadily in recent years) and, yes, the blurring of lines between generations.

This was to be a book, I promised myself, that would include strong and beautiful writing by Jewish women whether their names were readily recognizable or not. There would be room for new voices if we left out some of the mother/daughter stories that are the staple of so many other collections. I hoped for a gathering that might feel fresh to even the most voracious reader of Jewish women's literature, not simply another new combination of old work.

As the book began to take shape, I found that though narrative styles and poetic forms have changed to reflect the fractured and chaotic nature of the times, certain consistent patterns remain. Many Jewish women continue to write out of an unself-consciously assimilationist background. Others dramatize the sense of the Jewish woman as outsider, both as a Jew in America and as a woman in Judaism. Some younger women write out of a Jewish experience that has become so diluted in America that this fact itself becomes a subject of the work, while others depict moving from non-observant upbringings to the search for a home in more traditional Judaism. In an effort to reconcile what are often polar opposites, Jewish women of different generations struggle to balance their own integrity with what they see as allegiance to their heritage. Both mothers and their feminist daughters explore Jewish spirituality and the quest for a moral meaning in Jewish life; their discoveries pass like precious heirlooms from one to the other and back again.

We learn what it is like to grow up in small-town America as an outsider, a member of a minority, and of what coming of age in a big-city Jewish ghetto entails. Sephardic and Ashkenazi, working-class, middle-class, and upper-class Jewish life—all are depicted here. An American Jewish woman sets a story of motherhood in Israel; other experiences span our own country from Florida to Michigan and from one coast to the other.

Daughters write of frustration with what they see as their mothers' limited lives; their mothers write of fears that their daughters have taken upon themselves other kinds of limits, perhaps more destructive than their own have been. In one story a daughter becomes aware of her own mother as a sexual being; in one poem a mother imagines her daughter's first lover. A mother speaks of discovering her daughter is a lesbian; a daughter writes about coming out to her mother. Here are the experiences of daughters whose mothers died young, and representations of mothers who lived on and were lost to their daughters in spite of it. Holocaust survivors, both mothers and daughters, describe the recurring dark visions that invade their lives by day and by night. The guilt of surviving daughters adds complexity to the already tangled skeins of mother/daughter relationships.

And, as I had predicted, the shadow of the Holocaust in symbol and metaphor hangs over these stories and poems and essays no matter how far from the event their subject matter seems to lie. (There is a looking over the shoulder in many of the works, a sense of uneasiness that no outer semblance of being at home in America can dispel.)

I expected intergenerational conflict and I found it. Daughters have a bone to pick with their mothers, and Jewish daughters are no exception. There are silences to breach and disappointments on both sides. The knife blade of a mother's death or a daughter's untimely dying leaves wounds that are a long time repairing. Yet there is also the divine prodigy of birth and expectations bright as snowfall, unsullied yet by experience. Daughters puzzle out their mothers' lives and with the road map of their own suffering find their way to understanding. Many of the strongest selections patch together a bright quilt of reconciliation wide enough to enfold writer and reader as well.

The book is finished now. Like the proud mother of an adopted child, I can kvell at its beauty, since I am caretaker, not creator.

Recently my mother has begun to come back to me in dreams. Her hair is brown like my daughters' and the part crooked as mine so often used to be when four small children left me little time or energy for primping. In the dream my mother caresses my arm with strong fingers that are twins of my own. She calls me *"faygeleh," "mammeleh,"* and "little daughter"—"*tochterel.*" I can hear her voice. She says, "You have been a good mother. You did what you could, and so did I." I forgive my mother for everything, as I pray my daughters will forgive me. When they look in their mirrors one day and my face appears, I hope they will love what they see.

PART ONE

ક•

WE GIVE BIRTH TO EACH OTHER

Immediately on our arrival in Hamburg, I became with
child, and my mother along with me. In good time the Lord
graciously delivered me of a young daughter. I was still a mere
girl, and unused as I was to bearing children, it naturally
went hard with me; yet I rejoiced mightily that the Most
High had bestowed on me a healthy, lovely baby.
My good mother had reckoned out her time for the same day.
However, she had great joy in my being brought to bed first, so
she could help me a little, young girl that I was. Eight days
later my mother likewise brought forth a young daughter in
childbirth. So there was neither envy or reproach between us,
and we lay next to each other in the same room. But, Lord,
we had no peace, for the people that came running in to see the
marvel, a mother and daughter together in childbed.

The Memoirs of Gluckel of Hameln, 1690

BRIT KEDUSHA

for my daughter

JODY BOLZ

Here is your first gift
(this blessing, this echo):
sound you'll answer to
turning, always, to see who spoke.
Here is your name.
which people we don't know
will call you years from now,
when your infant face
with its astonished look
is just a picture
and our huge, parental love
a blur of hands.

BORROWING THE KNOT

KARREN L. ALENIER

Mother stored her mad money
in a drawer with her lingerie,
socked away, she said, for
calamity, a *get*, or a gold lamé
evening gown. "First one
out of the house," she used to say,
"best dressed" — her younger
sisters were left with empty
hangers. She kept her nest egg
secret from the breadwinner
who worked three jobs. I hid cash
in the family Siddur. "*Mazik*,"
she'd call me, "let me borrow . . ."
Slumped like a golem in my father's
chair, I flipped the holy pages
when she put her hand out.

POKER

JOAN SELIGER SIDNEY

At eleven years old my daughter reads me
the rules, insists we play poker
on the Oriental rug, closing both doors
for privacy. In the first deal two aces

crowd my king. I bid five, she passes,
throws out two tens. I win. Not like the first time.
Next-door in Flatbush, two sisters taught me
strip poker. With each deal they giggled, waiting

for me to show them more. We sat in a circle.
Tossed clothes in the center. A pile of shoes,
socks, hankies, barrettes began to take
the shape of preteen girls. First to unbuckle

my belt, I slid off my woolen skirt, stretched
the turtleneck over my ears. The room
was cold. Like tonight, winter, my hair
has turned the color of coal dust and frost

laced across their windows above the cellar door.
My daughter huddles deep into her cards, her lips
parting to blow wisps of black out of her eyes.
I see myself in that other room, the radiator

coughing steam. No window quilts, no thermal panes.
I shiver, hug my shoulders with crossed hands.
down to my cotton panties, my first bra.
In their skirts and sweaters they stare. Their eyes

make me hot and cold at the same time. My cards
can't win: no flush, no triplets. They watch
my fingers unhook the bra. They stare at my secret,
tiny breasts, nipples like sentries in the cold.

I hate their eyes, their laugh, their warm clothes.
Two against one and I can't stop. Nor can I win.
Not with the cards they deal me, not in
their own room. I am naked in my panties

when their mother opens the door. She tells me
to get dressed, to go home, a memory that still
makes me cross my arms and hug my shoulders, shivering
tonight in my pine-paneled room. I hear the furnace

hum below us in the basement, my husband and sons
gallop the stairs outside my door. For these few moments
we sit warm and safe inside our house. My daughter
deals me another hand, asks softly why I want her to win.

LINES OF WORK

JODY BOLZ

I am no archivist,
crying over
figures cut from magazines
sixty years ago

because my mother picked them out
and pasted them
and wrote each caption
when she was a girl

in North Bergen, New Jersey.
It's a project book on jobs:
she's thought about it,
chosen four she thinks she'd like

I. *Diplomacy*
II. *Social Work*
III. *Horticulture*
IV. *Dressmaking*

and written a report on each.
Underneath a picture of two men
on a city street
she says:

The U.S. has an ambassador to Cuba
and his name is
Harry F. Guggenheim.
(A Jew like her?)

Then outlines
Personal Qualities
Required for Success
in this Occupation:

A. *Good Judgment*
B. *Broad Mind*
C. *Absolute Integrity*
D. *Imagination*

and includes a photo:
Doctor Dumba and Count Von Bernstorff,
the Austro-Hungarian and German ambassadors
during Wilson's time.

A picture of Prajadhipok, King of Siam.
A map of Poland.
A Europe whose borders
are just about to change.

My mother is in eighth grade,
top of her class.
She thinks
she'd like to be

A Social Service Worker.
She does the research,
compiles a list—
Professional Responsibilities:

1. *Makes homes for the homeless*
2. *Loves children and directs care of the adopted*
3. *Seeks jobs for the jobless*
4. *Reads character, makes a study of people*

She's sent away for booklets,
application forms,
job descriptions.
Qualities Required?

A. *Self-forgetfulness*
B. *Courage*
C. *Sympathy*
D. *Tact*

And here's a letter from the newspaper—
the mayor of New York writes:
I earnestly believe this new year . . .
will bring us back to prosperity.

It's 1931, Joyce.
You're done with Miss Tartikoff's
elocution class in Woodcliff—
done declaiming

monologues:
"The Blind Princess,"
"Betty at the Baseball Game,"
"The Organ Grinder's Daughter."

But still there's piano at Juilliard,
music theory and ballet.
You want to be an actress.
but you don't say that here.

Instead, you analyze
Mechanical Injuries to Fruit
and next to illustrations
of the seventeen-year locust,

other cicadas and lantern flies,
you write:
Enemies of the Horticulturalist.
You paste in a map of Central California,

all of it still green—and there's
"Salinas"—the town you'll move to
thirty years from now
but haven't heard of yet.

I see you leaning over these pages
in the half-gloom of your parents'
well-appointed living room,
smooth-limbed, black-haired:

a beauty without knowing it
Some very smart dresses for street wear
in the warmer months in love
with the boy downstairs, who's older

If the air is bad in your shop
you may get certain diseases of the lungs
unable to sleep when your parents stay out
late, unable to stop worrying *New Organdies*

and Chiffon Frocks;
Blouses Taken to Sheer
Lingerie Effects
self-forgetful, sympathetic

    A. *Cleverness*
    B. *Light Touch*
    C. *Eye for Style*
    D. *Patience*

you never liked to sew.
You'd finish knitting sweaters
after I'd outgrown them.
Mother, here you are,

fourteen years old—
your parents laughing in the kitchen,
your brother on his bike in the street below.
You hold the scissors in your right hand

the paper in your left.
You cut it straight across,
turn it on its side
and cut again.

You hold it up
(even now you're nearsighted)
and look
at the picture:

the husband you haven't met,
the daughters you haven't had,
your grown-up arms around us,
holding us together.

MATRUSHKA DOLLS

JUDITH HARRIS

How many coats of darkness can there be,
as the child falls asleep,
like a story within a story;
or a doll within a larger doll
like the wooden dolls
my mother wrapped up in two small boxes
and carried home from Haifa.

Green dresses, bowed kerchiefs,
and painted faces,
bellies halved and shellacked
in baker's aprons,
they had girths wide
as the earth itself,
belted with a tiny crack
at the middle.

My mother never told me
how babies were born,
only that the body
unscrewed itself like a jar
and that the shell peeled open;
and inside was the seed that would
begin the child, like a sprout, growing:

a girl within a finished girl
as a maze uncoiled upon the map
or a bobbin of thread unwinding,
or a branch unravelled

from the licorice twist of wind
or the sky lifting up
yet another hollowed mask.

Now I have my own daughter,
a scroll of flaxen hair laid
in the spread palms of afternoon
and I wonder
what my daughter dreams:
as she falls back inside
the dark orchard I meant
to plant inside her,
and the darker orchard underneath—

And there a gardener gathers
under the base of the tree;
more red and gold in airy baskets
until, one day, she will eat the flaky seed
that will split her in two
and break the sky
with a cranny of thunder.

My daughter was born in summer
among the lemons and roses.
What my mother told me
whispered again in my ear:
how a child snaps out
from the tree,
and how the cored world circles
and circles around
the black mouth of its own equator,
sealing itself back together again.

HAPPY BIRTHDAY

ALICIA SUSKIN OSTRIKER

Happy birthday, a gray day like the first one—
You were so brave to enter our world
With its dirty rain, its look of a sepia photograph.

I call you at college, early and drowsy.
I hear you describe the party last night,
How you danced, how dancing is one of the things

You love in your life, like thinking hard. You are
All right, then, and on the telephone
Hearing the high snaredrum of your voice

I can feel you about to be born, I can feel
The barriers yield as you slide
Along the corrugated glitter,

Like some terrible rubbery ocean built of blood
That parts at a touch, leaving a path.
"What should I do," you wonder, "after I graduate?"

Now I imagine you curled under your quilt
As a cold light begins to enter
Like a knife in a pirate's teeth. Dear salt flesh,

I am ready if you are, I am afraid if you are.
I still ask: will this hurt, will it give pleasure,
Will I survive it? On your mark, get set,

We give birth to each other. Welcome. Welcome.

PART TWO

IN ANGER AND LOVE

As is the mother, so is the daughter.

Ezekiel 18:20

SURVIVOR

BARBARA GOLDBERG

They say I should feed you,
child with the gift of tongues.
But darting through woods of dark pine
hounds chase the scent of sandals.

Days spent under cover
in a field of eiderdown,
my fingers search for traces
of my own lost mother.

At night, when the bulb shines through
the parchment, and I scrub
my body down with soap,
I think of her parting lace curtains
looking for Father to round the corner.

A small patch of pine presses against the north
side of this house. Here, by Union Turnpike,
a car is parked in the driveway.
We'd all fit in, all, if we had
to make a quick journey.
I keep a bar of gold under my pillow.

They bring you to me, my locket
clasped in your fist. I want
to feed you.

It's those spiked needles that scrape
against the glass, those shadows
that won't sleep behind the drapes.
It's that woodsman walking
through this forest
swinging his ax.

THERE WAS MY VERY SCARY MAD PERIOD

SANDRA BERNHARD

*T*here was my very scary, mad period which lasted for at least thirty years. Sudden depression, melancholy, loneliness. You know, the usual—bursts of anger accompanied by intense sadness.

It was one night in particular when everything came to a head. Memories of childhood traumas, people who had left me, sirens screaming in the distance. A dog hit by a car, a little puddle of urine forced out, a dribble of blood running out of its mouth. The retarded kid who waved her hands above her head behind the chain-link fence in Flint. Sunday afternoons winding down into night, my mother's fragility, my father's obsessiveness, my brother's fears, the sweetness of Yiddish grandparents, timeless modern furniture, leaping down five stairs in an act of triumph, a thousand endless conversations with fictitious comrades, lovers, and business partners, wasted relationships, abandoned plans and dreams, rewards, successes. You know, the usual.

It started coming faster and faster. The thoughts wound around one another like the inside of a baseball, rubber bands of thought wrapped around a hard rubber core. I let it all go, to unravel without judgment or regret. Numb, at times vomiting, shaking, shitting, contemplating razor blades in a dramatic moment to produce some blood, not much, just a little something to leave a scar on the top of my arm, nothing more than a deep scratch, but that passed and was overlooked for the predictability of it.

Finally I managed to call my mother, who by this point had garnered an amazing amount of strength for someone who was like a leaf hanging onto its tree for dear life. She listened and I could feel her gentle hand on my forehead, like my grandmother's hand scratching my back until it turned bright red. Hands, oh, I remember everyone's hands, and I felt my mother's love then like I never had before, it soothed me and I wanted so much to let go of my demons, my dybbuks. When do you release them, when do they let you rest? I asked her. And she told me that they just do when you don't need them anymore, and I prayed for that moment because there have been times when they went away for a while. My mother's words soothed me, everything receded back into some serene spot. I slept, finally, dreaming about round edges and my mother's hands. I try to stay there whenever I can, until I have a child of my own to soothe and take away the madness and the pain.

FAMILY FEELINGS

JUDITH VIORST

*I*ndeed, it has often been said that in becoming parents ourselves we now understand what our mother and father went through and thus can no longer blame and denounce them, as once we could easily do, for all that we have suffered at their hands. Parenthood can be a constructive developmental phase in which we heal some of the wounds of our own childhood. It also may allow us to recast our old perceptions of that childhood in less alienated, more reconciling ways.

But parenthood—our parenthood—can also serve a reconciling function by giving our parents better parts to play, by freeing them to be—as grandma and grandpa—more loving, indulgent, tender, patient, generous, you name it, than they had ever been as mother and father. No longer concerned with instilling moral values, no longer in charge of discipline and rules, no longer dedicated to building character, they become their best selves, and we—in our pleasure at all they can offer our children—begin to forgive them their sins, both real and imagined.

Here is how this played out between one woman—my mother, Ruth Stahl—and her daughter Judith:

I remember always wanting an enormous amount from my mother, though no more than my mother wanted from me, and entangled in disappointment and hurt and anger and frustration and passionate love, we— my mother and I—grew up together. And struggled together. And enjoyed some measure of happiness together. But it wasn't until I had children that we finally found the roles that allowed us to suit each other perfectly: I as the mother of her glorious grandsons, she as terrific as any grandma could be.

Within this special relationship I first began, I think, to know my mother, to understand something of her history, to note that she could be brave and that she could be funny and that she could recite every word of

"Annabel Lee." To love her for instructing me in the pleasures of lilacs and books and female friendships. To love her for loving her grandsons better than me.

Not deeper, perhaps. Not necessarily more. But certainly . . . better.

For to me my mother had always been the most alluring and most vexatious of women. For me the cost of loving had always come high. With all of my children, however, my mother had only one face and that face always smiled upon them. To them she gave free love till the day she died. "Grandma says I'm completely great," reported my oldest son, who viewed her just as unambivalently. But between my mother and me ambivalence was, for many years, the name of the game.

I had lived with my mother in anger and love—I suppose most daughters do—but my children only knew her in one way: as the lady who thought they were smarter than Albert Einstein, as the lady who thought they wrote better than William Shakespeare, as the lady who thought every picture they drew was a Rembrandt, as the lady who thought that whatever they were and whatever they wanted to be was . . . completely great.

My mother asked nothing more of my sons than the pleasure of their company. My mother had had a more stringent agenda for me.

"Be better," she said. "Try harder," she said. "Do it," she said, "my way. Or else you'll get hurt, you'll get sick, you'll fall in a hole." "Don't do anything bad," she said, "or you'll break your mother's heart. Be a good girl."

And I yearned for her love and approval and I yearned to be her good girl, but I yearned for freedom and autonomy. And the pain of growing up was recognizing that I could not have it all. And so when my mother pleaded, "Why don't you listen to me? I only want what's good for you," her rebel daughter, shaking her head and drawing the battle lines, replied, "Let *me* decide what's good for me."

But my mother had no dreams to lay on my children. She had tried . . . and succeeded . . . and failed with my sister and me. She was done with that now and her grandsons couldn't defeat her. Or disappoint her. Or prove anything—anything good or anything bad—about her. And I saw her free of ambition, free of the need to control, free of anxiety. Free—as she liked to put it—to enjoy.

"Grandparenthood," writes psychoanalyst Therese Benedek, "is parenthood one step removed. Relieved from the immediate stresses . . . grandparents appear to enjoy their grandchildren more than they enjoyed their own children."

And enjoy them my mother certainly did.

For she had at last come to a place in life where happiness wasn't yesterday or tomorrow, where happiness wasn't elusive or remote, where happiness wasn't what should have been or might still be someday, but now—in her kitchen—eating lunch with her grandsons. Or on the living-room couch, reading books to her grandsons. Or buying double-dip ice cream cones for her grandsons. Or trying to catch a pigeon with her grandsons.

How lucky for them. How lucky for her. And how lucky for me. For with the children between us we had found our optimal distance, not too close and not too far apart. Linked by Anthony-Nicholas-Alexander, my mother and I had made a new connection.

OLD PROS

PATRICIA VOLK

$\mathcal{F}$rom thirty-three thousand feet in the air the clouds look like cauliflower and I can't help wondering if Mammeleh will look familiar. I haven't seen her since the last face-lift. I haven't seen her since Eddie became disenchanted with the building business and decided to find out what he really wanted from life and if what he really wanted included me.

The pilot releases and lowers the wheels. Something in my stomach gets released and lowered too.

I walk through the umbilical cord that connects my plane to my mother. Everybody's walking at window-shopping speed like there's something to see. Humming with power, I leave them in my wake. I whiz by so fast that the air lifts my crazy, viney, "is-this-child-blessed-or-what?" hair. My khaki skirt is two years old. What Mammeleh will make of this is: my daughter is trying to irritate me; my daughter is poor; my daughter wants to shop; didn't my daughter learn *anything*? All of the above.

I want to spot Mammeleh before she spots me, but the people at the end of the ramp are blurred together, waving, calling, reaching. They look like *Liberty Leading the People* in actionwear. I search their bodies, their postures, their colors for a hint of Mammeleh. The last time I saw her, Mammeleh's hair was Lucille Ball red. That was after the second face-lift. Now, whenever I think of her it is with the hair color of the second face-lift and the face of the first face-lift. The style itself, beehive, never changes, but I can no longer remember Mammeleh's face as it looked leaning over me, pulling up the covers and saying good night, or Mammeleh's face in the bathroom bending down to meet mine, saying "Plié" so she could wipe between my legs after a bath. My mother's face is gone.

In the end, it's posture that defines Mammeleh. A woman is holding her head up and slightly to the side. According to Mammeleh, this is the most flattering pose a person can take. It eliminates strange shadows around the neck, or a double chin, and, most important, gives the illusion of a nothing-to-hide head-on shot. Everyone, Mammeleh likes to say, is prettier from the side than the front. With the exception of Ava Gardner, whom Mammeleh thinks was perfection from any angle.

Mammeleh likes to tell the story of how she went to see a man from Ava Gardner's past in a nightclub act during the seventies. She went to the club not so much to see the performer, who was wearing love beads and sadly past his prime, but to feel a kinship with Ava. The act was not going over well, and out of nowhere the man from Ava Gardner's past signaled the band to stop playing. He walked over to the floodlights and leaned into the audience. "Folks," he said, "I've had a very colorful life. Very colorful. So you know what? I'm not going to do my act tonight. No, that's right. I'm going to cancel my act for tonight. And you want to know why? I've led a very colorful life. You all know that. A lot of women. A lot of problems. And so tonight, instead of doing my act, I'm going to give you, the audience, the chance to ask me anything about it." Pause. "Anything you want to know about me and my past, ask away." Pause. *"Anything at all."* No hands went up and the band began to look fidgety, but the old pro in his love beads and turtleneck slid up and down the stage and kept talking. "No kidding, folks. There isn't any question I won't answer. Nothing is too personal." He squinted at the audience, hand above his eyes like a visor, and kept up the patter. He discussed his alimony payments, near-adventures with organized crime, bouts with alcohol, bouts with women, bouts with the alcoholic husbands of the women he'd had bouts with, and the whole time, no questions. No one in the audience had a thing they wanted to know. "Nothing is too personal," he kept explaining. "Ask away." Finally, a flash of pink emerged from the crowd. The old pro spotted Mammeleh's hand and thrust his microphone toward it. "Yes!" he shouted. "What is it? What would you like to know about my life?"

Mammeleh cleared her throat and spoke:

"How tall was Ava Gardner?"

"What was that?" The old pro cupped his hand behind his ear.

"How tall was Ava Gardner?"

The old pro stopped pacing. "How tall was Ava Gardner?" He lowered his voice. "Well, this is going to come as a shock to a lot of folks. Let me tell you, a lot of you are going to be very surprised. But standing in her high heels, and Miss Gardner always wore high heels, Ava Gardner was"—he paused for effect—"Miss Gardner was . . . *five-feet-two-inches tall!*" The audience gasped. The old pro pivoted on his heel and pointed to the band. They launched into a full-blown "Roses of Picardy" and the man from Ava Gardner's past sang along, scatting where he forgot the words. With the music still up, he bowed, leaving the stage before the applause had a chance to start.

As it turns out, Mammeleh always wears high heels and in them she is five-feet-two.

"Mammeleh!"

"Sukeleh!"

We lean toward each other for the Dade County kiss, left cheek almost touching right cheek, right cheek almost touching left cheek, so as not to smudge Mammeleh's makeup. The smell of it clouds my nostrils, a damp cake applied with a foam sponge, discontinued years ago. (Mammeleh has stockpiled a supply from three states. She keeps the stuff in her freezer, cryogenically preserved. "My greatest fear," she likes to say, "is to outlive my makeup.")

I steel myself for a look. Her skin appears to be stretched over a bowl like a piece of Saran Wrap.

"Well?" She smiles a new smile with her head up and slightly to the side.

"You look gorgeous, Mammeleh. Like always."

"Your mother's a regular knock-out," says a small scrubbed-looking man with a jaw like a glove compartment. He is wearing a baby-blue leisure suit with dark blue stitching on the lapels.

Mammeleh grabs the man's arm with fingernails made possible by the miracle of plastic.

"This is Sy," she says. "Sy, did I tell you?"

"The apple don't fall far from the tree."

There is a lot of play in the Cadillac. Sy is able to keep the steering wheel in continuous motion without any repercussions on the tires. Pulling away from the airport, he reads a sign:

"'SIX MILES TO THE BASS MUSEUM.'"

"Are you hungry, Sukey? Sy and I couldn't decide whether to take you for stone crabs or give you a nice home-cooked meal."

"'HOWARD JOHNSON'S MOTOR LODGE. CLAM FRY EVERY WEDNES-DAY NIGHT.' What's tonight?" Sy turns to Mammeleh.

"Tuesday. So we decided to compromise. We got fried chicken."

"'OCEAN WORLD IN KEY BISCAYNE. SEE HUGO THE KILLER WHALE.'"

"So let me look at my baby." Mammeleh twists in her seat.

She studies me as if I'm her reflection in a mirror. She takes me in. She feels the bottom of my hair with her palm as if she is weighing it. She squints, cocks her head, straightens the chain around my neck, then looks at the hollow heart that hangs there.

"New?"

My fingers fly to my throat. I never thought of taking it off. If it weren't for a mall in New Jersey with sewage problems, I wouldn't be here.

"'FLYNN'S DIXIE RIBS. EAST OF U.S. I AT 152ND STREET.' 'FLOR-IDA,'" Sy adds, "'SEE IT LIKE A NATIVE.' 'SEMINOLE INDIAN VILLAGE. TEN MILES WEST ON TAMIAMI TRAIL.'"

Side by side we work in the kitchen.

"Making them happy, so what's the big deal?" Mammeleh offers as she gets out the cucumbers.

I run cold water over the romaine.

"'WHAT YOU SHOULD DO IF YOU SWALLOW A HEARING-AID BAT-TERY,'" Sy reads from the living room. "'CALL YOUR LOCAL POISON CONTROL CENTER OR THE NATIONAL BATTERY HOTLINE'"

It turns out that a swallowed hearing-aid battery can cause death. Sy comes into the kitchen and checks to see if he has the local Poison Control 1-800 number on his list by the phone. He does.

"'POT SCRUBBERS AID COW DIGESTION,'" he reads on his way back to the recliner. I decide not to ask what happens if a cow that swallows a pot scrubber then swallows a hearing aid. Mammeleh interrupts her cucumbers and inspects the white spines of the romaine leaves, finding black dots I missed.

"Here." She thrusts the peeler and takes over the lettuce. She is wearing her duster, or model's coat. Like the Victorians, Mammeleh changes her clothes to match her activities. This is the work-in-the-kitchen outfit. Later, an eating-at-home-fried-chicken outfit.

"Want an apron?"

"I'm fine."

"Want to call Eddie and tell him you're in one piece?"

"He's not where I can reach him."

Mammeleh runs a gleaming talon down the romaine. "So . . . tell me something I don't know."

By this she means, I'm worried about you.

"I got new dishes. For every day. Plain white."

By this I mean, I appreciate your interest.

Mammeleh is not a lover of eating in, so my guess is we're home because Sy does something truly terrible in restaurants. A Sweet 'n' Low thief? A "You-didn't-fill-the-cup" kind of guy? A sender-backer? Maybe he reads the menu out loud. His manners are fine though. He does eat impeccably. Not everyone knows that the correct way to eat fried chicken is to cut off as much as you can first. Only then is picking up acceptable. All these men. All that training. How does she do it? How come she never calls me Sarah?

"This is your vacation," Sy says when I rise to help clear. "I don't want you should think we asked you down here to work."

We.

In the kitchen, he runs water for tea. Mammeleh concentrates on removing a smudge of grease from the glass-topped table. She rubs it until the skin around her fingernail turns white, as if she can burnish the stain into the glass. Rubbing grease into glass is worse than useless, but I keep my mouth shut. I check her out but can see no scars. Could a stranger tell it's a new face? Or does it only look new if you're familiar with the first two? My hand slides up my neck. I feel the beginning of loose flesh under my chin. How did that get there? Looking at Mammeleh, I discover I'm the "before" picture.

"'SARA LEE CHERRY CHEESECAKE,'" Sy calls. "'LEAVE IN REFRIG-ERATOR FOR TWO HOURS OR AT ROOM TEMPERATURE FOR THIRTY MINUTES.'"

"Want to try Eddie now?" Mammeleh says.

She knows everything worth knowing. "He's out to dinner."

"So, Sukey." Sy brings in the tea.

"Sarah."

"So, whatever. You tell me. I want to know. What do you think first attracted me to your mother?"

He waits a moment as if he expects me to say, Talent? Money? The biological imperative?

"Her hair!" He smiles at Mammeleh. She glows and tilts her head. "That's what gets me. A gorgeous head of hair. I can take it if they're flabby. I can take it if they're old. But if the hair don't have flair, toot-toot-tootsie, good-bye!"

"Oh, Sy." Mammeleh smiles.

In the tub, I feel all my emotions coming together into something big and new I can't identify. But I can feel it, hot and tight, in the center of my chest. My shoulders and knees break the water, primordial islands. Steam condenses above my lip. My back was born to fit into the hollow of my mother's tub. I add more hot and distribute the heat with a flutter kick. I release the drain and run more in again. This time I go under, holding my breath, and as I do, it occurs to me that maybe in modeling myself against my mother I have made myself manless. I can't keep one man and Mammeleh has so many. Unless, unless, it suddenly hits me, Mammeleh has so many because she can't keep one either. Maybe we are not so different. Maybe we're like that political circle Eddie once drew for me. When the right goes so far right and the left goes so far left they wind up in exactly the same place. I come to this underwater. I am my mother, my mother is me. This whole idea forms itself on a single breath of air. Finally I decide to surface, and when I do, there she is, looking down at me. She stares at what's changed since the last time she has seen her daughter in the tub.

"Here." She pulls a plump towel off the bar. What does the *B* in the monogram stand for? Sy Baumgartner? Sy Blumenthal? Sy Brontosaurus? Are these towels left over from the cigar-smoking Herman Brill?

She closes the door behind her and I flip the drain lever with my toe. I dry my legs, longer than Ava Gardner's. I remember all the different towels Mammeleh's had, the sculpted florals, the velour period, the extinct Vigo-Rubs, each one monogrammed in good faith.

On the terrace, Mammeleh is in an emerald silk djellabah. Her hands clasp the railing in the clawlike way people with extraordinarily long nails have to clasp things. I'm in my nightgown with a sweater buttoned over it. I clasp the railing too.

"You know you can always . . ."

"I know."

"If ever there's something . . ."

"If there was I'd tell you."

"I'm not the type to . . ."

"Yes, Mammeleh. I know."

We stare out at the sky. Together we stare at the quivering lights and the abrupt black of the ocean beyond. Miami's nighttime skyline is nothing compared to the shimmering of my mother's hair beneath her yellow bug bulb. I look at the stars. From far away they look as close to each other as we are. Closer. They are light years apart, but I can block out a constellation just by closing one eye and putting the tip of my pinky in front of the other.

In my room, Mammeleh has left me the local paper. When I get to the page with the crossword on it, I see she has missed two words. For as long as memory, Mammeleh has started her day with a cup of coffee and the puzzle, which must be why I don't drink coffee and never do the puzzle. She's missed two words today. The winner of the Preakness in 1942 bisects a four-letter word for Saberhagen. Saberhagen. I don't know what Saberhagen means either. I have no idea who won the Preakness. My mother and I don't know the same things.

I turn out the light and, lying in bed, picture Sy waiting for Mammeleh under the sheets. I swallow and wonder if I'll feel the tightening in my throat tomorrow that comes from going to bed with a wet head. I fluff the pillow and turn onto my side. I hear nothing but see a white line of light appear on the wall I am facing. The white line gets wider. It gets wide enough to accommodate the shadow of a woman with tall hair. It's a shadow I'd know anywhere. It stays in the light stripe, not moving. Then it teeters on tiptoe, looming larger and larger, blocking out more light, until it raises a hand, lays it gently on my damp hair, and reaches over to close the window. It pulls the covers up high on my shoulders. "I love you," the shadow whispers, then gets smaller, smaller, smaller until, at last, it is gone.

OUR WOUNDED

for Gina

SHIRLEY LATESSA

Wearing their loss
like makeup
or hiding it in a locket

next to a tattoo
limbs made of twigs
bodies tree-houses

they can't climb into
my daughter's friends stumble
through our home

They don't say why
they shrug off
the on-going sales pitch

and look for fun
crazy stunts
a way to stall

the death years
bearing down
like a ten-ton truck

delivering unwanted changes
Perhaps they fear losing touch
with that half-sensed heart-space

where blood swirls into a vortex
before it is veined
madly out again

where a new thought
sense-free can arise
or an image not found on t.v.

not found in the violence
Hollywood cradles them in
Like walking willows

they droop through my kitchen
saying who they are
Hi, mom, they say

and unfurl into
my daughter's room
skirting the piles of t-shirts

wild mushrooms
blooming on the floor
safe for a bit

in an electronic forest
of hard music
some with shaved heads

some with hair like a
madonna-blue annunciation
and each, each, each

with wounded eyes.

LOVINGKINDNESS

(EXCERPTS)

ANN ROIPHE

*W*hat do we know about mothers and daughters? If there is a recurring myth of matricide and usurped power, who tells that story? If mothers and daughters form a unit that crackles and splits and sends particles out into the universe, particles of hate, revenge, and passion, where do we hear it? Mothers are not afraid of their daughters (except for the wicked queen in "Snow White"). Our power is so oblique, so hidden, so ethereal a matter, that we rarely struggle with our daughters over actual kingdoms or corporate shares. On the other hand, our attractiveness dries as theirs blooms, our journey shortens just as theirs begins. We too must be afraid and awed and amazed that we cannot live forever and that our replacements are eager for their turn, indifferent to our wishes, ready to leave us behind. For women too it must be a struggle to honor, to love, to respect, not to fear, not to be cruel, not to exercise too much power when you have it, to accept its loss with grace. To maintain affection while dying is as complicated for women as for men. The daughter cannot help having this urge to get on with it, to get away, to pull apart and fly off, leaving the decaying old lady on the ground where she is free to crawl after her disappearing child, dragging herself along with longing, hope, unsatisfied tenderness. Mother and daughter tales are not apt to have bloody sacrifices at their apex. They will be about minor acts of treason, a tablecloth burned accidentally, a recipe given without its crucial ingredient, a desertion to another city, to another country, to another group, a sticking out of the tongue, a teasing good-bye poke; a daughter whose mother was the chairperson of the local chapter of Planned Parenthood has eight children, the daughter of an opera buff plays the drums, the daughter of a horsewoman in Connecticut raises miniature poodles in a penthouse apartment in Hong Kong. Between mother and daughter the affair is fraught with small needles, little pinpricks, an occasional bloodletting, a wrenching away from exactly the unity that was once so desired, so needed, so always imperfect. As the mother withers, her need for her daughter mounts. She pours herself into her child. Each triumph, each flash of beauty, each step in the wider world is enjoyed as if it were one's own. But exactly this stickiness, this gluing of completeness onto incompleteness, drives the daughter to secrecy, to abandonment, to a ferocious fight for her own skin, her own destiny. If she succeeds in shaking off her mother, she will remain a glorious self—but only briefly, just until the moment she forgets what she has learned and gives birth herself to a daughter who will call her in the night, press hot skin against hers, and frighten her with myriad misfortunes, and as it started so it repeats with daughter racing toward freedom and mother running behind, "Wait, wait, tell me what is happening, speak to me, darling, don't you remember when I was the ocean and you were the fish, when I was the night and you were the moon?"

Persephone had to die in order to escape Ceres. She married the King of the Underworld and all the earth turned brown with Ceres' grief. But was Peresphone sad or was she gloating in her palace on the dark side of the river? Is death or life a matter of point of view? Was Ceres the first grasping mother whose daughter was willing to leap even into oblivion to remove the annoyance of a parent who rejoiced too much in her presence?

If God had come to Sarah and asked her to take her daughter to the mountaintop and tie her to a rock and slit her throat because God commanded it, there would have been no chosen people. The Jews would have wandered, nomads in the desert without the law, dancing before golden calves, idling through the centuries indistinguishable from their neighbors. No mother would give back her daughter, which may be the explanation for patriarchy. But on the other hand, if God were a woman would She ever have considered giving Her children free will, would She not have created a more harmonious, closer, loving family in which one small bite of an apple could be forgiven and the gates of Eden be sealed so that exit was impossible?

Precisely because Sarah could not, even for the Deity, even for the welfare of all humanity, sacrifice her daughter (the daughter she didn't have because if a miracle is to be a real miracle it shouldn't produce a second-class baby), our mythology about mothers and daughters is thin and low on plot. There is a reason why the Ten Commandments have placed so prominently the words "Honor thy father and thy mother." It is clear that no one, naturally, easily, without the force of law, wants to honor their father and mother. Dishonor to the elders is the natural human inclination.

I don't understand this clearly, but I am thinking about Andrea and missing the flush of her skin, the way her legs move across the room, the way her eyes glare at me and sometimes she makes me laugh. I will have to see her, the new her, the one that I do not know. I will have to follow her since she will not come home to me.

&

*W*hat does Andrea look like now? When she left home she was so thin her collarbone was almost an offensive weapon. Her legs were spindly and when she raised her arms you could see her ribs under her shirt. Why did she have to be so thin? What was so disgusting about the rounded shoulder, the full arm, the bodice that announced itself? I was at a NOW strategy meeting with a group designing a campaign to counter abortion clinic bombings when someone in the room asked how many of our daughters had had abortions. All over the room hands went up. I asked how many of our daughters were either grossly overweight, or underweight, or threw up their dinners in the toilet each night. There was a shocked silence and then hands went up, a forest of hands. One woman who did not raise her hand called out, "I have only sons, but my niece is in the hospital being force-fed."

What is it? I asked. We are the ones who freed women from the beauty parlor, from waxing their legs, from doing their nails, from feeling that their worth lay in conformity to some model who was shown in soft focus on a magazine cover. We were the ones who said you shouldn't squeeze your stomach into a merry widow, you shouldn't have to mince around in uncomfortable shoes. All by yourself, as a natural woman, you are beautiful whatever the shape of your nose or the color of your skin; that was where we began, but look at our daughters. They diet, they diet too much and end up on the psychiatrist's couch or in the hospital. They gorge and they binge and they hate themselves and they vomit till their teeth fall out. This abortion issue is just the tip of the glacier that's coming to run us over.

Someone shouted out that I was off the subject, and so I was. But I'm still thinking about it. There is something in the air that makes women unable to accept their shape, that makes of puberty a nightmare, that makes so many girls hide their breasts in folds of fat or diet them out of existence, or exercise them into flat muscle. Is it still a shame to be female, does it promise so little or offend so greatly? We underestimated the problem. We were romantic in our belief that men would accept women if women would just like themselves. Maybe, like a dog in heat, the female of the species changes her chemistry to attract men. Women, our daughters, do not like their natural selves any better than we did. Perhaps equality was never the real issue. We talked of opportunities, ignoring the roar of biology, the odors of sexuality that could neither be banished nor harnessed for our lofty purposes.

ONLY A PHASE

LESLÉA NEWMAN

I.

At 11:30 in the morning, Miriam Rosenfeld sat in the brown vinyl reclining chair she had bought her husband fifteen years before for Father's Day, with her feet up and her head tilted slightly back. The TV was on, the curtains were drawn, and the burglar alarm was set. There was a cup of lukewarm instant coffee perched on a nearby end table, a lit Marlboro cigarette smoldering in an ashtray balanced on the arm of the chair, and a remote control for switching TV channels lying in her lap.

Miriam was knitting a tiny sweater. There was also a ball of yellow yarn in her lap, attached by a thin strand to the knitting needles she held in her two hands. The needles were constantly moving, and their incessant clicking was both comforting and annoying to the various members of Miriam's family, none of whom were home at 11:30 on a Tuesday morning except for Noodles, the family dog. Noodles lay in his customary spot, under the extended part of the recliner upon which Miriam rested her green fuzzy-slippered feet.

Every so often, Miriam pulled out more yarn from the ball on her lap by raising both her arms high over her head. Then she would lower her arms and wrap the loose strand of yarn around her left index finger, which she kept stiff and pointing skyward as she continued to knit, barely missing a beat. Occasionally Miriam interrupted herself to take a sip of coffee, puff on her cigarette, or change the TV channel by aiming the remote control at the set and pushing a button. Then she would squint at the screen across the room, ignoring the glasses that dangled from a chain around her neck and rested contentedly on her bosom. Miriam wore a green velour bathrobe that matched her slippers. There were dark circles under her eyes.

At exactly noon "The Price Is Right" was over and the news came on.

Miriam had no interest in the news—wars, killings, muggings on the subways—you call that news? she'd ask her husband, who always protested whenever Miriam pointed the remote control at the set and zapped the evening news into "Laverne and Shirley."

In between the morning game shows and the afternoon soaps, Miriam ignored the disasters of the world, and instead let the dog out, took in the mail, made herself a fresh cup of instant coffee, and sometimes made a phone call or two. This week she had to call the exterminator to take care of the ants in the kitchen, the floor waxer to do the downstairs floors, the electrician to fix the light over the garage, and the mechanic to see if he had time to give her car a tune-up. Sighing, Miriam put down her knitting and started to get up from her chair. Then, changing her mind, she settled back down again and held her work up to the light for inspection.

"Not bad, if I do say so myself," Miriam said to no one in particular, pulling at a small yellow sleeve. She was making a sweater for Esther's grandchild, her third, due in two weeks. Miriam wondered whether it would be a boy or a girl, and hoped for a boy for Esther's sake. Boys were so much easier. She futzed with the sweater a minute longer, then put it down, and with an oy! heaved herself out of the reclining chair, which snapped into an upright position. Noodles bounded out from under the chair, his tail high in the air, his head tilted slightly to one side. A walk maybe? Or better yet, some lunch? Perhaps both. This was the extent of the possibilities that existed in his little canine mind.

"Oh Noodles, I'm ti-re-d." Miriam let out a big yawn, stretching her words instead of her body. "Come here, Noodles. Where's that Noodle-Poodle? Let Mama see her good boy. Such a good boy." She bent down and stroked Noodles's curly grey head. Noodles, lulled by Miriam's voice, lay himself down and rolled over, presenting his belly to her as a token of undying, everlasting love. Miriam petted the dog for a minute, and then with another oy! straightened up. Noodles leapt to his feet.

"Good boy," Miriam repeated. "Wanna go out?" At those words Noodles made a dash for the front door and stood there waiting, his little pompom of a tail wagging furiously and an occasional impatient yelp escaping from his mouth.

"I'm coming, Noodles. Mama's coming. Hold your horses." Ignoring the advice she used to give to the children—pick up your feet, walk like a mensch!—Miriam shuffled down the hallway to the front door.

"OK, OK. Does Noodles want to go out?" Miriam turned to a panel on the wall, where a small red light glowed eerily through the semidark hallway. She turned a key that changed the light from red to green, signaling that the burglar alarm was disengaged. Then she opened the front door and stood in the doorframe, one foot inside the house and the other on the cement path. Noodles ran past her and commenced his morning ritual of cautiously sniffing the shrubbery and raising his rear left leg every few feet.

Miriam shifted her weight so she could reach into the mailbox for the mail. Cradling it in her arms, she narrowed her eyes at the day, waiting for Noodles to finish his business. It was mid-April and there was still a chill in the morning air, though here and there a bird sang sweetly, and a few crocuses had already popped their little purple heads up in the neighbor's front yard.

After a minute Miriam called out, "Nu, Noodles? C'mon, boy. In the house. Let's go." The dog appeared in a second, his tail high and his walk bouncier than it had been a few minutes before.

"Did you make? What a good boy. You're such a good boy." Miriam held open the door as Noodles trotted past. Turning her back on the day, Miriam entered the house, shut the door firmly behind her, and turned the key in the wall, resetting the burglar alarm. Then she walked into the kitchen, where Noodles was waiting expectantly.

"Do you want your crackers, you good boy? Is that what you want?" Dropping the mail onto the kitchen table, Miriam reached up into a cabinet for a red box. She pulled out three crackers shaped like firemen and tossed them to Noodles, who promptly devoured them and then, tail high and nose low, proceeded to conduct a thorough investigation of the kitchen, searching for stray People Cracker crumbs, signs of last night's dinner, or remnants of the sesame seed bagel Miriam's husband had eaten for breakfast that morning.

Left to her own devices, Miriam took a cup down from the cabinet, dumped a spoonful of coffee and emptied a packet of Sweet 'n' Low into it, and turned the flame on under the teakettle. She put a cigarette into her mouth and bent over the stove to light it from the burner. Then she sat down to sift through the mail.

There was the *TV Guide*, a flyer from JC Penney's announcing their annual spring sale, the synagogue's monthly newsletter, an invitation to Irma and Stanley's thirty-fifth wedding anniversary, a bill from the oil company, and a letter from Deborah.

Miriam exhaled a long stream of smoke from her nostrils and stared at the envelope in her hand addressed to Ms. Miriam Rosenfeld and Mr. Seymour Rosenfeld. Would it kill Deborah to stick in that little *r* between the capital *M* and small *S*, and address her mother by the title she so rightfully deserved? No, Deborah had to do everything her way; she was as stubborn as the day was long.

Miriam took another puff on her cigarette and stared at the handwriting on the envelope for a moment, as if it held some clue to the contents inside. It was the first letter Deborah had written them in a long time, in almost a year. Maybe she was writing to tell them she had met a nice Jewish doctor and was bringing him home for Pesach. Maybe they were even engaged. Miriam doubted it, but you never know. She hoped Deborah wasn't sick, or, God forbid, pregnant. She opened the envelope, unfolded the letter, and held it away from her at arm's length, as though it were something distasteful to the touch. She squinted at Deborah's curly handwriting, which was not unlike her own, trying to make out the words. After a minute she gave in, unfolded her glasses, slid them up her nose, and began to read:

Dear Mom, Dad, and Noodles,

Hi! I hope you are all well and happy. I know I haven't written for a while and I'm sorry about that. I know it must have hurt you, but that's not what I intended. I just needed some time to figure some things out.

I haven't been exactly honest with you lately. I haven't lied exactly, but I haven't told the whole truth either. You know when you call and ask me how's everything and what's new, and I say everything's fine and nothing's new? Well, that's not exactly so. Everything is fine. As a matter of fact, I'm happier than I've ever been. And a lot is new. I went through a rough period for a little while, but I am doing what I think is right, and what I believe in, just like you always taught me to.

What I am trying to tell you is this: I am a lesbian. I've known it for a while and now I want you to know it too. I'm tired of hiding the things that are important to me from you. I'm tired of the silence and distance that has grown between us. I hope that my taking this risk will bring us closer. I want you to know who I am. I trust that your love for me is real, and that you will accept me as I am, even if that is different than how you want me to be.

I'm happier than I ever imagined I could be, ever since I came out, and I know that is what you want for me (to be happy I mean). I still love you, that hasn't changed. Please write or call me so we can discuss this, or anything else.

Love to Grandma and Grandpa.

Love,
Deborah

The teakettle was whistling shrilly, sending a blast of steam up through its spout into the still kitchen air. In fact, the water had been boiling for the last five minutes, but Miriam didn't seem to hear it. Finally she got up and turned off the stove, but she didn't pour the hot water into the open mouth of the waiting cup.

Instead she sat back down at the kitchen table, her feet flat on the floor, forming a perfect pillow upon which Noodles immediately lay his head. Miriam slipped her glasses off her nose and let them hang idly around her neck. She stared at Deborah's letter again, not seeing the words this time, but seeing Deborah's face—not her twenty-six-year-old face, but her two-year-old face, with her auburn hair in tiny wisps around her head, her green eyes fringed with long dark lashes, and that toothless grin that even strangers in the street would stop to admire.

"My baby," Miriam whispered, reaching out her hand as if she could somehow enfold Deborah into her arms. My only daughter, my baby girl. Miriam remembered the day Deborah was born, and how she had cried with joy to have finally produced a girl—a little miniature of herself, with ten perfect fingers and ten perfect toes, and those huge green eyes, though God knows where she had gotten them from, certainly not from Miriam's side of the family. Miriam was crying now as well, big fat tears streaming from her eyes. She wiped her face with the back of her hand and stared at the letter again, seeing Deborah's face once more.

This time, though, Deborah's tiny infant face dissolved and then reappeared as adult Deborah, looking somewhat hostile and somewhat vulnerable, as she had when she came home to visit two Pesachs ago. She had cut off almost all her beautiful auburn hair, and she wore a red T-shirt under black overalls with no brassiere underneath. Miriam had been so excited that Deborah was coming home for the holidays that she had resolved not to nag her about anything, and she was all ready to greet her with a big hug and kiss. But when she opened the door and saw her daughter looking like something the cat had just dragged in, she had been forced to greet her coldly and bring her upstairs to change her clothes before, God forbid, any of the relatives got a chance to see her looking like that. Miriam had made Deborah borrow one of her own dresses to wear to dinner, but with her black sneakers she had still looked ridiculous. Why couldn't she be more like Esther's daughter, Miriam often lamented. Esther's daughter, Irene, had married a nice Jewish boy, an engineer, and had already given Esther two grandchildren, both boys.

But not Deborah. She had been trouble from the first—always wanting to do things her way or not at all, insisting on going to that meshuggeneh college way up in Maine in the middle of nowhere, where they didn't even give out grades for all the money they charged, then living in that filthy hippie commune, and now . . . now this.

She has absolutely no sense, Miriam thought, suddenly feeling angry. Never did and never will. Always trying the newest thing; putting three holes in each earlobe, smoking marijuana, and now this. Why, if the latest thing was wearing a frying pan on your head and walking up Fifth Avenue stark naked, that kid would probably do it.

Miriam folded the letter carefully, returned it to its envelope, and put it in her bathrobe pocket. I'll be damned if I'm going to show this to Seymour, she thought, stacking the rest of the mail into a neat pile. As if he doesn't have enough on his mind. It would kill him. She was always his favorite, Daddy's little girl. How dare she write us such a letter? Hasn't she put us through enough? What a rotten kid. She never thinks of anyone but herself.

Miriam sat at the kitchen table with Noodles dozing at her feet for a long time, not making her phone calls, not drinking coffee, not knitting, not smoking cigarettes. She just stared at the yellow oilcloth covering the table. Once the phone rang and Noodles picked up his head, but Miriam didn't answer it.

At 3:00 the familiar voice of Mike Douglas, blaring from the TV set in the next room, seeped into Miriam's consciousness. Seymour would be home in two hours. She had to get dressed, straighten up the house a little, make supper. I'm not going to let that lousy kid ruin my life, she thought, placing both hands on the table and pushing herself up into a standing position. It's only a phase. She'll get over it, she told herself as she took two sirloin patties out of the refrigerator. Then she shuffled down the hallway toward the bedroom to get dressed, the dog, as always, right at her heels.

II.

At exactly 4:31, Deborah Rosenfeld looked back over her right shoulder, pulled her car out of its parking space, and headed for home. She drove with the windows wide open and the tape deck blaring out Alive's newest album so loudly that when she stopped at a red light the people in the car next to her turned their heads to stare. Ignoring them, Deborah kept her eyes fixed on the traffic light, her right hand on the stickshift so she could switch gears and peel out as soon as the light changed, singing along with Rhiannon at the top of her lungs.

As she drove along, Deborah felt along the passenger seat for a pack of Chiclets. She chewed gum constantly, a habit that was both annoying and endearing to her various friends and coworkers. In addition to the box of Chiclets, a pair of mirror sunglasses, a pen, three quarters, two dimes, and a parking ticket lay on the front seat. Without taking her eyes off the road, Deborah's right hand located the box of gum, opened the flap, removed two pieces, shifted the car into fourth gear, and popped the gum into her mouth. Then she shifted her weight forward and pushed the box of gum down into her hip pocket. Deborah was wearing tight black chino pants, a white button-down shirt, a jeans jacket, and a pair of red Reebok sneakers. She also wore five earrings: two silver studs, two small hoops, and a silver snake that slithered from her left earlobe almost down to her shoulder.

The music ended when she was almost home, and the tape deck automatically spit out the tape and switched the radio on. Deborah groaned and turned it off. She hated listening to the news—war, killings, rapes—the same thing every day. It's too depressing, she always said to her girlfriend, who liked to listen to the six o'clock report over dinner.

Deborah drove the rest of the way in silence, compiling a mental list of all the phone calls she had to make when she got home. She had to call Fotomat to see if her pictures were back yet, call Wendy about the Gay Pride posters, call the phone company about last month's screwed-up bill, and call Anita to see if she could reschedule her acupuncture appointment. She swung into the driveway, turned off the car, and pulled up the emergency brake. Then Deborah gathered up her shoulder bag and a magazine from the back seat, opened the car door, and thrust first one leg and then the other out of the car. Standing up, she inspected the day. The sun was low in the sky, but the day still had some warmth left to it. One of the neighborhood kids rode by on a bicycle, his jacket balled up in the handlebar basket—a sure sign of spring. Deborah wished she didn't have to miss the best part of the day by being stuck in an office from 8:30 to 4:30, but, at least for the time being, that's the way it was.

As she walked toward the back steps that led to her apartment, a grey-and-white cat ran up to greet her.

"Sushi! Hi there, Sushi. How's my Sushi-Pushi?" Sushi rubbed herself against Deborah's ankles, and Deborah bent down to scratch her between the ears.

"How's my girl, huh? How's my Sushi? Are you my best girl? Are you hungry? Come. I'll give you some supper. Let's go in the house." Deborah rubbed Sushi at the base of her spine, causing her tail to stick straight up in the air. "Oy, I'm tired," she said, straightening up. Then she headed up the steps with Sushi following behind.

Deborah stood on the back porch for a moment, fumbling with her keys. Sushi, not being big on patience, calmly pushed open the hinged cat-door Deborah had installed for her and went inside. A minute later Deborah entered to find Sushi sitting right next to her supper bowl, her big green eyes staring at Deborah's hands, which she knew would eventually hold a can opener and a can of Nine Lives. Would it be chicken and cheese tonight? Or tuna and egg? Perhaps both. Sushi narrowed her eyes to concentrate on all the possibilities that existed in her little feline mind.

Deborah threw her keys and magazine on the kitchen table and slung her shoulder bag on the back of a chair. "Did you make today, Sushi? Let's see." She went into the bathroom to inspect the litter box. "What a good cat. Clean as a whistle. Did you go outside? Good girl," Deborah crooned, bending down to scratch Sushi behind the ears again. Then she walked down the hallway into her bedroom to see if anyone had left a message on her answering machine.

The red light, glowing eerily through the semidark room, blinked three times, then paused, then blinked three times again, signaling three calls had been recorded. Deborah sat down on the edge of her bed, rewound the tape, and turned the knob to Playback Messages. Then she sat back with a pen and notebook in her hand. Sushi, realizing that dinner was temporarily postponed, sauntered into the bedroom, jumped up on Deborah's lap, and began to purr.

"*Beep*. Hello, this is Joan from Fotomat calling. Your pictures are ready. Thank you."

"*Beep*. Hi, Deb, this is Marcia. Wanna go see *Desert Hearts* tomorrow night? We can go to the late show. I'll even cook dinner for you. Call me. 'Bye."

"*Beep*. Deborah, you're never home, I'm sick of this machine. Kvetch, kvetch, kvetch. Listen, I'll be over at 6:30 with a surprise for you. What's for dinner? Can't wait. 'Bye. Oh, in case you're wondering, this is your girlfriend."

"*Beep*." A long dial tone followed, and then silence. Deborah turned the knob to Answer Calls, and the little light on the machine turned green. Then she shifted her weight and gently nudged Sushi off her lap. Sushi, annoyed by this gesture and by the fact that her dinner had yet to appear, turned her back on Deborah in a huff and started lazily licking her right front paw.

"Oh Sushi, don't give me the cold shoulder. C'mon, let's see if we got any mail." Deborah opened the front door and walked down the steps that led to the lobby of her apartment building, Sushi trotting after her. She opened the box, took out the mail, then reached all the way inside, making sure she didn't miss anything. Satisfied, Deborah climbed the steps and waited for Sushi, who was busy sniffing around a dusty corner of the hall. Deborah stood in the hallway, cradling the mail in her arms. "C'mon, Sushi. C'mon. Here, Sushi-shi-shi-shi-shi. You're a good cat. Let's go now." Sushi bounded up the stairs and walked through the door Deborah was holding open, her tail swishing behind her.

"Do you want your supper, you good cat? Is that what you want?" Deborah followed the cat into the kitchen, dumped the mail onto the table, and finally took off her jacket. She reached up into a cabinet for a can of Nine Lives, opened it, and plopped two spoonfuls into Sushi's dish. Sushi crouched in front of the bowl and began eating noisily, her metal pet tag clinking against her glass bowl.

The cat taken care of, Deborah took a mug down from the shelf, threw an Almond Sunset tea bag into it, and poured in a spoonful of honey. Then she turned the flame on under the teakettle, popped a fresh piece of gum into her mouth, and sat down at the kitchen table to sort through the mail.

There was the latest issue of *off our backs*, a flyer from the women's book-store announcing their annual spring sale, the Lesbian Alliance's monthly newsletter, an invitation to Melanie's thirty-fifth birthday party, a bill from the gas company, and a letter from her mother. Deborah cracked her gum extra loudly as she stared at the envelope in her hand addressed to Miss Deb-orah Rosenfeld. Would it kill her mother to write *Ms.* like the rest of the human race? It's the 1980s for God's sake, Deborah thought. Even the office where she worked used *Mr.* or *Ms.* on all their forms. But no, not her mother. She had to do everything her way. She was as stubborn as a mule.

Deborah stared at the handwriting on the envelope as if it held some clue to the contents inside. She had never expected her mother to write back so soon; she had sent her parents the letter only a week ago. Maybe her mother was writing to say "Mazel tov! You're gay! Why didn't you tell us before?" Maybe she would even offer to throw her a coming-out party. Deborah doubted it. But you never know. She hoped her mother wasn't going to dis-own her or, God forbid, sit shiva for a week. She opened the envelope, un-folded the letter, and held it up close to her face, trying to make out the words written in a curly handwriting that was not unlike her own. After a minute she gave up, reached into her shoulder bag, and pulled out her glasses from a black case that had a lavender women's symbol embroidered on it. She slipped the glasses onto her face, picked up the letter, and began to read:

Dear Deborah,

Thank you for being so honest with us. As you have set such a fine example, I will be honest as well and tell you that you are the most self-centered, self-absorbed, selfish person that I have ever met. I don't understand how two such decent people like your father and I could have raised such a daughter. Don't you ever think about anyone but yourself? How could you do this to us? You do not live in a vacuum you know. If you would only stop and think for a minute, which I suppose is too much to ask, you would see that your actions have serious consequences.

I will not call you to "discuss this or anything else." Thank you very much for the invitation. I have not shown your letter to your father, nor do I intend to do so. The least you could have done was think about him. He has enough things on his mind right now.

Grandma and Grandpa are fine. I trust you will have the decency not to say anything about this to them. Deborah, where is your head? You never did have any sense.

Noodles is fine and sends love.

Be well,

your mother

The teakettle was whistling shrilly, sending a blast of steam up through its spout into the still kitchen air. In fact, the water had been boiling for the last five minutes, though Deborah didn't seem to hear it. Finally she got up and turned off the stove, but she didn't pour the hot water into the open mouth of the waiting mug. Instead she sat back down at the kitchen table, her thighs pressed together, making a perfect bed for Sushi to hop up onto and lie down on. Deborah took her glasses off and put them upside down on the table. She stared at her mother's letter again, not seeing the words this time, but seeing her mother's face. Not her fifty-year-old face, but the young face that had hovered over two-year-old Deborah, like the brightest star at night, singing a special lullaby just for her.

"My mommy," Deborah whispered, reaching out her hand as if she could somehow find her mother's skirts and cling to them. Deborah remembered all the times her mother had kissed away her tears—when she fell in the park and cut her knee on some broken glass, when the boys at school teased her for being a carrot-top, and the time the science project she had worked so hard on placed only third in the school's science fair. Deborah was crying now as well, big fat tears streaming from her eyes. She wiped her tears with the back of her hand and stared at the letter again, seeing her mother's face once more. This time, though, Deborah saw her mother as she had looked two years ago, the last time she had seen her, when she went home to visit for Pesach. Deborah had resolved to be pleasant to her mother and not criticize her about anything. She had even bought a black velour sleeveless jumpsuit and a red shirt to wear, which Roberta assured her looked just fine. But when her mother had met her at the door with that look of absolute disgust on her face and then actually made her put on a dress that was way too big for her and looked ridiculous with her unshaved legs and high-top sneakers, Deborah had had no choice but to remain cool and aloof for the entire visit. Why couldn't her mother be more like Melanie's mother? Roxanne didn't care that her daughter was a lesbian. In fact, she had marched in Gay Pride last year carrying a sign that said "Hip Hip Hooray, My Daughter's Gay!" She'd probably even be at Melanie's birthday party.

My mother's always been impossible, Deborah thought. Always trying to make me do things her way—go to an Ivy League school, marry a nice Jewish boy, have a bunch of kids. She was completely closed-minded, Deborah thought, feeling angry. Why, if chastity belts were still around my mother would probably make me wear one. And if she'd really had her way, she probably would have gone to a *shadchen* and arranged a match for me a long time ago.

Deborah folded the letter carefully, returned it to its envelope, and put it in her back pocket. How dare she write me such a letter, she thought, glancing for a minute at the rest of the mail. She's called me names my whole life. She's the one who's selfish, always thinking about herself—herself and what the neighbors will say.

Deborah sat at the kitchen table with Sushi snoozing on her lap, not drinking tea, chewing gum, or making phone calls. She just stared at the texture of the two straw place mats on the kitchen table. Once the phone rang and Sushi's ears twitched in her sleep, but Deborah let the answering machine get it.

At 5:45, Deborah looked up at the clock. Roberta would be over in forty-five minutes. She had to get out of these work clothes, straighten up the house a little, and make supper. I'm not going to let my mother ruin my Friday night, she thought, as she lifted Sushi off her lap, placed both hands on the kitchen table, and pushed herself up into a standing position. It's only a phase. She'll get over it, she told herself as she put on a pot of water for the spaghetti. Then she walked down the hallway toward her bedroom to change her clothes, the cat, as always, trailing right behind.

THE BAD MOTHER

JANE SHORE

When we play our game, my daughter
always saves the best parts for herself:
the princess, the mermaid, Cinderella.
Pushing her toy broom around the kitchen,
Emma puts up with the dust and the suffering
because she knows she'll be rewarded in the end.

When we watch the Disney video *Cinderella*,
the part when the wicked stepmother
locks Cinderella in the attic
and refuses to let her attend the ball,
Emma will turn from the screen and say,
"But the stepmother's *nice*, not mean!"
though she'll learn better, later.
When she's fifteen, she won't give the mother
the benefit of the doubt.

After the movie's over, we act out the scene
where the wicked stepsisters
tear Cinderella's dress to shreds:
the dress she's about to wear to the ball,
the dress sewn from scraps
of her own dear dead mother's clothes.
(Emma makes me play *both* sisters at once.)
In my wicked stepmother voice, I hit her
with a long list of chores, leaving poor Cinderella
to waltz at home with her broom.
That's her cue to fling herself to the floor
and sob and weep so convincingly

that the fairy godmother (also played by me)
must restore the world to her, only better,
with a ball gown tiered as a wedding cake.

Crammed into her twin bed, I'm turning
the pages of *Little Red Riding Hood*,
and Emma reassures me,
"But wolves are very *nice* animals."
Four years old, she doesn't want to believe
that people are *all* bad.
When she was two, and mesmerized
by *The Wizard of Oz*, her first movie,
swaying before the TV screen,
she would kiss the witch's luminous green face
the way my mother used to kiss
the little silver hand
she wore on a chain around her neck
to ward off the evil eye.

We've become ancient adversaries, she and I.
We run through our repertoire.
evil parts always reserved for me.
I'm Snow White's stepmother
begging at the Seven Dwarves' door;
I'm a Fuller Brush Woman of sweet deception,
selling Snow White—no, giving away for free—
my entire inventory of poison bodice, apple, comb,
to a heroine so innocent
she gets instant amnesia
when evil is about to strike.

And I'm the thirteenth, vindictive fairy
who makes Sleeping Beauty
prick her finger on a spindle
and fall into adolescence's deep sleep,
from which she'll awaken, years later
as I did, as a mother.

Over and over, I must watch my daughter
fall into a faint, and die.

"Rapunzel, Rapunzel," I call from below,
eye-level with the hem of the dust-ruffle,
"let down your hair!"
And Emma solemnly flips her long beige braids
over the edge of the bed,
a pair of my pantyhose pulled over her head.
The nylon feet softly brush the floor.
Now I am witch, now prince, now witch,
climbing the pale ladder of Rapunzel's hair.
Pretending my two fingers are scissors,
I lop off her braids, cutting off
the source of my daughter's power,
her means of escape, her route to loving
someone other than myself.

Is it better to be the daughter—
young, beautiful, virtuous, and innocent forever?
Sometimes when I vacuum the living room
or fume in the kitchen
or shout commandments from my throne,
I dream I'm the princess again—
a girl who grew up and left the palace
for a palace of her own.

THE DRESS

RACHEL PASTAN

*F*or days my mother lay on the bed in the dark, fully clothed, so entirely motionless that she didn't even wrinkle the spread. She would do this at unpredictable times, moaning and holding her temples if you so much as cracked the shades. Then one afternoon I got home from school to discover her restlessly circling the powder-pink living room, her coat and one es-padrille on, crimson lipstick shining like a beacon on her pursed lips. Seeing me come in, she said, "I can't find my car keys."

"They're not on the hook in the kitchen?"

Her eyes lit up and she hurried from the room. I followed.

"Hey, Mom, where're you going?" I asked, alarmed by her sudden verticality.

"I think I need a new dress," she said. "I'm running down to Tyson's." She hesitated, her pale blue eyes widening, imploring. "Why don't you come, too?"

I sighed. She looked so pale and dishevelled, her stockings doing ele-phant legs at her ankles, a stain on the leather of her purse—I couldn't bear the idea of being anywhere near her.

"Come on," she wheedled. "It'll be fun. We'll buy you something pretty."

Pretty. The word made me clench my teeth. Cheerleaders and daisies were pretty. A glitter of ice was what I wanted to be, a motorcycle—a black rose.

Tyson's was not the nearest of the many malls, but it was the biggest of the big three: White Flint, Montgomery Mall, and Tyson's. In earlier years my mother and I had haunted them together, she thin and freckled in her A-line skirts and shirtwaists, me in the flowery, frilly, baby-doll clothes that in those days we both loved. As a baby I'd been blond, and though my hair had darkened, my mother and I continued for years to believe that it was still the color of hay, or at least honey.

In the car I sat as far away from her as possible in the front seat, pulled down the sun visor, and examined my hair in the mirror. It was uneven and spiky, the way I liked it, and I worked at it constantly with a pick when no one was looking.

Mom leaned over the steering wheel like an old lady, her eyes fixed furiously on the road. But gradually she relaxed, sat up, and started glancing over at me. "I don't know why you want to look like that," she said.

"*Mom*," I warned.

"Really, Leanne. You're so pretty. I don't know why you want to disguise yourself like that. When I was a girl I was so—you know, bony. And my hair, it just hangs down limp as a fish. You're the lucky one, sweetie."

"Mom—let's not talk about it, okay?" I wanted to scream it, but I spoke quietly, thinking of her lying on the bed, her yellowy skin against the baby's breath–patterned quilt, her mouth opening and closing soundlessly.

"All right," she said, her forehead wrinkling. "But I don't know *why* any boy would want to take out a girl who has no respect for her own looks."

Her words made the ugly red zit on the side of my nose throb like a tiny heart.

The mall was a dazzling maze of benches, towering ficus trees, aerobics demonstrations, glass elevators, and women pushing small children in rented carts. Afraid of seeing kids from school—or rather, of having them see me—I alternated between keeping my head down and throwing twitch-like glances over my shoulders.

Beside me, Mom had retreated into herself. She walked the shining floor like a zombie, her blue eyes blinking in the bright lights. I led us up to the second level and down toward the most obscure arm of the place. The crowd thinned out here, and my mother seemed a little better. She stopped before the window of Williams Sonoma and looked in. I followed her gaze to the back wall, where the bright copper pots hung in every size, like Russian dolls. Mom's eyes filled with tears. My stomach shriveled and I took a step away from her, then a step back. I pretended I wasn't there. She took a hankie from her purse and wiped her eyes, blew her nose sharply and started walking away. I trailed behind her to the coffee shop, where we reunited without a word. She had tea and I had a Coke and we sat in not uncompanionable silence in a booth in the back. When she was finished she set the tea bag in her saucer and poked at it with her spoon until it broke open. She dumped the soggy leaves into her cup and stared at them.

"Here." She passed the cup across the table. "What do you see?"

I looked down. "A compost heap?" I tried to joke, but her lips trembled.

"Before I was married, you know what I thought marriage would be? A kitchen hung with shining copper pots." She nodded to herself. "And do you know what? Your father bought me a pot like that—a small one was all he could afford—the first year we were married. But it was so heavy! So much heavier than I had thought. It was all I could do to pick it up."

The store we went to was called Junior Miss, and everything in it was very expensive. The clothes were frilled and frocked, pastel colors only, as though the spectrum ceased at rose.

The dress she picked out was yellow with a small waist and a full skirt, and a delicate pattern of flowers. My heart sank when I looked at it. Even puffed sleeves. It cost $115, though, and I didn't think it was likely Mom would make me buy it.

In the dressing room I unbuttoned my jeans and tugged them down. I yanked my T-shirt off and settled the dress over my head. It was so light it seemed to float slowly through the air as though it were made of feathers. Its silkiness caressed me, and I zipped it carefully up.

But it was too big—it hung stupidly around my bony shoulders. "I'll go get a six," Mom said.

While she was gone I turned slowly in front of the triptych mirror to look at myself from every view. The dress was certainly too big, but still I could see how it would be if it were the right size. I could see what I would look like—balletic, confident—poised and buttery as morning. And suddenly I longed to be transformed.

But when my mother returned, it was with a rushed, apologetic step. "It's the last one, sweetie," she said. "The line's been discontinued."

Reluctant as a child at bedtime, I took it off.

I had begun to walk out of the dressing area when my mother said thoughtfully, "You know, I'm just a bit bigger than you." She hung her purse on a hook and began to undress.

I was appalled. The very idea was revolting—my old mother with her sagging belly trying on this yellow dress! "Mo-om," I said with all the disgust I could muster.

She didn't pay any attention. She slipped the dress onto herself like a shoe onto a waiting foot.

The dress fit—the skirt snug at the waist, the tight bodice pushing up her breasts. The color was perfect—her skin glowed golden. I stared at her, but although she faced the mirror, her own eyes were shut. Her expression rapt, she stood perfectly, radiantly still. Her arms were slightly lifted, palms open like Shiva, as though she were frozen in the act of reaching for an invisible dance partner. I knew just what he looked like, that suave, handsome man—ready to waltz her into a world of pretty girls and weightless copper pots, a world in which I would never have been born.

SELFISH

PHYLLIS KOESTENBAUM

On a soft spring Saturday, Mother takes the local to Cortelyou Road to Snow's Hardware (she works for Uncle Mac), Daddy gets the black DeSoto, I lock up the apartment and meet him out front. He smokes a cigar, like Uncle Eddie. I wear purple lipstick. We drive across the bridge where you smell coffee to his pupil's father's blouse factory. From beaming Sidney Goldfarb he buys twelve blouses I've chosen, two he's chosen for Mother. We don't eat lunch out.

Mother comes home at 4:30. Daddy is writing on a yellow lined tablet in their bedroom. I am sitting on my pink chenille spread in mine, reading poems in the Louis Untermeyer. The bleary light smears the spread, my arms, the book.

Mother opens the door, open a crack, all the way. She is wearing a gray skirt, a gray blouse with silver threads. Her hair has a gray streak in front like an animal. We have the same colorless plastic glasses. Through her thin lenses, for once, her eyes meet mine.

"You selfish girl"—she doesn't raise her voice. "You selfish girl"—like a folk song. "How could you have been so selfish? Don't I buy you enough?"

PLASTIC FLOWERS

CAROLE L. GLICKFELD

$\mathcal{M}$y whole spring vacation from P.S. 152 my mother spent getting ready for Passover. She redid the foyer closets, vacuuming the back corners and putting in a fresh bunch of mothballs. She laid down new oilcloth on the kitchen shelves and washed the whole inside of the Frigidaire. Roaches came out half dead from behind the stove where she had put a lot of roach powder.

One morning, on account of the garbage truck, I woke up early and found my mother kneeling on the kitchen floor with my father standing over her, yelling the way he does, which was real scary.

I saw them from the foyer. My mother couldn't see me because my father stood between us, but I saw her hand spelling out, "B-u-s-y l-a-t-e-r."

My father exploded. "NOW!" he barked, signing at the same time. "R-u-t-h sleep now, l-a-t-e-r t-o-o l-a-t-e!" When he moved to one side my mother saw me. She waved her arm, making him turn.

I explained about the garbage truck, looking at the giant freckles on his shoulders. I wondered why he didn't have his shirt on yet, since the rest of him was dressed. He didn't say anything, just walked out of the kitchen.

I sat down on the linoleum where the soup boxes and cans of vegetables were all spread out. My mother let me help her dust them off. Usually I had to beg her to do anything, such as dry dishes. At my best friend Glory's it was just the opposite. Her mother, Dot, always made long lists of things for Glory and Roy Rogers to do. Once, when I asked Dot if I could help her water the plants, Glory got mad and almost stopped speaking to me.

When the things were put away, I had cornflakes and milk, then I got dressed. My mother changed her slippers to shoes and put her raincoat on over her housedress. We took the shopping cart with us to the A&P to do the Passover shopping.

My mother knew just what she wanted, even though she never made lists because her writing wasn't very good. We got two of the ten-pound boxes of matzo, six of the big jars of gefilte fish, two jars of herring in sour cream, and six cans of macaroons, half almond and half chocolate. There was more to get but that's all we could fit in the cart. Going up the four flights of our building, she held the front end. I had the back end.

My parents didn't talk to each other during lunch, which was our main meal because my father worked nights at the post office. The only sounds were of the forks and knives on the plates and my father's chewing.

When my mother was done with the dishes, she said the plastic flowers needed a bath. That didn't surprise me. She washed them right after we had bought them at the Five and Ten, before school started, and then again before Chanukah. I went and got the flowers from the vase in the foyer and the three vases in the living room, tiptoeing so I wouldn't wake my father, who was taking a nap in his chair, like he always did before work.

While I sat at the kitchen table reading the Inquiring Photographer in the *Daily News*, my mother swished the flowers around in the soapy water in the deep sink next to the regular one. "Full dirt," she said. "Look black." As she signed she accidentally spritzed me with suds. "Sorry," she said, smiling with her lips closed and her dimples showing. She let the water go down and then put more Vel in and filled up the sink again. The third time she didn't put soap in. When she held up the flowers to shake the water off, I hardly recognized them. Instead of the loud reds, oranges, and blues we had picked out at the Five and Ten, there were only pastels.

"Wash make f-a-d-e," I told her.

She shook her head. "Sun f-a-d-e. Wash make bright."

But the flowers looked sick. The green plastic leaves had yellow spots as though they were about to die.

"T-o-o f-u-s-s-y," she said to me, but she was always saying that, like when I put the flowers in the vases according to the colors. I couldn't stand colors clashing, which I learned about from Mrs. Drucker, my art teacher in school.

My mother put the flowers on the drainboard to finish drying and said she was going to get dressed. It always took her a long time to put on her good brassiere and corset and nylon stockings and a real dress (instead of her housedress). I asked if I could get the rest of the Passover things at the A&P while she got ready. I could hardly believe it when she said okay.

At the A&P, I got the matzo meal, kosher coarse salt, and farfel, then stood in line with my cart, looking to see what everyone else was buying. I could tell a lot about someone from what was in their cart, like if they had a dog or a bird, or if they were Catholic, since Jews didn't eat bacon or pork chops.

I was straining my eyes to see what the label said on a package in the cart over on the next aisle when I heard a voice say, "Is your mother all right?" I looked up and saw Mrs. O'Meara, her freckled face and a bit of red hair sticking out from her white kerchief. "I never seen you alone in here before," she said.

I told her my mother was getting dressed to go out.

"Passover's almost here," she said, looking at my cart. "Easter is this Sunday already." In her cart there were two packages of hot cross buns. My mother always got cake at Goldin's Bakery on Dyckman, which didn't have stuff with white icing on them. I asked her what was in the package that looked like a giant sponge.

"Tripe," she said. "Pig's stomach."

I giggled. Once Glory had tried to tell me that the tongue my mother cooked was a real animal's tongue. That wasn't as silly as a pig's stomach, though.

Mrs. O'Meara and I walked back to Arden Street together. On the stoop she made a big sigh. "I'll be doing the windows this afternoon," she said. Then she smiled. "If it wasn't for Easter, the O'Mearas'd be living in a dirty pigsty."

That surprised me. I didn't know that people who weren't Jewish did extra cleaning. I wasn't even sure that all Jewish people did it, because I thought my mother had a thing about it.

Mrs. O'Meara went up to her building, across the stoop from us. I ran up the four flights three steps at a time. As soon as I opened the door I heard a funny noise, like a strap hitting something. My father was yelling "Never, never" while the thwackthwackthwack got louder. Then I saw him hitting the edge of the sink with the plastic flowers.

"Spoil," my mother said.

My father shoved the window open and threw the flowers out. He slammed the window down so hard I could feel the floor shake. My mother made a funny sound, like deaf people make sometimes, like a doll saying "Ma-a-a-a."

Not knowing what else to do, I went in and put the bag on the table. My father came up to me and hugged me with his right arm. Out of the corner of my eye I could see his left hand spelling out to my mother, "A-l-w-a-y-s b-u-s-y." Then he let go of me and went out of the kitchen.

"Think himself," my mother said. "Never help." She meant he never helped her around the house.

"Go down flower?" I asked, meaning should I go down and get the flowers from the alley, but she wrinkled up her nose. "D-o-g pish," she said, meaning dogs pished down there.

"Buy new?" I asked.

"A-l-b-e-r-t fault," she said, meaning it was my father's fault we didn't have enough flowers now and she wasn't going to do anything about it. I followed her into the bedroom and watched her put on lipstick, first making the outline and then filling it in before she rubbed her lips together and blotted them with tissue. The lipstick was too orangey for her dress.

I waved good-bye to my father and we went out, first to Fort Tryon Park, where the deaf people met around the sandbox in the playground. "Things d-o," my mother told them, so we didn't stay long.

At the kosher butcher's on Dyckman we got two chickens. I was hoping we'd go to the Five and Ten for something, but we crossed Dyckman and went to Goldin's and got a rye bread, sliced with seeds.

"Last bread," my mother signed to me, while they were slicing, meaning it was the last rye we'd be getting before Passover, when we had matzo instead.

At Nick's Fruits we got some bananas and apples, then we turned the corner onto Nagle. Right away we both noticed there was a new store where the glove store had gone out of business. We went up to the window. There was a cardboard sign with black letters: MAHMOUD'S GARDEN. There were also vases in the window with flowers. Plastic flowers. A woman came out of the store with red roses sticking out of a brown bag.

"O-n-l-y look," my mother said, starting to go in. "J-u-s-t look," she said again as soon as we were in the door.

It was dark inside, probably because the lights on the ceiling weren't spaced close together. Lots of ladies were crowded next to each other, bending over the barrels of plastic flowers lined up against the walls. Each barrel had a different kind and color of flower.

When I started signing to my mother I realized she wasn't next to me anymore. Then I saw her down the aisle, digging in a barrel of red tulips. The chickens and fruit were on the floor between her legs. She looked up. "Ask how much," she signed.

I went up to the man at the cash register and asked him. He stared for a moment like he didn't hear me. His face was large and the color of a Nestle's bar. He had thick black eyebrows and a mustache much bigger than my father's. My father's was a reddish blond.

"Is that your mother?" the man asked me. "The deaf-and-dumb lady?"

"She's not dumb," I said. "She's a deaf-mute."

"Don't get me wrong. I didn't mean nothing," he said. "Explain to your mother that because she's so beautiful I give her the flowers twenty for a dollar and five for free. For everyone else, it's ten for a dollar."

I didn't tell her the part about being beautiful. I wondered why the dark man said that. My mother was short, only four-feet-eight-inches. Already I was taller than her. She had light brown hair pulled back from her little round face, made into large pompadours on both sides, which she stuck big combs into. She had to hold in her huge bust and stomach with a brassiere and corset. Otherwise the front of her was like two stacked beach balls. But in a dress she didn't look fat. She was wearing her red-and-white checkered two-piece and black laced oxfords with medium heels from Red Cross Shoes on Dyckman.

We took our time, walking up and down the store, looking into each barrel. All around us ladies were grabbing at the flowers and calling out to each other. Then the dark man came up to us and whispered in my ear, "Tell your mother she is the most beautiful flower in my garden."

My mother was curious what he said. "You pretty," I told her.

She smiled at him with her teeth showing. She had a funny look on her face, like she was trying not to show her feelings. I don't think she liked him. "Clever make friends," she signed to me.

He asked me what she'd said.

I shrugged my shoulders. "Nothing."

"Come on, little sweetheart, what did your mother say? Does she like me?"

"P-e-s-t," I told my mother.

He tried to talk to her himself. Without saying it out loud, he mouthed the word "beautiful" and pointed to her eyes.

My mother has brown eyes, nothing special.

"What is her name?" he asked me.

"Hannah Zimmer," I said. "Know your name," I signed to her.

She smiled.

"You German?" he said. He looked kind of funny. So I said, "My mother's Russian. She was born there."

"My name is Mahmoud Abdullah," he said. "I spell it for you, so you can tell your mother."

When I got done spelling it, my mother said, "T-o-o long, can't remember."

That almost made me giggle.

A lady yelled from the cash register about who was going to take her money. "Sweetheart, I'm coming," he yelled, walking away from us. I could see him watching us as he rang the register. By the time he came back we had picked out three yellow tulips. He sort of pushed his way between us and reached into the barrel. He stuffed a whole handful of yellow tulips into a brown paper bag. "What else? What else?" he asked. "What does she like?" he asked me. He walked up the aisle, grabbing handfuls from different barrels and putting them into the bag, then he gave the bag to my mother.

"How much?" My mother asked him herself, mouthing the words.

He waved his hands.

"Think f-r-e-e?" my mother signed to me. She was smiling so that all her teeth showed.

I don't know why, but I felt squirmy inside.

Another lady was yelling by the register, so Mr. Abdullah excused himself. My mother and I just stood there. "See ring," my mother said, pointing to her wedding band. "Know me married," she said.

When Mr. Abdullah came back, he gave my mother a card that said "Mahmoud's Garden" on it. He mouthed to her, "You come back tomorrow morning."

My mother nodded. I could tell she didn't get what he said.

He pointed to the shelf. "I give you a vase tomorrow. Any one you want."

I told my mother.

"Maybe feel sorry, me deaf," she said, blowing him a kiss with her hand to say thank you.

I looked at the shelf to see if there was anything nice. There was a vase with a Chinese lady on the front of it. Her blue-and-pink dress had lots of material so there were waves at the bottom of the vase and around the sides. The top of the vase was green and orange. A lot of different flowers could go in it.

He saw me looking. "Tell her she should come back in the morning," he said.

Halfway up Arden Street my mother said she had left the bread at the flower store, so I ran down the block to get it. Mr. Abdullah held up the bag when he saw me. "Where do you live?" he asked.

"Sickles," I lied. "Twenty-two Sickles." I wondered if he'd find out, because that was where Marilyn Jaffe lived and I went to her house sometimes after school to help her with long division.

"I'm saving the vase," he said before I took the bread and ran up the street.

When I told my mother he wanted to know where we lived, she shook her head and closed her lips so you could hardly see the lipstick.

I asked if we were going to get the vase tomorrow.

She thought for a second. "Handsome man," she said.

I didn't see how she could think he was handsome, but then she thought my father was handsome. That's why she married him, she told me once.

As soon as we got upstairs I counted the flowers. There were fifty-seven, more than five dollars' worth at the regular price. My mother washed them while I had milk and rye bread with butter. My father had already left for work. When the flowers were dry, I laid them out according to the colors and put them in vases. I had a lot left over, which made me wish for the Chinese Lady, but I didn't know if I wanted my mother to see Mr. Abdullah again.

Still, when I woke up the next morning the first thing I thought of was how to make her. I went to the kitchen but she wasn't there. She wasn't in the bathroom either, so I went to the other bedroom where my father was probably still sleeping. I figured she was in there, cleaning drawers or something. I couldn't believe my eyes when I opened the door. My father was lying on his back and my mother was sitting on the edge of the bed next to him. His hands were on top of her breasts. She jumped up when she saw me. "Go k-i-t-c-h-e-n," she said.

I poured my own cornflakes and milk in a bowl and read the Inquiring Photographer. The question was about what people were giving up for Lent. I knew Glory was giving up desserts. Then my mother came in and I asked her why my father was touching her bust, but she said he wasn't.

"Saw," I said.

She shook her head. "Know too much. Like grown-up." That meant she wasn't going to tell me anything.

It was ten-thirty. Mr. Abdullah said she should see him in the morning, but she was still in her housedress. She never went anywhere in her housedress except the A&P with her coat on over. She never put her real dress on till the afternoon. I wondered if he would wait.

After lunch, though, my mother didn't get dressed. When I reminded her about the vase, she said, "B-u-s-y, see l-a-t-e-r." I went down with her to the washing machines in the basement. We sat on the folding chairs waiting for the bedspreads to get done. Then we pulled them through the wringer, my mother standing on one side and me on the other. We carried the cart upstairs after that.

Just as I was done handing my mother clothespins to hang the bedspreads out on the washline, my father came in looking for a toothpick. That's when he noticed the flowers. "Buy new?" he asked my mother.

"F-r-e-e, man give," my mother said. "Crazy."

"True?" he asked, like he thought she was lying.

I waved at him. "Man like Mama, give flowers," I said.

For some reason, that made him even madder. He grabbed my mother's arm and pulled her out of the kitchen. "I-n-n-o-c-e-n-t," she spelled out to him before they turned the corner.

Since I knew my mother was going to wash the kitchen window and curtains, I climbed up on the windowsill and got down the rods, then put the chintz curtains into the big sink. I listened for angry sounds from my father, but I couldn't hear any.

Soon my mother came back. She noticed the window right away. "Thank help," she said.

"Daddy mad?" I asked.

"Cool," she said, meaning he had cooled down. She handed me some money, but not for shopping. "Go movie," she said.

"Today?" It was Thursday and usually I went on Saturdays. She gave me thirty-five cents, even though the movie only cost a quarter and I never got more than a nickel for candy.

"E-n-j-o-y." she said.

When I got outside I started toward where the Loew's was, but on Nagle I crossed the other way and went into Mahmoud's Garden. Mr. Abdullah came running up to me and asked where my mother was. He called her Mrs. Hannahzimmer, like it was all one word. I pretended to smile and said she was busy. Then real quick I asked how much the Chinese Lady was, holding out my hand with the quarter and dime in it.

He looked kind of funny all of a sudden and then I realized he was looking outside the store. A dark woman with a brown scarf around her head and some dark children with her were crossing Nagle toward us. It had to be Mrs. Abdullah.

He took the money out of my hand and put the vase in a brown bag and kind of shoved it at me. "Tomorrow," he said, and went to the back of the store.

I held the door open for Mrs. Abdullah. The kids were all fat but she was real skinny. Beautiful and dark, like my friend Glory, without being Negro.

I sat in the library all afternoon, looking at the magazines and trying to read a book, but I kept thinking about Mahmoud Abdullah. I wondered if he was looking for white slaves. Marilyn Jaffe's big sister had told us about white slaves and she wasn't kidding. I tried to imagine how he would get my mother and me into the back of his store to chain us up before he took us away. I got real mad at him because he must have thought my mother was dumb, just because she was deaf.

At three-thirty, when I figured the movie was over, I went home. My father was napping in his chair, even though he was taking the day off from work. My mother had done the kitchen window, top and bottom, and was washing the curtains. Right away she asked me what was in the brown bag, so I opened it up and took out the Chinese Lady.

She put her fingers over her lips. "Tell A-l-b-e-r-t," she said, meaning I shouldn't say anything to my father. She looked like she was going to say something, but she started rubbing the curtains against the washboard. I put the leftover flowers, as many as I could fit, in the Chinese Lady and waited for my mother to turn around. But when she did, she didn't notice.

"Not t-r-u-s-t." she said, meaning Mr. Abdullah. "Touch you?" she asked.

She had told me before about letting men touch me. "Me not stupid," I told her.

"Careful," she said, then took the rubber plug out of the sink. She wrung out the curtains and pointed to the overhead drying rack, which I let down because the washline outside was full. When she was done hanging, I pulled the rope until the rack was close to the ceiling again. My mother still hadn't said anything about the vase.

"Pretty?" I asked her.

"Give f-r-e-e?"

I told her it cost me thirty-five cents.

"N-o movie?"

I shook my head. "L-i-b-r-a-r-y read."

"Devil," my mother said to me, but I could tell she wasn't mad. "Help rug last," she said, meaning I should help her with the rug and that was the last thing we were going to have to do before Passover. First, though, she made me put the Chinese Lady in my room.

We rolled up the rug from the living room, careful not to wake my father, who was snoring. She took one end and I took the other and we carried it up to the roof. She took out a rope from the pocket of her housedress and strung it across, like a washline, between two posts, and we put the rug over it. Then my mother went and got the brushes.

She showed me how to beat on the rug to make the dust come out. Soon we were almost choking and my eyes were burning from the dust. The sky was a bright pink and way above there was a dark gray cloud which I pretended was made from the dust that came out of the rug, to keep from thinking about how my arms were killing me. Switching the brush from one hand to the other didn't help.

The wind started to blow and things were creaking all around us, which of course my mother couldn't hear, so it didn't scare her. I heard a noise like someone was opening one of the doors to the roof. What if it's Mr. Abdullah, I thought, coming to take us away? But it was only Glory and Roy Rogers. She was going to show him her secret hiding place for special rocks, which I already knew about.

"Haven't seen you all week," she said. "You angry or something?"

"I've been helping my mother," I said. "A lot."

"Big deal." When I didn't say anything, she asked if I could come down after supper.

"Okay," I said. I was dying to show her the Chinese Lady before my mother washed it.

"What'cha doing?" Roy Rogers asked.

"Getting the dust out," I said, beating harder to show him.

"A poison cloud!" Glory screamed. Both of them went running across the roof to get away.

My mother stuck her head around the rug. "Give e-x-t-r-a flower G-l-o-r-y," she said, meaning the four red tulips and two white carnations I couldn't get into the Chinese Lady.

I nodded, thinking that maybe I could trade her for a chocolate Easter egg, the kind that had flowers on top in different colors of icing.

Soon the dust stopped coming out. The cloud above was gone, too, and the sky was almost purple. We got the rug off the line and started rolling it up, when I heard a lot of creaking, then heavy footsteps. I told my mother, but I was too scared to look myself. Behind me the footsteps were getting louder. My mother got an expression on her face like she saw something she didn't expect. I was dying.

"S-i-l-l-y," she said. "Daddy."

"Daddy?" I turned around.

"N-e-e-d help?" my father said.

While my mother got down the rope and wound it up in a ball, my father gave me one end of the rug to hold and he took the other. Then we carried it downstairs. Behind us I could hear the heels of my mother's slippers flopping open on each step. I was glad they had made up with each other while I was gone. But I was sure my mother wouldn't let him touch her again you know where.

ON ROCKAWALKIN ROAD

for Hannah

JEAN NORDHAUS

Two in step, we walk
beside the sea, you
in my body, blue jeans
wet to the crotch, your t-shirt
lettered with the name
I gave you

though I'd take it back now,
stuff you down inside
until we're warm, you

pirate, stealing my life
with your two-moon
buttocks, wing-stubs
small and sharp.

Fly, robin, fly,
I sing. *You're in my heart,*
you're in my soul, you answer.
Line of driftwood from a passing
song.

It's wrong. My body
will be walking down the beach
without me, long
after my name is gone
spelling me out again
in bone and limb
in daughters rocking
daughters

walking, fly, robin, fly.
Half-drenched in salt
and singing, some girl
will be dangling my legs
in the white
mouth of the sea.

PART THREE

ﻉﻟ

SURVIVING, PRESERVING, BELONGING

There is a certain place where dumb-waiters boom, doors slam, dishes crash; every window is a mother's mouth bidding the street shut up, go skate somewhere else, come home.

Grace Paley,
"The Loudest Voice"

LISTENING TO MYSELF
ON MY DAUGHTER'S
MESSAGE MACHINE

BETTY BUCHSBAUM

This is your mother—at two in the morning from London
I'm calling—just back from Rome—Thought I'd quick
try to catch you—Maybe a little later—again I'll try—
'til seven they still charge less to talk—But
I don't want you should depend on me staying up . . .

It does me strange justice, this voice my daughter saved,
taping it off her message machine
so she can store it away for her children.

Was it the rain those months in London that made me speak
like that—washing off outer layers so you heard
the Yiddish flavors of my Lower East Side grandparents?

And the rain that Roman Easter as I stood outside
St. Peter's—bells tolling in the downpour
the resurrection of the spirit—

did it waken in my ear the spectral tongue and cadence
of grandmothers Kate and Leah who kept urging
the next day on my return to London—

I should go—pick up a phone—and give a call
to the children scattered in Denver, Philadelphia,
Boston. And early morning when I connected,

not with a daughter but with her message machine
(one beep at my back and another about to silence me),
did the grandmothers purse their lips and whisper

about this latest tyranny, did they roll up
their sleeves and show me how to work against time
with dignity: starting slow, like an update

on weather, reporting my foreign movements at some
crazy hour, yet at the canny moment
tying loose ends up with a flourish:

. . . *read your letter, read your card (kiss).*
Love you darling (kiss), and as if shutting a door
for a brief turn round the block, *bye-bye.*

PLUMBING

ADA JILL SCHNEIDER

I don't want to talk about plumbing;
plumbing is just in or out.
I want to talk about the thunderous
cascade of a rain forest in your shower
that numbs your skull, leaves you limp,
lets you slip like soap into the moist,
humid recesses of your tangled mind
to breathe freer—clear
of appointment books, obligations,
incessant demands of humanity
on whose snapped plumb line
you hang stunned
by indecisive reverberations
like a clapper out of control—
bonged, gonged, donged
relentlessly between generations;
tolling in time to everyone's wants—
chipping your features blunt,
becoming a frenzied, thudding
lump of response, hanging
on for dear life, clinging
to a translucent stream of water
that runs down the drain
when the phone rings.
I don't want to talk about phones.

IN MY MOTHER'S HOUSE:
EPILOGUE

KIM CHERNIN

AUGUST 1981

$\mathcal{S}$he calls us on the telephone two times the day before we are due to arrive in Los Angeles. The first time she says, "You know that spinach loaf I make? You think Larissa would like it?" "The spinach loaf? With carrots and wheat germ? She'd love it." "Good," says my mother, "I already baked it."

Our second conversation is like the first. "I found a recipe," she says. "I made kugel. Just like Mama used to make. But now the question is, should we go out instead for dinner maybe?"

Her third call comes the next day, a few hours before we are leaving. "Maybe we should go out after all," she says. "How many times in a life does a person get accepted to Harvard?"

"Mama," I say, "are you kidding? I told Larissa about that spinach loaf. We didn't eat since yesterday morning. Just to have a big appetite when we arrive."

"You don't say," she sighs, "since yesterday." And then she realizes I'm kidding. "You," she says, "you can't fool me. Didn't you just tell me you were cooking breakfast?"

On the way to the airport Larissa is silent. She drives fast, moving the car easily between the trucks and buses on the Bayshore Freeway. I remember teaching her to ride the bus alone, going back and forth with her between home and school. As we are passing the Coliseum, she says, "What if I have a boy someday?"

"We'll love him, of course. It goes without saying."

"But what will happen to our pattern?"

I try hard to keep my voice casual. She doesn't like it when I get melodramatic. "I've heard it takes four generations to make a gentleman,"

I say. "Maybe it takes four to make someone really at home in a new country."

"Me? The goal of all these generations?"

She has a way of jabbing at my inflations. I like it, but it doesn't keep me from talking. "I've been to Europe at least six times since you were born. I've been to Israel. Always looking for my 'real home.' When I first got interested in feminism, I had the feeling every time I went to a women's event that I'd found a homeland. I've never been able to settle in."

"I didn't like it when you went to Israel," she says, ignoring my outburst.

"You could have come. I wanted to take you."

"Peter Minkov told me there was a war. I was afraid." She always refers to her father in this way, formally.

"You were eight years old, the war had ended at least five years earlier. And anyway, why didn't you just tell me?"

"Because I was eight years old."

She turns the wheel sharply, moves out into the fast lane, and passes a few cars.

"You remember that time we went back to Dublin and you left me there with Moira?"

"Yeah?"

"You didn't say good-bye. How old was I then?"

"Five or six. I'm not sure. Why?"

"You told me you'd wake me up from my nap. But when I got up you were gone."

"I let Moira convince me. I thought it would be easier that way."

"How did I know you'd come back?"

She reaches up to adjust the rearview mirror, giving me a pointed look. But then her mood changes and she begins to reminisce. She can, when it pleases her, set aside her sophistication and chatter like a much younger girl. It's one of her most lovable traits, and I find myself hoping she will never lose it. "Moira told us she was a witch. I guess I was only five. She said she was two hundred years old. And we believed her."

"You wouldn't believe something like that at the age of six."

"Did you ever think," she says, "all that work to make the fourth generation into an American? And I was born in Dublin."

Her laughter reminds me suddenly what it is like to be this young. There is something in it still so trusting of life.

"I don't think I want to be a writer," she says, changing her mood.

"What then?"

"I don't know. Science is a dead end. There's nothing left but smaller and smaller particles. Maybe philosophy. I want something"—she takes her hand from the steering wheel and stretches it out, defining a large space—"where you can still *do* something . . ." Her voice trails off. "Lasting, original, immense," are the words I hear, but she doesn't speak them. She's the same age I was when I went to Moscow. She's the age my mother was when she left Waterbury and went to New York. I'm glad she too is audacious.

"When I tell people I might study philosophy they say I'll end up being a computer programmer. Everyone knows someone who studied philosophy at Harvard and ended up selling stockings in Macy's."

"Don't you believe it." I know I should retreat from this intensity, but I don't want to. "I don't care how many people end up doing nothing. It doesn't have to happen to you. It didn't happen to Grandma. It didn't happen to me. There *are* exceptions. Why not you?"

She raises her eyebrows, mocking me. But finally she says, very quickly, before leaving the whole discussion, "I'm glad you think that. It's a relief."

"Do you believe me?"

She looks at me for a moment, vaguely sardonic. But then she says, "Yes," very firmly, and the conversation is closed.

The plane is late, of course. We hang around in the magazine shop, waiting. She slips her arm through mine and we stroll out to the gate. Twenty minutes pass, a half-hour. We're silent, but our shoulders lean together, almost touching. "Do you think I have a good memory?" she says. It's an airport mood.

"Of course. Are you kidding? You remember everything you read."

"I don't mean that."

"You used to be able to remember things that happened when you were one or two years old. It was extraordinary."

"I can remember all the houses we lived in since Peter Minkov left. After Stanyan Street we moved to Sausalito. Then to Berkeley, before you went to

Israel. Then I lived with Peter and Susan in Fairfax. When you came back we lived with Bob in Belvedere. Then we lived in the Raleigh house, in the collective. And then you and Bob bought the house on Euclid. Seven houses. Before I was nine years old."

Suddenly I realize what all this is about. We are separating again, now that she is planning to leave for college. And no doubt it is intensely painful. But I know not to say anything directly. She has her own way with these things, and her own wisdom.

"I gave you a hard time with all those moves, didn't I?"

"That's not what I'm saying."

"Maybe not."

She takes a few restless steps toward the ticket counter. People are beginning to line up for the plane. Then she comes over and puts her book bag over her shoulder. "When I went for my interview they asked me how I was going to make a living if I studied philosophy. Did I tell you? I said I would probably teach and the man said, 'What about getting married?' "

I pick up my overnight bag and look at her. Never again will there be a little girl racing to me across the school playground waving a drawing. "What did you say?"

"Well, I told him it never had occurred to me. And you know, it hadn't."

We wander out across the landing field. A dry wind is blowing. I can feel the drift of something unspoken. "And maybe I don't want to have children," she says, as we climb the stairs to the plane.

"I didn't think I'd have kids. And just look what happened."

"Wish you could change your mind?"

"What? Are you kidding?" My arm goes out and wraps around her. "The way I love you?"

We crowd past the stewardess and enter the plane. Larissa smiles happily, and I see that this burst of feeling was precisely what she wanted.

When we arrive in Los Angeles I look around for my mother. Even while we're waiting for our Avis car I keep glancing around. But when we're driving out of the lot and I take a sharp right and head out along Airport Boulevard, I remember living in this city. And I'm scared suddenly that maybe she's really ill, and not just overworked and exhausted.

"It seems funny that Grandma didn't come," Larissa says.

"You think it was easy to keep her at home? She doesn't listen to doctors. 'I'm almost eighty years old,' she says. 'I figured out how to live this long, so you think maybe I know something more than they do?'"

"You really don't have a great Yiddish accent."

"But you have quite a tongue."

The streets grow more familiar as we turn on Century.

"Are you going to get along this time?" Larissa asks.

"We've never been better."

"The great reconciliation scene?"

"Something like that." I wait, all due respect to her playfulness. "You know what she did when she read my last chapter?"

"Tore her hair? Rent her garments? Covered herself in ash?"

"You're not always the easiest person in the world to talk to."

"I know. Other people have told me that."

Now I'm irritated and it's hard to get going again. "I'll tell you later. I'm not in the mood." But I want to tell her the story.

"I wish you'd try. Really." She looks serious now.

"Well," I say, drawing it out, "I left the manuscript downstairs, the way I told you. The minute I got back to bed I fell sound asleep and I didn't wake up until eight o'clock the next morning. Then I heard her in the kitchen. And I was scared. I knew it was all right, and then again I didn't know. I went down there. She was making tea, setting out the dishes on the table. The minute she sees me she starts to talk. 'There used to be a bookstore on Fifth Avenue,' she says. Just like that. 'It was called the Classical Bookstore,' she says. 'I went in there one day. You know how it is, I liked the name. The owner was a crippled man and that, too, interested me. Later, he even came to visit and had tea. That was before I married Paul Kusnitz . . .'

"Then she stopped talking. Well, I know better than to ask her questions, so I waited. And finally she says, 'I wanted to get a copy of Dante's *Purgatorio*. I don't like to read in translations, and I figured, I've had four years of Latin, maybe I can translate for myself. I talked to this man, and he found me a dictionary and he found a copy in Italian. I was working then in a lady's garment shop. But after work I'd go home and sit at the table with the dictionary and read the *Purgatorio*.'"

"That's it?" Larissa says, trying to figure it out.

"That's it. She wanted me to know she understood what made me into a poet."

"You'll never argue again?"

"I'm not saying that. We're both very passionate. Secretly, we wish anyone we love will think exactly the way we do. For her, the entire meaning of her life depends on the success of the Russian Revolution."

"Well," she says, still keeping it light, "isn't that what it means to be a Communist?"

"I think you can admire her life no matter what you feel about Soviet Communism."

Larissa looks skeptical, then she says, "When I went for my Harvard interview I told them my grandmother was a Communist."

"Are you kidding? You're lucky you got in."

"They asked if I was interested in politics," she says with a knowing smile. "I started talking about Grandma. I felt proud of her." She pauses here to think it over. "It's hard to believe my own grandmother has lived that kind of life. When I was little I used to want the kind of grandmother who bakes things. But not now."

"You can't imagine what it was like growing up in my mother's house," I say, overjoyed suddenly to be bringing her home with me. "We had the most amazing social life. Barbecues in Griffith Park when the Armenian community was holding a national celebration. Korean banquets at the home of her friends. We knew Greeks and Latvians and Bulgarians. We had a friend named John who wore shorts and sandals even in the winter and rode his bicycle all over Los Angeles. And that, remember, was in the late forties. He brought us a wonderful yogurt culture from Bulgaria. My father used to make it in a huge green crock."

"I remember when you tried to make pickles in that crock. They came out all covered in dill, with no taste. You forgot the salt."

I can see her eyes in the rearview mirror. They have a fine, deep glow of love in them. Suddenly she looks right over at me.

"If your mother heard you talk about her life like this she wouldn't be happy? She'd still want you to believe in the socialist revolution?"

"Maybe she's been able to do what she's done because she believes so strongly in something. There are hundreds of people who would have been jailed or deported if it weren't for her. Or some other organizer with the same system of belief. It makes you wonder, should you judge a life by the ideology that inspires it? Or by what that ideology, true or false, inspires the life to do? It's a whole different way to measure truth."

"Or to measure your attachment to your mother."

This time I look at her. She's smiling, and I can see she's uncertain about how far she can go with me on this point.

"I have a feeling you're going to be crying soon," she says, but her voice is much more gentle than she would ever imagine.

During dinner the phone keeps ringing. "I can't talk now," my mother says, standing next to the table. "My daughter and my granddaughter are here."

Then, setting the phone down, she says, "If you would dream a life could you dream something better?"

Larissa goes into the kitchen and turns off the teakettle. My mother leans over and whispers in my ear. "I'm almost eighty years old," she says. "Look at my life. My mother, the one literate woman in our shtetl. And today, my own granddaughter going to Harvard."

While we are drinking tea she stand up suddenly and goes off into her bedroom. She has moved since Gertrude's death and has bought herself a little house in a beautiful project at the foot of the Baldwin Hills. My high school is three or four blocks away. Now black people are living in those hills we can see so clearly from her patio. All the others have moved away.

She comes back into the room wearing a little pair of knit slippers. The doctor has told her to rest and she is trying. "I have some money for you two," she says. "What do I need it for? At my age, the needs are little. If I get sick I know you won't let me die because of a few dollars."

"I'm glad you know that about me," I say, strangely relieved that she does.

"I know you. A mother knows her child," she says.

After dinner Larissa goes out for a jog. We can see her, in her red running shorts, looping around the lawns, past the roses and camelias, beneath the olive trees. But then we turn back into the room and my mother sits down in her large chair, near the bookcase. I look at her balancing her checkbook. She has developed a child's very deep concentration. To open her purse, to look through it searching for her glasses, takes time, a deliberate focusing of attention. It removes her from me, sets her apart in her own world, with that serious frown which makes a kingdom out of a sandbox.

She crosses her legs and takes off one slipper. She is the size of a ten-year-old child, but her head is large and her expression very grave; it gives to this woman, born in a shtetl, who has lived her whole life among the people, a curious air of nobility.

Since I saw her last she has entered into old age. The masks have been thrust off and she has regained the ability to pass rapidly from one pure state of feeling to another. Above all, she loves with such intensity that she cannot keep still. And so she cries out, "What shall I do with all this joy? Do you know how happy you have made me? How will I keep it inside?" And then she presses her hand to her heart and squeezes down, her eyes spilling.

At ten o'clock we make up a bed in the living room. Larissa falls asleep quickly, but I hear my mother moving about in her room. Drawers open and close, there is a patter of feet and then I see her peeping in at me, trying to determine if I am sleeping. I wave to her, and she crooks her finger at me, beckoning.

Her room is large and perfectly ordered. There is a bright afghan on the bed, crocheted for her by a deportee from her committee. On the wall near the window a large oil painting of two Chinese women soldiers sitting with their guns and reading together from a book. On the dresser there are photographs. And then I see something new. She comes over to stand beside me. "That's what I wanted to show you," she says. "I found it. In the drawer with the letters. My friend Anna Gloria is a printer. She made this for you and put a frame on it." She reaches up to take it down from the wall. "So read," she says, pushing it into my hands. Her love for me has taken possession of her face. She shakes me lightly by the shoulder. I remember a large hall; hundreds of people there, at long tables covered in white cloths. I came all dressed up, and I went up to the stage when my name was announced. I talked into a microphone. And even before I opened my mouth I saw the old women, sitting together, nudging and whispering, the handkerchiefs coming out.

"Shall I recite it for you?"

"Oy," she says, pressing her hand to her heart, "would you do that?"

I glance down at the page, but I realize at once that I don't need it. For more than twenty years I have remembered every word of this speech I gave at her birthday celebration after she was released from jail.

I would like to greet you on my mother's fiftieth birthday, and tell you what her great fight for freedom and equal rights for all peoples has meant to me. All my life she has taught me to fight for my rights and for the rights of other minority groups. . . . My mother has been a guiding light and a strong influence. . . . I also know now that more than anything in the world I would like to follow in her footsteps and earn from you people the love that she has earned.

I stop, remembering how true these words once were for me. And now, as I go on reciting, I can for the first time in my life acknowledge the longing which even then I saw in her face.

She has been sitting on her bed, her legs drawn up and her bathrobe tucked carefully around her. When I finish, she holds out her hand. "There it is," she says, "there it is. Always the people."

I notice that she has taken a small drawer out of her dresser. She pats the bed next to her and I sit. Then she reaches into the drawer and takes out a little velvet box. "This is my wedding ring," she says, handing me the thin silver band. "And here's the ring your father gave me when we were married twenty-five years." She reaches over and opens my hand. "It's time for me to divest," she says.

My hands shake as I receive the rings. "Look inside," she whispers. "You'll see the dates." I turn it and hold it up to the light. Inside, in a delicate script, it says: *P. K. R. C. June 21, '26.* She is rummaging in the drawer again. She takes out a beautiful silver necklace and hands it to me. "Heirlooms we don't have in our family. But stories we've got." As I put it around my neck she begins to rock herself, her hands gripping her knees. Softly, she hums a tune I remember from many, many years ago. "It's the story of Stenka Razin," she says. "You remember? The great peasant leader. This necklace your father got for me when we were traveling down the Volga."

She goes back to looking in the drawer. "Good, here it is, I thought I lost it maybe." The drawer yields up a pin with a hammer and sickle. This, too, is passed on to me. She brings out a gold pendant in the shape of a triangle. It holds a red stone set in gold and I can see at once that it is valuable. "This one, a lady gave me after a speech. She came up, she took it from her neck and put it on mine. 'Because of the work you've done, Rose Chernin,' she said. You see this inscription? G 12732. That was her number from the concentration camp." She reaches over and puts the pendant around my neck. "You'll take good care," she says. "This is my life here."

I realize that Larissa is standing in the doorway, watching. She has been asleep and she looks very young, her hair tossed about, her cheeks flushed. Is it really true that she is going away from home in a few months? My mother opens her arms and to my immense surprise my daughter comes over, lies down on the bed and puts her head on my mother's lap. I take her feet and hold them, squeezing tightly. My mother says to her, "When you were a little girl you'd come to visit. I'd give you a bath, dinner of course, and then I'd pick you up to put you to bed. And you'd say, 'When I grow up I'm going to carry *you* around. Because *you* are a little grandma.'"

As she says this I remember a dream. I was walking about all over the world carrying a burden in my arms. In the beginning I was afraid that the burden would be too much for me. But then, as I kept walking, I found that the burden was growing lighter and lighter and I could not tell, looking down, whether it was my mother or my child.

Larissa stretches herself and turns over onto her back. "I remember Grandpa Kusnitz," she says, in a sleepy voice. "He used to spin me around in the air. And I remember Bill Taylor," she says. "He was huge. A black man, and he took me with him one time on the plane to Los Angeles. You remember, Grandma?"

My mother strokes her hair, humming the Russian lullaby she used to sing to me. "*Spe moi angel, moi precrasni, bayoushki bayou. Ticha smotret mesyats yasni, callibel twayou.*"

Larissa goes on talking. "I remember walking in a carriage, with Mama and Peter in Dublin. We saw trees and Mama gave me a green leaf with prickly edges."

My mother gestures to me and takes my elbow and pulls me down so that she can whisper in my ear. "Think of it," she says, "a mother and daughter together like this."

Larissa says, "And a granddaughter."

She curls up against me and puts my hand on her head. It's the last time, I think. The last time. It'll never happen again. And my daughter says, "I remember when we came to America. I was one year old. We stopped in New York. In the Bronx. We stayed with Sonia Auerbach and she made me a bed in a drawer."

My mother reaches up for a pillow and puts it under Larissa's head. *"Ti-cha smotret mesyats yasni,"* she sings. And Larissa says, "I know what it means. The bright moon looks on quietly."

My mother goes on humming, Larissa's eyes open and close. And my mother says, "Did I ever tell you about Zayde?"

We have both heard this story before. She told it seven years ago, when I first began to write down her life.

"Well," she says, taking a breath, "when we lived in the shtetl, Friday was always the longest day of the week. And why? Because, of course, we were waiting for Zayde . . ."

But this time she talks with a voice so gentle it will run, I know, right into Larissa's dreaming.

And then it is Sunday, the last day of our visit. Larissa has gone over to see some of my mother's friends who live in the project. A few houses down there is a woman I've known since childhood, a professor of Marxism at the university. Dorothy Healey, who was in jail with my mother, will be moving in next year. Yesterday, when we went out for a walk, an older man came over to meet me. "A comrade," my mother whispered, taking my hand and placing it in his.

These people have lived their whole lives caring about the world. Little by little the dogma has dropped away, and now only the sense of human possibility remains. It makes them tender, in spite of their militancy. And for me they make this housing project strangely like a shtetl.

We are sitting on the little patio behind her house. It is spring, but leaves are falling. A breeze rises suddenly and my mother says, "Do you know the poem by Lermontov? I remember it from when I was a girl."

I look at her, unable to talk.

"Wichaju adin na darogu," she recites, very grandly. *"Skvoz tuman krem-nesti poot blestet / Noch ticha pustenya vnemlet bogu / E zvezda zvezdoyu gavareet."*

She puts her two hands on her cheeks and rocks herself. "Do you know what it means?" I nod, but she translates anyway. "I walk out on the road alone. The path shines through the fog. The night is still. The desert is aware of God. And the stars speak to one another. Why do I feel so lonely?"

There are tears in her eyes. I wonder what she is thinking when she falls silent. I do not dare to say a word and finally she says, "It is as beautiful today as it was seventy years ago."

There are words but I do not speak them. I wonder whether in this struggle to become myself I have become what she was as a girl. I say, "Do you remember when you used to recite that poem to me?"

"Do I remember?" Her eyebrows fly up, her eyes sparkle. "You used to climb into my lap. You'd say, 'Mama, tell me.' 'What,' I'd say, 'what shall I tell you, child?' And you, very serious, used to answer, '*Wichaju*, Mama, *wichaju* . . .'"

We do not move. We do not look at one another. But I feel the way something is imparted to me, palpably, passing between us. And then, grabbing my hand, pressing it against her heart, she says, "You remind me of Lermontov. Did I ever tell you that?"

I look around me in this garden behind my mother's house. It has become a wave of light, an affirmation that rises not only beyond sorrow, but from a sense of wondering joy. I glance quickly at my mother, who has fallen silent, and I watch with disbelief the way the distance between us, and all separation, heals over. We are touched by a single motion of forgiveness. Her hand touches my cheek, she calls me by my childhood name, she says, "The birds sing louder when you grow old."

It has grown dark; the breeze is growing cold and yet we sit on here, where the shadows gather, my mother and I together. Above us, on the hills, lights are shimmering in a dusk that seems to be falling earlier for them.

My mother says, "There is a saying I learned in Russia, when I was a child. '*Da nashevo berega, dabro nie daplievot.*' Do you want to translate?"

"Nothing good ever swims to our shores."

"*Da, da,*" she says, "a peasant saying. And do you believe it?"

"Not anymore."

"And yet the people are wise."

"Sometimes a life can grow beyond wisdom."

"So it seems. So it seems."

It is late. My mother is tired. She reaches over to hold my hand. Suddenly she speaks familiar words in a voice I have never heard before. It is pure feeling. It says, "I love you more than life, my daughter. I love you more than life."

SURVIVING

(EXCERPT)

Los Angeles, 1977 / Princeton, 1985

ALICIA   SUSKIN   OSTRIKER

X

Mother my poet, tiny harmless lady
Sad white-headed one
With your squirrel eyes
Your pleading love-me eyes
I have always loved you
Always dreaded you
And now you are nearly a doll
A little wind-up toy
That marches in a crooked circle
Emitting vibrations and clicks.
Mother, if what is lost
Is lost, there remains the duty
Proper to the survivor.
I ask the noble dead to strengthen me.
Mother, chatterer, I ask you also,
You who poured Tennyson
And Browning into my child ear, and you
Who threw a boxful of papers, your novel,
Down the incinerator
When you moved, when your new husband
Said to take only
What was necessary, and you took
Stacks of magazines, jars
Of buttons, trunks of raggy

Clothing, but not your writing.
Were you ashamed? Don't
Run away, tell me my duty,
I will try not to be deaf—
Tell me it is not merely the duty of grief.

POCAHONTAS IN CAMELOT

MAXINE RODBURG

*L*ike all parents, mine always worried—about taxes and money, about a possible upsurge in anti-Semitism, even about the weather—but the year President Kennedy was shot my mother also worried about Thanksgiving, only days away. She was afraid her sisters might think her uppity because Pop had convinced her to get a few things from Tabatchnik's for the family dinner we were hosting. She was cooking the turkey herself, but since we'd moved so recently she couldn't do everything else. Half the pots and pans weren't yet unpacked.

"Everyone knows Tabatchnik's has the best food in the world," my father told her. From my hiding spot just outside their bedroom, I was using the TV's bluish light to cut an old blouse into fringes. My mother had cried when she picked me up at school on Friday and my father had cursed when he came home from work, but now the President's murderer was also dead, and I was hoping that things might get back to normal. School would start again and I would wear the fringed blouse when I presented my report on Pocahontas. "We'll eat like kings," Pop told my mother. "Believe me, honey, your sisters will thank you for it."

"It's not the taste of the food." Mama turned on the hot water in their bathroom and as the sink filled she held her arms above the steam. Then she creamed her arms clear up to her elbows. These nightly treatments kept her hands as soft as butter. "It costs a lot of money, and I don't like to rub their noses in it."

"Buying a little potato salad and cole slaw isn't a crime in New Jersey," Pop said when the water stopped running. He lit a cigar and settled in for the night as Mama went and pulled from her sewing pile the taffeta dresses she had bought Sue and me downtown at Hahne's, Newark's nicest department store. She tore the gold labels from the collars and got into her side of the bed with the sewing kit.

"You know what I've been thinking lately?" she asked him in a tired voice. "I've been thinking that maybe we shouldn't have bought this house."

The smack on the mattress was his hand, all frustration. Mama scrounged through her sewing kit, pulled out two plain white labels, and tossed the gold ones in the wastebasket. She threaded a needle and started sewing the plainer labels into the collars of our new dresses. Pop leaned over and put his hand on hers, so she couldn't go on without stabbing him. She stopped sewing but kept her eyes down as he talked to her.

"Honey, listen to me. Maybe my parents should have stayed in Russia and waited for the next pogrom. Maybe yours should have, too. Maybe your sisters would have liked that. But it's not like we bought a plantation down in Alabama or a villa in the south of France," Pop said. "It's not like we moved into a mountainside palace in Shangri-La. We've got six rooms and a screened-in porch, plus two tiled bathrooms and a disposal in the kitchen sink. All right, we're doing well. We're doing very well. Still, it's not like we moved into the White House."

Mama bit the last thread between her teeth and folded up our dresses. She stood at the window and stared out at the silhouettes of the other houses on Keer Avenue, pushing the sleeves of her nightgown past her elbows. Outside, the last city bus rumbled by and the air took on a deeper silence. Keer Avenue was a street we'd always admired, driving up and down on Sundays when we still lived on Schluy Street. My father would slow the car at houses we found especially attractive and we'd try to guess which window led to which room, how high the ceilings might be, whether the layouts were quirky or typical. The colonials on Keer Avenue were brick or frame, or a mixture of both. Each had three bedrooms and most had at least one oak or maple tree on the lawn. All the yards were fenced, with swings.

After a few minutes had passed, Mama turned back to my father. "You're not taking this seriously, but it is serious," she told him. He glanced at her for one split second, which evidently was enough to read her mind and see what she was planning. "They won't see you cleaning," he told her in a quiet voice.

"I know that," she said. "But maybe I'll feel better if I do a little work."

She kissed him on the cheek and I backed into the darkened hallway as she went downstairs. When I heard her reach the kitchen I leaned over the bannister. She was sprinkling baking soda into the sink and around the edges of the garbage disposal. She cleaned the tiles along the sink with vinegar, and when she had finished she walked into the living room with a bottle of ammonia and two clean rags.

On the far wall, near our breakfront, there was a floor-to-ceiling mirror that was actually a knobless door leading back into the kitchen. Because the mirror was so hard to clean, we never used it as a door, but in the last few days dust had gathered on the surface. Now my mother sprayed ammonia all across the mirror. She rubbed one rag along the top and then, bending on her knees, she rubbed along the bottom, first in tiny circles and then in widening ones. Soon the ammonia's acrid smell had made her cry.

She kept rubbing her rag at the mirror, wiping the tears from her cheeks with the other rag. One spot on the bevel of the mirror wouldn't come clean, but when my mother rubbed some more, the glass began to gleam. She was on her knees, but I could see her face reflected perfectly, and her long fingers on the other rag, turning red beneath the cream that she had carefully rubbed into them.

In the weeks before we moved into our new house, my mother had so carefully packed our things in excelsior it was as if she thought that every single piece were a bomb that might explode when we got where we were going. But in truth we moved only six blocks from the brick apartment building in which I had been born. Our new block was half in Newark, half in Hillside. From my bedroom window I still could see my grandparents' building and the roofs of the buildings where my aunts lived with their families. Along Broad Street, Weequahic Park kept its name from Newark's Claremont Diner past our corner and beyond into Hillside's deeper wilds, as if confident that anyone who chose to live along its landscaped paths must be a Newarker at heart. And Bergen Street remained our lifeline. My mother still bought all our meat and poultry at the kosher butcher, Dumbroff's. She bought our bread and cake at the Bergen Bakery and our smoked fish and delicatessen at Tabatchnik's. That way, my aunts couldn't say we'd changed in more ways than our address.

Bergen Street was where we went the next afternoon to pick up the food for Thanksgiving. After finishing at Kaminsky's fruit place we paused on the sidewalk in front of Miss Elsie's Belles Modes Dresses. Miss Elsie herself had come out of the shop and was standing with us. As children she and my mother had lived in a poorer section of Newark; they had gone to school together and knew each other's families.

"Come on, Lillian. Wholesale, either one." Miss Elsie had small eyes that disappeared when she laughed and a French twist of hair whose color seemed to vary depending on the season. That day it was a deep, glowing orange. "Take the plunge and I'll have my people make the alterations overnight. And for you I'll forget about the tax. Let Uncle Sam go out and work for a living, just like everybody else."

"That black suit you sold me will last at least another season," laughed my mother. She was holding a bag full of apples, plums, grapes, and tangerines—a cornucopia she purchased twice weekly so that our growing bones would never grow weak with scurvy or rickets or polio or any of a myriad of diseases. "I've barely ever worn it."

Sue snickered at a dress of royal blue with pearly beads dangling from the bodice and real feathers at the hem. She had wanted my mother to buy herself a new dress for Thanksgiving and I had pointed to the mannequin in the window of Miss Elsie's shop. I had said that my mother would look like Pocahontas in it.

Sue gazed dreamily at the other mannequin, a mess of frills the color of cough syrup. For three years she had worshipped our First Lady, her haute couture and slender figure, and of course her Frenchy name, but she seemed to lack respect for the original American princess, Pocahontas. "You've got a strange ideas about the clothes that Pocahontas wore," she told me for the tenth time. "She didn't wear tops, for one thing. Anyway the pink is ten times prettier and the one that Mama should buy. She'll look like Jackie, but in blond. Jacqueline Bouvier Kennedy would never wear feathers," she added, savoring the exotic lilt of the middle syllables.

A tangerine rolled onto the sidewalk as Mama shifted her bag of fruit and moved to stop me from jabbing Sue with my elbow. "Jackie's not First Lady anymore," I reminded her. "It doesn't matter what she'd wear."

"Look, girls. Instead of quibbling, watch this." Mama reached into her bag and plucked a bunch of grapes from their tiny tree. She widened her mouth and stretched back her neck so that her thick blond hair tumbled past her shoulders. She was wearing the new ring that Pop had bought her on the night that she agreed to buy our house, but the stone was turned inside her palm so that people wouldn't see its size. As her hand went up to toss the grape, the ring flashed blue and orange, like the lowering sunset. "Aaah," she said. The grape hit the side of her nose and tippled along the sidewalk, as if too much sun had turned it into a tiny cask of Manischewitz wine.

The second grape bounced off her forehead. She tossed the third a little higher, several inches from her, and then she gave a kind of hoot as she ran forward. The grape landed right on her tongue.

"Bingo." Mama held her bag of fruit in one hand and put her other hand behind her back. She swallowed the grape and took a bow on Bergen Street. Miss Elsie munched an apple as she peered along the sidewalk as though the area might be filled with spies who would arrest her if they heard what she was saying. "Let me tell you something, Lillian, and cut my own throat while I'm at it. Silk, chiffon, brocade, or sackcloth—you could wear a housedress and still look like a million dollars."

"Stop," said Mama, blushing. "That's not true."

"Your mother was the most beautiful girl in all of South Side High School," said Miss Elsie. "Next to Betty Grable, everyone wanted to look like her. Everyone still does."

For years Miss Elsie had been Newark's uncontested fashion expert, but she wasn't telling me anything I didn't know. Wherever we went, people always were saying that Mama's skin was like cooled peasants' bread, that her eyes were the color of fresh celery, that her bearing was as regal as a queen's. They said she should have been a movie star or model, or a Rockette over in Manhattan at Radio City Music Hall. But for a woman of such beauty my mother was painfully modest. Her elegant hands, long and graceful as a pianist's, were her only vanity. Once a week she had a man-icure at the Bergen Beauty Parlor, but she never used makeup or colored her hair, and everything she wore was black or beige or white, and perfectly tailored.

Of course Miss Elsie knew all this, just as Sue and I did, but whenever we passed the Belles Modes Shoppe she joined us in pretending otherwise.

"You'd look spectacular in either of those dresses," she said on that No-vember day. "Oh Lillian, just imagine. Can't you imagine?"

My mother looked up at the window—reassessing the beautiful blue dress, then the awful pink. "Well," she said. "The truth is I can't see it."

"You're not even trying," I complained.

"Don't be silly," Mama laughed. "I'm always trying."

That night I was sitting cross-legged on my bed, my Pocahontas books and papers sprawled around me, when my sister came into my room, her wet hair wrapped around six empty orange juice cans borrowed from a friend because my mother always squeezed our juice by hand. "Here," Sue said, holding out one of her old crinolines. "You can put this around your neck when you're talking about Captain Smith. The Virginia colonists always wore those getups. I've seen pictures."

She dropped the white crinoline on the bed and it stood up stiffly, by itself. I got off, crinkling my papers, and scrounged around in my dresser drawer while she plopped herself in the rocking chair near the window. "I've got some money in here somewhere," I told her. "I can pay you."

"Don't be silly," she said. "It's a present."

"Really?"

"Really."

I got back on my bed and sat waiting. Her face looked fuzzy through the crinoline's mesh. "You know," she said, rocking slowly, "I really wish you'd stop calling me Sue. I've gotten Mama and Pop to call me Susan. And all of the relatives. You're the last holdout."

"It's okay." I shrugged. "I don't mind."

"That's not the point."

"What's the point?"

"The point is that I don't like being called Sue. It sounds like a little kid's name. I'm thirteen, I shouldn't have a little kid's name."

"If you think Susan sounds French or something, it doesn't. It sounds Jewish. Susan Shumofsky. Susan Bluestone." I closed the book and named all the Susans I knew. "Susan Laskowitz, Paula Eisenberg's cousin. If you want to change your name, then I can't stop you. But I don't have to call you by it, either."

She came and sat behind me, twisting her neck to see my writing. She frowned as she read a few paragraphs of my report. "I think you have that part wrong. Pocahontas didn't marry Captain John Smith. She saved his life, but she married John Rolfe. We learned all that in history."

"I learned something different. Something true." I pointed to my library books. "Do you think I'd make this up? It's a report. It's not a story."

She shrugged and yawned as she got up to go into her own room, the juice cans on her head quietly clacking. "Enjoy the crinoline." She shrugged. "Just don't come complaining later on that no one warned you about Pocahontas and John Smith."

"I won't, Sue," I told her. "I promise."

When school resumed the teachers all looked older, drawn and weary. Mrs. Powderly greeted us in dark glasses perched tight on her nose instead of dangling from the chain around her neck, but that day none of the jerky kids whispered "Four-Eyes" when she turned to the blackboard. I had liked her ever since school started and never called her names behind her back. It wasn't her fault if she wasn't beautiful. Lady Bird Johnson wasn't beautiful either and she had been the Vice President's wife. Now she was our First Lady.

That day no one gave Mrs. Powderly any trouble at all and for the first time that autumn we said "please" and "thank you" at lunch. In the morning we read aloud from our history books, but midway through the chapter on Plymouth Rock she seemed to lose interest and switched abruptly to arithmetic; we slid our history books into the desks and no one made a wisecrack. She chalked a few subtraction problems on the blackboard and Mr. Philip Genius Davidoff got the first one wrong, but she didn't notice and no one waved a hand to point out that the little angel wasn't perfect after all.

In the afternoon Mrs. Powderly gave up on lessons and had us push our desks into a circle while we crayoned paper turkeys and cut pilgrim hats from cardboard, talking quietly about where we'd been when the President was shot. Every one of us had been outside at recess when Dr. Krumbeigel walked onto the playground and made the announcement, but everyone seemed to remember something different. Ivan Shaperstein said that his basketball seemed to spin around the orange rim for hours. Karen Shumofsky couldn't stop thinking about this little baby chipmunk she'd been watching. It seemed to have lost its mother and kept running in and out of the wire diamonds of the fence. I couldn't remember very much at all, only that Dr. Krumbeigel's news could not be true—that everything he said could be undone, the way Pocahontas had thought that Captain Smith was doomed to death and then gloriously won his freedom for him.

Mrs. Powderly wore those dark glasses all day. Above the hissing radiators at the windows the sun had disappeared and the sky was turning colorless. "It will snow," she told us when our class went out for recess, and no one pointed out that it was still too early in the season. "Can you smell it?" We just stood around her, breathing quietly, and didn't go near the places we had been the previous Friday.

At the end of the afternoon I went into the supply closet, changed into my fringed blouse, and gave my report on Pocahontas. When it came time to explain about Captain John Smith I slid my sister's crinoline around my neck. After I finished the marriage scene my classmates applauded—a loud, welcoming sound that kept on going as I took three bows.

When everyone stopped clapping I waited for Mrs. Powderly's words of praise. "Well, Debbie. You've certainly read your speech very well," she said. "You have excellent enunciation. But I'm sorry to say that you've gotten the facts wrong." Mrs. Powderly removed her dark glasses as she told me this, and like everyone else in the room I looked at her red, rheumy eyes and wondered what she possibly could mean.

"Pocahontas saved Captain Smith from being murdered." I shrugged. "Her father, Chief Powhatan, was all set to kill him. He had his hatchet ready and the funeral pyre was burning when she ran up and put her own neck to the blade." I wasn't sure about the pyre part but had seen the word in print and figured it would stop her. "That's it. That's what happened."

"Yes, I know." Mrs. Powderly nodded. "And her courageous act did save his life. But Captain Smith didn't marry Pocahontas."

And that's when she said that he had handed Pocahontas over to John Rolfe, just as my sister had warned me. She said that John Rolfe took the Indian princess back to England, dressed her in a satin gown, and got the Queen to call her Lady Rebecca. And Pocahontas never again saw her beloved Virginia or heard her true name spoken.

By now the dismissal bell had rung. I was tentatively smiling as my classmates gathered up their things and raced away—I assumed that Mrs. Powderly must be joking. But when the halls had quieted and we were left alone, something in her face confused me all over again. And then she repeated what she had said: that only for the sake of peace between her tribe and the colonists had Pocahontas laid her yearning throat beneath her father's hatchet while the tom-toms begged for war.

"Then you don't think Pocahontas saved John Smith because of love?" I finally asked, and even I could hear the quaver in my voice as I waited for her to take back what she'd said. But of course teachers never did that. Once they said a thing, then that was it. And Four-Eyes was no different. Teachers could tell you ten times ten was ninety-nine and you were supposed to believe it. "I could have sworn the book I read said something about that."

"I'm sorry, Debbie," she repeated. "I know how hard you worked."

In fact I'd read three library books and I didn't believe a word that Mrs. Powderly was telling me. I was sure that Pocahontas had wound up in a Virginia teepee with Captain Smith, not in a damp English manor with dull John Rolfe. Or, if somehow a cruel twist of fate had really trapped her on a boat in the Atlantic, then I figured she must have died of a broken heart at sea.

The next morning was Thanksgiving, a cold and glassy sky. In the dining rooms along Keer Avenue the bay windows had frosted up. The oaks and maples were completely bare now and only the hills of dead leaves raked to the curb proved that they'd ever been different. By the end of the meal I had spilled gravy and a glob of cranberry sauce down the front of my taffeta dress. Our table was strewn with empty plates that had been full of potato salad, cole slaw, sour tomatoes, chopped liver, three kinds of breads, all kinds of pickles. My mother's home-cooked turkey had been picked to the bone.

By then my cousin Kitty was chomping on her second plum. "Kennedy started the Peace Corps," she was saying. "When I'm old enough, I'm joining it."

"Me too," Sue said. "Either that or be a stewardess. I'd like to go to Africa, or South America, and do some good for mankind. *Peut-être* Bechaunaland," she added dreamily. "Or Sierra Leone. I could use my French there."

My mother's three sisters—Vivian, Jean, and Carole—sat on one side of the table. Mama sat on the other. Vivian, the oldest, leaned across to Sue. From time to time Vivian stood all day on her aching arches and handled the cash register at her husband's grocery store. She said her feet always swelled up like a pair of salamis. "If you want to marry a *schvartze*, then you don't have to go to Africa. Just walk across South Orange Avenue," she told my sister. "Plenty of *schvartzes* on South Orange Avenue."

"That's not funny," Mama said. "Not at all."

My aunt Carole glanced at her and winked at Jean, who occasionally answered the phone for Dr. Blumenthal, our dentist. Luckily for her, Dr. Blumenthal was getting old and couldn't take many patients. "Look at that face! That beautiful face, all twisted up like a loaf of challah."

One of the uncles pulled a few cigars from his pocket and distributed them to the men. To my father he said, "Here Vic, try one of these. Havana—smuggled up just last week. Let the kids forge ahead and try to change the world. Let them learn the hard way how much worse it could get."

"Kennedy wasn't a saint," said Dickie, the oldest cousin and a notorious bookworm. "Look at the Bay of Pigs. Look at southeast Asia."

Sue rolled her eyes and elbowed him. "Look at Alan Shepard and John Glenn," she said.

My uncle took a long puff on his cigar. "Kennedy obviously wasn't a cigar-smoker, or he'd have used kid gloves with Castro."

"You're confusing JFK with Eisenhower," Pop told Dickie. "Ike's the one who started it. Though of course he had his reasons."

"Actually," Sue mused, "I think I'd rather go to Paris."

Pop's remark about Eisenhower had made my aunt Vivian indignant. "How ridiculous! Kennedy had a full head of hair, thick and beautiful as Lillian's. Everyone in that family has good hair, even the children." She peered over at my mother. "Actually yours looks lighter than usual. You're not bleaching it, are you, Lillian?"

Mama's face went blank, as it often did when the family gathered. "I'm not bleaching it," she said quietly.

"It looks a little blonder." Vivian shrugged. "I thought maybe you were having it done."

In the kitchen a geyser of steam shot to the ceiling. Mama went in and came back with the kettle and a platter of strudel. She poured the tea and coffee, but instead of sipping hers she held a hand above the steam until her flesh was damp, then turned her hand and stared at it.

"I feel sorry for Caroline and John-John," said my cousin Kitty. "They're nearly orphans now."

"Johnson will be good for the Jews," said an uncle. "If he can just keep a lid on the *schvartzes.*"

"Negroes," Pop said. "Call them Negroes."

"Maybe the ones who go into your diner are Negroes," laughed my uncle. "The ones who come into my grocery store are *schvartzes.*"

"Their money is as green as yours or mine. So you ought to call them what they want to be called."

"Maybe if I had your money then I could afford to," laughed my uncle.

"I feel so sorry for Jackie," said Sue. "I can't stop thinking about her."

My aunt Vivian snatched Kitty's next plum. "That's enough with the plums. You're always getting diarrhea from Lillian's wonderful plums. Last week I had to pump her full of Kaopectate," she told my mother. "All night I was up with her because of your delicious nutritious fruit."

I got up from the table and wandered toward the mirrored door. None of the aunts realized that it was actually a door, and I was standing there, thinking about how dazzled and jealous they would be if they knew, when Vivian turned back to my sister. "Don't you worry about Jackie. With her looks and her money she'll find another man in no time."

Mama stopped eating her strudel, clinked plates and glasses, and carried a teetering stack from the table. Spoons and forks fell to the carpet, but instead of picking them up she kicked them away and kept walking. And just as I was swinging through the beveled glass to show the aunts that things weren't always what they thought they were, or at least could possibly be different, I heard a scream, my mother's scream, and saw her arm in the sink, and the kitchen tiles turned into a singe of splattered red—my mother's blood.

All those tiles, sparkling and hand-cleaned with vinegar, bright with blood, down the hallway and out into the yard, where she ran screaming, trailing all that blood. I stayed frozen where I was, imagining the tips of manicured fingers as they swirled around and around in our stainless steel disposal. Behind me on the mirrored door, my own ten prints were clear as maps.

The adults began to yell and knock chairs over as I stood frozen, thinking, Now I will have to clean the mirror by myself. And I will never get it clean. Around and around and around. I'll have to clean it now myself. And I will never get it clean. Around and around and around.

And later, after Pop had disappeared with Mama moaning in the front seat of our car, I furiously scrubbed my fingerprints from the mirrored door while the aunts tried to make me stop. I wouldn't go in the kitchen for ammonia, so I used water from the pitcher on the table and two cloth napkins. The aunts' sobbing sickened me; I wouldn't cry. The bevel at the mirror's bottom was the trickiest part and for that I kneeled, my back toward all of them. And in the reflection of the glass I watched my sister say that they could all go home, that being thirteen now, she was old enough to stay with me.

The next afternoon Pop took us to the hospital. Mama was sitting up in the bed, her hand bandaged to twice its size. I avoided looking at her, but my sister went over and sat near her feet until Mama told her to come closer. I fiddled with my jacket zipper and from the corner of my eye watched Mama stroke her palm and try to talk to her. My sister wasn't saying much.

"Don't you worry," Mama said. "It's my left hand, not my right, and just the tips of the last two fingers. The doctors say that except for the nails we'll never notice the difference."

The police had taken apart our garbage disposal and brought the whole thing to the hospital, but all that they had found there were some half-ground turkey bones and her diamond ring. The doctors had told them flesh could not survive those blades.

Mama winked at Pop, who was standing at the window fiddling with the shade. Outside, the sky was tough and heavy, cold blue with streaks of white. The snow still hadn't started.

"Maybe there's a silver lining," she said. "Maybe I can get the woman at the beauty parlor to give me twenty percent off on my manicures."

Pop's shoulders flinched, but he kept his face steady as he fiddled with that shade. After a while I didn't have much choice, and I had to go to Mama. Actually, my sister made me do it. She stood up and smoothed down her skirt; then she came and gently pulled my socks back to my knees. She took my hand and toured me all around the room, as if she thought we were in Europe or Africa or somewhere exotic. But then she showed me the tiny bottles of mouthwash and baby powder lined up on the sink, the rented television in the corner that looked just like ours at home, the bulletin board where Pop had tacked my crayoned turkey. And then we were sitting on the bed, on either side of my mother's elbows. My sister had taken the hand side and let me have the other, but I could see the gauze on Mama's arm was clean. No blood anywhere.

"What are you thinking?" I said, to any of them.

No one answered. Mama closed her celery eyes. In a quiet voice she said, "Oh, nothing. I wasn't really thinking of anything." Then, because she never had been able to pretend and because we all knew anyway, she exhaled and said, "I was thinking about my sisters. I was thinking how different things would be if they wished me well."

When she leaned back and eased her arms out against the pillow I took it as an invitation to duck under. On her other side, so did my sister. There, enfolded in her, several moments passed—and not a sound. Mama's skin was pale but smooth and smelled as fresh as bread. Finally I said, "It would be different, Mama. So different that you can't imagine it."

And then I told her how at first Pocahontas thought she couldn't survive without John Smith, or her angry family in Virginia. I told how at night she cried herself to sleep and dreamed of maize and wild cranberries. How eventually she had new friends and children of her own, who helped her to go on.

And she began to love her life. Periodically she dressed in silks and satins and went to meet the Queen for tea. In Buckingham Palace they spoke of books and music, the latest restaurants, and gardening. At dusk she often rode her chestnut mare along Pall Mall's calming paths. John Rolfe adored her, and, content together, they lived for many years and knew their grandchildren, and great-grandchildren.

I had reached the great-great-grandchildren and even Susan seemed transported when something in my mother began to make a steady beat within her body, like a heart, or tiny drum. My father kept on fiddling with that shade until the whole thing snapped up against the window frame. The afternoon had faded now, deepened into dusk. Above Newark's old familiar buildings I saw Pocahontas galloping, galloping safely, through the English mist. She wore a beaded riding dress and held the reins lightly in her fingers. And on the back of her blond crown a pillbox hat bobbed lightly. My eyes began to sting and finally to tear, as if God was somewhere up there on His knees, cleaning the whole universe in preparation for the colder months that seemed so certain, so inevitable, now.

POLAND, 1944: MY MOTHER
IS WALKING DOWN A ROAD

IRENA KLEPFISZ

My mother is walking down a road. Somewhere in Poland. Walking towards an unnamed town for some kind of permit. She is carrying her Aryan
identity papers. She has left me with an old peasant who is willing to say
she is my grandmother.

She is walking down a road. Her terror in leaving me behind, in risking the
separation, is swallowed now, like all other feelings. But as she walks, she
pictures me waving from the dusty yard, imagines herself suddenly picked
up, the identity papers challenged. And even if she were to survive that,
would she ever find me later? She tastes the terror in her mouth again. She
swallows.

I am over three years old, corn-silk blond and blue-eyed like any Polish
child. There is terrible suffering among the peasants. Starvation. And like
so many others, I am ill. Perhaps dying. I have bad lungs. Fever. An ugly
ear infection that oozes pus. None of these symptoms are disappearing.

The night before, my mother feeds me watery soup and then sits and listens
while I say my prayers to the Holy Mother, Mother of God. I ask her, just
as the nuns taught me, to help us all: me, my mother, the old woman. And
then, catching myself, learning to use memory, I ask the Mother of God to
help my father. The Polish words slip easily from my lips. My mother is
satisfied. The peasant has perhaps heard and is reassured. My mother has
found her to be kind, but knows that she is suspicious of strangers.

My mother is sick. Goiter. Malnutrition. Vitamin deficiencies. She has skin
sores which she cannot cure. For months now she has been living in complete isolation, with no point of reference outside of herself. She has been
her own sole advisor, companion, comforter. Almost everyone of her world
is dead: three sisters, nephews and nieces, her mother, her husband, her in-

laws. All gone. Even the remnants of the resistance, those few left after the uprising, have dispersed into the Polish country-side. She is more alone than she could have ever imagined. Only she knows her real name and she is perhaps dying. She is thirty years old.

I am over three years old. I have no consciousness of our danger, our separateness from the others. I have no awareness that we are playing a part. I only know that I have a special name, that I have been named for the Goddess of Peace. And each night I sleep secure in that knowledge. And when I wet my bed, my mother places me on her belly and lies on the stain. She fears the old woman and hopes her body's warmth will dry the sheet before dawn.

My mother is walking down a road. Another woman joins her. My mother sees through the deception, but she has promised herself that never, under any circumstances, will she take that risk. So she swallows her hunger for contact and trust and instead talks about the sick child left behind and lies about the husband in the labor camp.

Someone is walking towards them. A large, strange woman with wild red hair. They try not to look at her too closely, to seem overly curious. But as they pass her, my mother feels something move inside her. The movement grows and grows till it is an explosion of yearning that she cannot contain. She stops, orders her companion to continue without her. And then she turns.

The woman with the red hair has also stopped and turned. She is grotesque, bloated with hunger, almost savage in her rags. She and my mother move towards each other. Cautiously, deliberately, they probe past the hunger, the swollen flesh, the infected skin, the rags. Slowly, they begin to pierce five years of encrusted history. And slowly, there is perception and recognition.

In this wilderness of occupied Poland, in this vast emptiness where no one can be trusted, my mother has suddenly, bizarrely, met one of my father's teachers. A family friend. Another Jew.

They do not cry, but weep as they chronicle the dead and count the living. Then they rush to me. To the woman I am a familiar sight. She calculates that I will not live out the week, but comments only on my striking resemblance to my father. She says she has contacts. She leaves. One night a package of food is delivered anonymously. We eat. We begin to bridge the gap towards life. We survive.

GARDEN

NADELL FISHMAN

In rich brown soil under
the tall pine that stood
in front of my parents' red
brick house, my mother half-planted
spatulas, butter knives, soup ladles,
all the luckless utensils of her orthodoxy.

Not the happy spoon of the rhyme,
who ran away with the dish,
her patterned stainless fell
folly to our forgetfulness. We knew
meat and milk don't mix,
but between the knowing
and the doing an innocent spoon
was banished to dirt
until harvest. Burdened by a role
in religious life, two separate
armies of kitchenware lined
the shelves and drawers on opposite
sides of the sink.

        Why is it,
my friends would ask, your mother
plants her silver? This question
sat long among the odd behaviors
that bloomed like cutlery in our garden:
the Sabbath darkness we groped in
rather than affront God with electric
light, the bacon

we shunned—the stuffed derma
we savored, the menorah in the window
at Christmas.

Venerable roots ground such faith
in this plant that does not bend.
The heavens and I as witness, my mother
upside-down interred those shafts,
serrated   pronged   and bowled,
exhausted her shame of us, in earth.

BELONGING

JUDY GOLDMAN

$\mathcal{I}$t didn't matter that we were Jewish, every Easter my mother would take me to Rock Hill Feed & Supply to choose a baby chick, its soft first plumage dyed blue or pink, sometimes lilac. I'd take that breathing inflorescence into my hands and the silk soon would be damp from the heat of my palm and the closeness of my inquisitive fingers. Usually the chick would be dead by May.

But one Easter, Mother bought me two and I promised to be careful, to keep them alive. They grew into Rhode Island Reds, marching through the yard like kings of the season, their combs a bright royal flush. I loved the feel of the glassy kernels of corn I scattered over the grass for them, the way they'd scratch the dirt, rumps high, sickle feathers flashing. I loved to carry those roosters around the neighborhood, one under each arm.

One night it rained so hard the truck delivering coal to the bin behind the house got stuck. Its huge tires were grinding scars deeper and deeper into the lawn. I could hear the engine revving and began to cry for my roosters, begging my parents to bring them in the house where it was safe and dry—first my father, who waved me off, then my mother, helpless in a sudden gasp of lightning. Finally, Mattie, who "lived in," waded out into the yard. From the kitchen window I watched her flashlight fling a path to my roosters.

Early the next morning my father and mother, my sister, brother, Mattie, and I heard the squawks and rushed down in our pajamas. The chickens were flying as far as their heavy bodies would allow, shattering the teapot, the iced-tea glasses, the pitcher next to the toaster. Spoons and forks were hitting linoleum like rain. I could hardly follow those birds with my eye, the way they flapped and skidded, the kitchen a stir of red.

In the glare of rising light from the window I couldn't see anyone's face, but I could feel Mattie's hand cool on the back of my neck. I knew my roosters would soon be gone, Easter over for this small-town Jewish girl. There was nothing to do but stand there trying to make out the dark knots of mud in the yard beneath the dogwood stripped of its blooming white crosses.

FRUIT CELLAR

ENID DAME

Bury your memories
like jars in a fruit cellar.
Let them mount high on the shelves.
Let them wait.
Dark jewels   in their cold nests
they will keep.

Unbottle them later,
if you can find that town,
if you can find that house.
If anything is left from that time,
break in. Smash windows,
lower yourself to the bottom.
Reach for a memory. Crack one.
Take what you need.

Now   hold your mother
lingeringly on your tongue.
Her fruit is still alive.
It tastes as it always did:
heavy   resonant   edgy.
It makes you think of old coats
fur-collared   camphor-scented
worn in another country.

Think of your mother preserving.
Think of your mother destroying.
Her stove: old companion,
turned against herself,

turned into an enemy,
that time she turned on the gas.
Good citizen,
the oven refused to cooperate.
Thirty years later,
she didn't need help to die.

Swallow this memory quickly.
The fruit cellar's silence
isn't empty.
It's a presence,
like a woman's disappointment
stored too long.

It can turn fruit sour,
fracture glass.

NO RETURNS

RUTH BEHAR

*H*undreds of hours of my girlhood were spent with my mother in the return lines at Alexander's, which used to be on the corner of Queens Boulevard in New York. My mother has always liked to shop at big department stores because they give you back your money without asking questions, without doing a smell test. I learned from her to boycott any store that allows no returns. Like my mother, I never buy anything that you can't take back to the store for a full refund. Like my mother, I try shoes on over and over in the shop, driving the salespeople mad. Like her, too, I cannot decide whether to keep a new blouse until I've worn it for several days with the price tag tucked under my wrist and enough deodorant to keep my sweat glands quiet. A chill runs down my spine as I snip off a price tag or step out into the street with new shoes that will never again be pristine enough to return to the store.

Our anxiety about keeping things has its roots, I think, in our exodus from Cuba. We left because of the Revolution, which promised, in the name of a Jewish theorist, to do away with materialism and capitalist greed. As a young girl I imagined them watching us with special Communist telescopes from the Port of Havana as we carried home shopping bags brimming with an ever new assortment of clothes, underwear, and shoes in our bleeding hands. Maybe because my mother also imagined they could see her, so many of the things we joyously brought home in our bulging shopping bags would later find their way back to the store, just a teeny bit sweaty, a teeny bit scruffy. Maybe, in a mysterious way, Communism infiltrated our souls, leaving its teeth marks on those things we played at owning but couldn't bear to keep forever. Maybe, if things could go back to their source, one day we ourselves would return to the country we had left behind because it had outlawed shopping.

* * *

It is a Saturday afternoon in July and my mother is asking if I'd like to go shopping. We have always done our shopping on Saturday afternoons, after the Jews who go to synagogue are done praying for the rest of us. Perched at the top of the stairs, she says to me in Spanish, "You don't want to go, right?" And she adds, "I have to return some things. I know how much you enjoy that." The things she has to return are marked-down rayon dresses and pantsuits she bought for me that I won't wear, even in Queens.

The truth is I don't want to go. I'm home for a few days with my husband and son and I'm in the attic bedroom working on my computer. I'm struggling with this piece and what I need is a quiet afternoon by myself. David and six-year-old Gabriel have gone with my father to his gym to play racquetball. So I'd raise a feminist eyebrow, my father said they were going to "look at the girls" (later David reports that there are no "girls" there, just aging men).

"Mami, I'm writing about you," I announce. I tell her I'm writing about how she returns so many things she buys.

"Okay, come with me so you can write about it," she says good-naturedly.

Nina, an old Cuban-Jewish friend of my mother's, gives us a lift to Filene's. "If only I could drive," my mother laments as we wave good-bye and wander into the store. My mother's deepest desire, now that she and my father no longer live in an apartment near a subway but in a tree-lined neighborhood of modest brick houses, is to get her driver's license and be able to drive. She has taken some driving lessons, but for the past ten years she hasn't been able to muster the courage to get her license. She's terrified of being behind the wheel alone. I understand her. I can drive fine, but once in a while, when I'm tired or frenzied, my mother's spirit gets into me and I panic in the car. I get dizzy, my heart beats too fast, I worry I'll black out. When I get really afraid I ask my husband to drive, but then I become furious at any sudden stop or start he makes and realize how awful it is to be driven around by a man. You feel incapable of taking life into your own hands.

"One day you'll learn to drive," I tell my mother. "It's not that difficult." As we head toward the return line at Filene's, I decide not to tell her about my own problems with cars. Our relationship has been based on our lack of resemblance. I have my Sephardic father's dark eyebrows and curly hair; *tienes un aire sefardí*, as my mother says with a certain pride, making me feel exotic. But I also have his fiery Turkish temper rather than her calmer Ashkenazi acceptance of limits. *Eres igualita a tu padre*, just like your father, she'd say when I misbehaved; she still finds many reasons to say it to me.

Yet throughout my girlhood we plotted together against my father's power, which to me often seemed as arbitrary as that of a sultan. At Asia Continental, the Cuban-Chinese restaurant on Roosevelt Avenue that we frequented (perhaps because it represented as comfortingly odd a mixture of cultures as our own Cuban-Jewish *arroz con mango*), I tasted shrimp and found it heavenly. My father looked the other way when I ate shrimp at the Asia, but he would not allow it or any other "unclean" food into the house out of respect for the memory of how Abuela, his impoverished mother, had tossed into a Havana street an unkosher cut of meat that Abuelo had once bought her. Now and then my mother would delight me by whipping out of the freezer a long-necked glass of shrimp cocktail that she'd hidden away for me, advising I eat it quickly and secretly before my father returned from work. I'd offer my mother a taste, but even though she loves shrimp as much as I do, she'd refuse in deference to my father's wishes.

Despite our plotting, the divisions between us run deep. I reaped the benefits of my mother's immigration, of her loss of language and country. She did all of my woman's work so I could become a woman who reads and writes books. My English is perfect, showing no trace of my birthplace in an island born of the counterpoint of tobacco and sugar. Her English is thick with a Latin accent that always shocks everyone in New York when they learn it comes out of a Jewish mouth. I became a *profesora* at a prestigious Midwestern university, with money enough to buy myself a spacious Wedgwood-blue Victorian house. She became a secretary who works in a basement office at New York University, checking for misspellings on diplomas and returning home to the brick house she and my father waited and waited to buy, never sure if they'd be staying in this country, never sure if they had enough for the down payment. Ay, if that *casita* weren't so little, *tan chiquita*, my mother is always saying, irritating the hell out of my father.

We unload our shopping bag, get our full refund, and are ready to start fresh at Filene's. At first I resist. I look around vaguely at the racks of clothes and can't imagine there is anything I'd want. My mother and I decide to start simple. We both need socks, I black ones to wear with boots, she white ones to wear with sneakers. After searching around, we find a bag of cotton socks in a mixture of different colors, which we agree to share. But my mother insists that I also pick out some individual packets of more expensive, lacy socks for myself. She always wants me to have more than her.

That task done, we gravitate toward the huge wall of silk blouses at the far end of the store. My mother is addicted to buying me silk blouses and suits that my gringo husband from Texas always ends up having to iron. We come across a rack of black silk blouses. Surely I don't need another one. But then I see that they come in a V-neck sleeveless style with ocean-gray mother-of-pearl buttons. That I don't have. My mother starts pulling out one size after another for me to try on. Then we see the baggy black pants with a snappy beige geometric design. "They're rayon. Does it matter?" my mother asks, knowing about my penchant for one-hundred-percent cottons and silks. "It's not bad for rayon," I tell her. They'll be great with the blouse, we both agree, and we nearly run, so excited are we, with the pile of clothing to the dressing room, where I try things on, complaining that I really didn't want to go shopping, that I wish I'd stayed home and kept writing, that I can't stand stuffy little dressing rooms, all the while enjoying how well things are fitting, but enjoying even more that I can come out to show my mother, who eagerly waits just outside the door for me, wanting so much for everything to be just right so she can buy it for me, like old times.

Hours have somehow passed, but we leave the store happy. Mission accomplished. Our spirits are high and we decide to walk the three miles home. I'm already thinking of how I'm going to write about this shopping trip. But there is another shopping story I need to tell, a painful story. I brought it up once, but my mother begged me then never to write about it. Out of respect for her I had abandoned in midsentence a piece I started years ago.

"Mami, what happened that time in Bloomingdale's?" I ask as we walk down a block of brick houses.

"You're not going to write about that, are you?" My mother's eyes plead for compassion. "It was so terrible. It happened because of my accent. Please, Rutie, don't write about that."

"I know you don't want me to," I say. I've never told her how much I actually know about what happened.

"They treated me so badly. I don't want to remember. Papi and I agreed never to talk about it." We keep on walking. "Ay, Rutie, look at those impatiens. That's what I should do in my front yard," my mother says, pointing to a row of hot-pink flowers.

I realize my mother is trying to change the subject and I begin to think I shouldn't tell that story. Why am I always dredging up sludge from the past? But then my mother surprises me. "Tell it if you want to," she says. And she adds, using one of her favorite English expressions, "I'm an open book."

It was the Saturday of Memorial Day weekend in 1982. I will never forget the date because it was a week before my wedding. Baba and Zeide, my mother's parents, had come from Miami Beach, and the six of us—they and my parents and David and I—had gone to the Bloomingdale's in Fresh Meadows to do some last-minute shopping.

That Bloomingdale's in Fresh Meadows represented many things to us. We had aspired to it, we had dreamed of it, during all those years when we had shopped at Alexander's, its poor cousin. To be able to live near the Bloomingdale's in Fresh Meadows had become a goal for us already in our early immigrant years, when we lived in a one-bedroom apartment in Briarwood, on the edge of Queens bordering on Jamaica, a neighborhood that had "started to go bad"—*que se estaba echando a perder*, literally "beginning to rot," as my mother used to say—code language for saying that blacks were moving in. It had remained a goal after we moved to a two-bedroom apartment in the much whiter, more Jewish, Forest Hills, where at least my brother and I could attend "good" public schools, if not the yeshivas to which the rest of El Grupo, the circle of my parents' Cuban-Jewish friends, sent their children.

But in Forest Hills, my parents, as Spanish-speakers, hit it off better with the Puerto Rican super than with many of their American Jewish neighbors, who viewed them as "Latins." Viewing themselves as Latins, too, they lingered in Apartment 9T, hesitating to acquire the brick house near the Bloomingdale's in Fresh Meadows until my brother and I were no longer living under their roof. Our family trip to Bloomingdale's, a week before my wedding, a year after my parents had purchased the house with the front yard, was a way of saying to ourselves that we had made it, that we Jews who had ended up across the border because the United States didn't want us back in the 1920s had arrived on this side, finally.

When we got to Bloomingdale's the men and the women split up into two groups. My grandfather, father, and David went to look at men's clothes. I went with my grandmother and my mother to purchase makeup. At the Estée Lauder counter we found a saleswoman who slathered different shades of eye shadow on me and then on my grandmother. Before we could turn to see where she was going, my mother said she wanted to try something on upstairs and would be right back.

After my grandmother and I selected eye shadow, face powder, blush, and nail polish, we began to wonder why my mother was taking so long. Neither of us could remember where exactly she said she'd be. We waited by the counter, and after a while I began to pace up and down the cosmetics aisles to look for her. Then I noticed the saleswoman who had smothered us with eyeshadow pointing me out to a tall, husky woman with nondescript short blond hair, drab blue pants, and a thin blue ski jacket.

The woman in blue came over to me and said, "I have a message from your mother. She wants me to tell you that she's fine and that she'll be home in a little while. She says that you and your family should go ahead home."

I was horrified by this strange messenger's words. "Who are you? Where is my mother? Why can't my mother talk to me herself? What have you done to her?"

The woman glanced at me coldly and said, "It's best if you just go home. Nothing's wrong with your mother. She's fine. Just go home."

My grandmother came over. "What happened?" she asked in her Yiddish-accented Spanish. "Is it something about your mamá?" I repeated the woman's message to my grandmother, and she too became afraid. How could we go home and leave my mother in the hands of a stranger? What if she had been kidnapped?

After the woman in blue walked away, I returned to the cosmetics saleswoman and asked if she knew the messenger. "She works here. She's a cop," the saleswoman told me. I still couldn't figure it out. "But why is she bringing me a message from my mother?" I said. "Maybe you'd better ask her," the saleswoman replied curtly, acting as if she'd forgotten all about the makeup she had just sold us.

I went running after the woman in blue and told her I had to know exactly where my mother was and why she couldn't speak to us herself. "She told me not to tell you," she said, her irritation growing. "So just go home." But I still hadn't understood. "No, please, I have to know," I said to her. Then the woman turned and looked at me, for the first time, with a trace of sadness in her eyes. "You really want to know? Well, I caught your mother shoplifting. She was trying to steal a jacket. They're going to bring her down soon and take her to the police station. Now go on home, because if she sees you when she gets out to the parking lot, it'll be worse." With those last words, the woman turned and walked away again.

I felt as though a tornado had ripped out my heart. In slow motion I started walking back to where my grandmother was waiting, clasping tightly onto our foolish bag of cosmetics, which I now blamed for all of our problems. What would I say to my grandmother? Clearly, my mother wished that the accusation against her remain a secret. As I was wondering what to do, I caught sight of my grandfather, my father, and David strolling toward the cosmetics counter. The three men had formed an easy relationship, even though each was so different—Zeide, a reticent Yiddish-speaking immigrant to Cuba who had lost most of his family in Byelorussia in the war; my father, a native *habanero*, the son of Turkish immigrants; and my husband-to-be, a recent convert to Judaism brought up on creamed-turkey casseroles, whose family had come to the United States on the Mayflower. They strolled toward me without a care in the world. I wanted to keep my mother's secret, but when my father asked where she was, I broke down in tears and told them all everything: that my mother was being accused of shoplifting, that the police would be coming for her at any moment, and that she didn't want us to know, so we had better leave right away.

We hurried out to the parking lot and got far enough from the back entrance in time to see my mother as she came out of Bloomingdale's, a police officer on either side of her. I wanted to scream, to pull out my hair, to run to her with my heart in my hands. My father told us to hide behind some cars so she wouldn't see us, but suddenly, as if pulled by an invisible string, he flew off, reaching my mother as she was being escorted into a waiting police car.

Like zombies, my grandparents and David and I stumbled back to my parents' brick house. We waited under the clock, which seemed not to move. Sitting at the glass and chrome kitchen table, my grandmother said, "Your mother would never do anything like that. It was a mistake."

"You think so?" I said.

"Of course," she replied. "Don't you?"

Just as a country stands between my mother and me, a country stands between my mother and her mother. Baba has the confident manner of a woman accustomed to fundraising for Jewish causes. Every year Soldiers of Israel sends her a calender displaying the muscles and guns she has helped to finance. Her dream was to become a singer in a Cuban cabaret, but she was the eldest immigrant daughter and her father put her to work selling cloth so they could make enough money to get her mother and six siblings out of Poland. All her life she worked selling cloth, first in the only Jewish family store in a forgotten sugar town deep in the countryside, later in the old section of Havana, where she and Zeide owned a lace shop, and in her old age as an employee at Gem Fabric, where the Brooklyn-Queens subway line ran overhead, rattling the walls. In Cuba, maids could be hired for nothing to do everything, and Baba spent very little time in the house caring for my mother and aunt and uncle. I wondered, sometimes, how well she really knew my mother. My mother, as the middle child, told me she felt her mother's absence, felt it as a loss. Coming of age in the 1950s, she wanted to be more present as a mother, luxuriously at home in a polka-dot halter dress, waiting for the children to come home from school for their rosy pink tropical *mamey* milkshakes. But a revolution had gotten in the way.

When my mother and father returned from Bloomingdale's we pretended that nothing had happened. "Just a little problem with my account," my mother said. Her face was tear-stained, her thick straight brown hair hung limp, and her beautiful long fingers were smeared with blue-black ink from the fingerprinting the police had done. How much I wished I could have caressed those fine hands in my own thicker ones that were just like my father's.

I never felt so sorry for her as I did then. I never loved her so much as I did then. And I never felt so cruel as I did then. I seemed to be watching her suffer inside a glass box. I could see in, but she couldn't see out.

In the evening my father took me aside and said I should never bring up the incident with my mother or anyone else. I begged him to tell me what took place at the police station. It's over, he kept saying. Forget it. Case closed. But I was deeply troubled and needed to find out for myself what had happened and why.

The following Tuesday I snuck out of the house with David and went back to Bloomingdale's. This time the store seemed garishly ugly to me, like a bad Halloween costume. I had to hold back my desire to smash the rows upon rows of perfume bottles, with their urine-colored contents, lined up on the cosmetics counters. I asked a saleswoman where I could find the head of their security squad. We were shown the way to a dingy back office, where I introduced myself as Rebeca Behar's daughter to the fiftiesh blond woman who seemed to be in charge. In hopes of impressing her, I said I was a Princeton graduate student about to get her doctorate. I told her my mother was innocent and that I was certain they had made a false accusation. I said I planned to take legal action against Bloomingdale's.

The woman listened to me with a smirk on her face. When I was done she shook her head and said, "Look, your mother didn't want you to know what happened because she knew she was guilty. She signed herself off as guilty. So there's not much you can do about it."

I was stunned. "But how is that possible?" I said. "She's never stolen anything in her life."

The woman looked at me harshly. "How do you know? We found out that she's returned a lot of merchandise to the stores." On that front, I couldn't argue. We had spent hundreds of hours at the return lines in Alexander's. But did that mean my mother was a thief?

"Look," the woman said again. "You should have left well enough alone. Let sleeping dogs lie. Your mother didn't want you to know. Why did you have to come snooping around?"

"Because no matter what you say, I know she's innocent. And because, because—" Tears started to form in my eyes. "Because I'm getting married in a few days." The woman still showed no sign of emotion; she was a cop to the bitter end. "I just don't think my mother would have done that to me a week before my wedding."

"Your mother is your mother, but your mother is a thief, young lady, whether you want to believe it or not. Maybe it's something she picked up in Cuba. . . ."

"I don't believe it. You're making it up!"

"Look, dear, I don't have to waste any more of my time on this. Your mother was stealing a jacket from our women's department. She was seen walking away with it."

"She was just coming down to show it to my grandmother and me. We were waiting for her at the cosmetics counter."

"That kind of behavior may be tolerated in Alexander's. But not in Bloomingdale's."

"You've ruined my wedding," I said, tears streaming down my face.

"Not me. Your mother," the woman replied, her face broadening into a full smile.

At the wedding, as we danced to a melange of horah music, salsa and conga, and Sephardic drumming, my mind kept being drawn back to the conversation with the head of security at Bloomingdale's. My mother couldn't be guilty. That was impossible. But why had she agreed to the verdict? Why was she so afraid to tell us the truth? And why, perhaps most disturbingly, had I, her daughter, a doctoral student at Princeton, been so inept at establishing her innocence? Why was I no better at talking back to the security chief at Bloomingdale's? She had practically convinced me my mother was a thief. Did I have no words to answer her with? What good had all my education done me? As my mother and father leapt to the floor to take the lead in dancing to a melancholy Sephardic love song, my mother motioned to me to join them and I thought I could still see the residue of the blue-black ink on the tips of her fingers.

For many years my mother refused to set foot in Bloomingdale's. She'd say, as we passed by, "They did something very ugly to me there and I'm never going back." I'd nod my head but keep quiet about what I knew. I, too, avoided the store and dreamed of vengeance. Then one day we heard the store wasn't doing well and it was closing. Too bad for the neighborhood, my mother said, but they deserved it. Yes, indeed, they did deserve it, for the injustice they committed against my mother, a Latina with a Star of David around her neck that didn't help her, a Latina who lacked the language to defend herself. On the ashes of my mother's shame they built a K-Mart.

A LIFE

CHANA BLOCH

She sinks
into the tub of herself
up to the neck,
an available warmth.

With one hand I can start her.
It's my pain.
Don't tell me what to do.
I was young too.

Once I stood on the table
to be her size.
She brushed my hair with her fingers,
stroking it like fur.

Damp, crumpled,
now she is mine.
I can stuff her into my pocket
and carry her home.

So this is America, she says
to the closet, a life
in camphor
with no one to talk to.

And in that darkness the fox-heads,
sharp-nosed,
amber-eyed,
dreaming her dreams.

BURGLARS IN THE FLESH

LORE SEGAL

$\mathcal{I}$t was February. Fishgoppel came into New York and took her cousin Ilka Weissnix to the wharf, where they stood in the cold drizzle and watched Ilka's mother carried off the boat. They brought her home to Fishgoppel's Manhattan apartment, and she looked so ill Fishgoppel asked her if she thought she should see a doctor.

"What does she want from me?" Ilka's mother, who thought Fishgoppel was speaking English, asked Ilka in German, and Ilka said, "She thinks we speak Yiddish."

Poor Fishgoppel could not afford this European kin for whom she had made herself legally responsible. Fishgoppel had never met either of them before last February, a year ago exactly, when she had come into New York to fetch Ilka from the airport, settled her into the small Upper West Side apartment, and caught the train back to New Haven. Ilka, with little English and no job, had promptly allied herself with—by any count—the wrongest man in America, and now here was this sick aunt with no English, and Fishgoppel had her examinations coming up. She told them, "*Ikh vel zayn tsurik in tsvey Vokhn*," and ran to make the last train to Connecticut.

"What did she say?" Ilka's mother asked Ilka.

"I don't *know*," Ilka said.

That was the night Ilka's mother first dreamed about the burglars.

"Who are really ants," she told Ilka, coming into Fishgoppel's little sausage-shaped kitchen in her tasselled jacquard dressing gown—a survivor, too, from pre-Hitler mornings of coffee and buttered rolls in Vienna.

Ilka was sitting at the table, fully dressed, her coat on her lap.

"Who rang on the telephone, already before breakfast?" Ilka's mother asked.

"A friend of mine," said Ilka.

"You are going out?" Ilka's mother asked.

"*Yes*, I am going out," Ilka said in a raised voice. Poor Ilka! Her emotion at seeing her mother again, seeing her mother alive, was already settling into the old irritations, for these also had come intact through persecution, emigration, via customs, into the New World. Thereupon Ilka bent over her mother's hand, which lay so amazingly here, in Manhattan, on Fishgoppel's kitchen table. The skin, spotted with the pale beginnings of age, was so finely grained it felt fragrant under Ilka's lips.

"So what did you dream?" she asked her mother, and laid her right palm over the face of her wristwatch. The wrongest man in America was sitting in his hotel room downtown, waiting for her. Ilka watched her mother pour herself a cup of American coffee, taste it, and grimace. Ilka's mother settled herself in her chair.

"I dreamed that the door opens—or Daddy opens it, or it already *is* open and Daddy is holding it . . ."

"And . . . ," Ilka said.

"And," said her mother, "these three ants walk inside, and Daddy is holding the door open for them. No, he's the one who opens it. I *think*."

"And . . . ," Ilka said.

"And they walk inside and they start to grow, and they grow and they grow and stand upright, and they are really men except they are ants—you know how ants have shiny black sections, head, middle, and tail end, like three shiny black beads, like black patent leather, only not really like patent leather . . ." While Ilka's mother sat staring into last night's dream to see what it is, exactly, that ants are black and shiny like, Ilka noticed the churning inside her chest. Ilka, who was twenty-two, still believed that the man sitting in his hotel room would be all right if she, Ilka, got there in time. Ilka wound her watch under the table.

"The biggest of the ants must be the father, because he makes them wash up. He asks Daddy where they can wash their hands, please—perfectly polite—and Daddy, very polite, too, bowing, nodding, shows them behind this white sort of folding screen and I'm surprised—this is so peculiar, *in the dream* I am surprised—that there is this row of bowls in the kitchen and they wash their hands and the father makes them dry *very* thoroughly . . ."

Ilka here openly looked at her watch.

"Then the father leaves," Ilka's mother went on. "At any rate, he is gone—you know how that is in a dream—and the two who stay behind have this black bag . . ."

Ilka had gotten up and put her coat on. Her mother followed her out into the narrow little foyer and said, "In my dream I'm wondering how I know, from this black bag, that they are burglars and I turn to ask Daddy, but he is gone—you know how in dreams someone is there, then they are not?"

"Not in dreams only," Ilka said. "*Muttilein*, this is Monday. I'm going to the Office of Unemployment before I come home. You should go out for a bit."

"Go where?" asked her mother.

"At least walk to the corner. There's a Polish refugee working at the butcher's. He speaks German."

Her mother said, "What do I do if the telephone rings and it's for Fishgoppel?"

"You say in English, 'I'm sorry, I speak little English.' Say it after me."

"I know, I know how to say that!" said her mother.

Ilka sat on the subway determined not to worry, but she walked the half-block to the hotel with the sensation that she was running, her anxiety at the pitch where it feels like pain.

Ilka knocked and listened to the stately tread behind the door, and he was all right. He was fine. He opened, a very large, very stout man with a look of density, as if he were heavier, pound by pound, than other men of equal bulk. His grizzled hair was cut unusually short to lie perfectly flat against an unusually large head. At rest, the large face tended to jaw and jowl. At the bridge of the nose, a small outgrowth of wild flesh suggested to the girl disastrous chances, moving accidents his youth had suffered.

Ilka felt herself seen. This man, whom in all the world Ilka liked best, was regarding her with the grave and total delight with which it had always seemed improbable to Ilka that she would ever be looked at.

He held the door and stepped back with a small, courteous formality, and Ilka, overwhelmed with shyness, came into the room and began helplessly to chatter. The man was so good as to lower his eyelids between his vision and her nonsense. When he raised them again, the comfort of their intimacy had been reestablished.

* * *

Ilka's mother went to sleep and dreamed that the two burglars rummaged in their black bag. She couldn't see them because they kept behind her, out of the line of even her peripheral vision, but she could hear one of them cursing—a low hiss under the breath: they had knocked something over. Ilka's mother supposed it was the kitchen stool, and she woke up and heard the front door closing: Ilka was home.

"You go already again out?" is the translation of what Ilka's mother said in the morning, which released in Ilka a thrill of exasperation.

"What do you mean, *again*?!" she shouted. Whereas Ilka's mother counted the number of times Ilka went out, Ilka counted every time she stayed at home. She said, "Again *what?*"

"Again you go out," her mother said—bravely it seemed to Ilka, because Ilka had the impression that her own too wide-open eyes were shouting at her mother. She normalized them.

"Again you go on the subway," her mother said.

"What's wrong with the subway?!" Ilka screamed. "It's better than sitting in Fishgoppel's apartment! *Mutti*, you're in America! This is New York . . ."

"I dreamed about the burglars again," her mother said.

"What did you dream?" asked Ilka with a substantial reluctance.

"That they have a black bag."

"So you told me."

"And they keep behind my back so that I can't see what they are doing. But I can hear everything. They knocked the kitchen stool over."

"In your dream," Ilka said.

"Yes," Ilka's mother said. "I dream I'm thinking one of them must be quite young, a boy, because I think it's the other one who says—you know how hard it is to remember what people say when you don't understand what is going on—something like 'Hold this *here*, idiot!' or maybe 'Hold it by this, *here!*' very impatient, which makes me think he's talking to a boy. When will you be back?" she asked Ilka.

'It's Thursday, *Mutti*. I have my class. *Muttilein*, if I register you for Beginners' English, will you go, too?"

"Go where?"

"Just three stops."

"On the subway!" her mother said. "What do I do," she came out to the foyer to ask Ilka, "if the telephone rings for Fishgoppel?"

The two burglars moved around in the kitchen behind Ilka's mother and she listened to the small clanking of metal and tried to understand what kind of instrument it was that they seemed not to know how to assemble. She kept meaning to turn around to look; however, she did not turn. It seemed to her that they were bungling it, and she wished their father would come back and stop them. She kept looking toward the door and heard the key and awoke, and it was Ilka in the foyer.

"*Her* trouble," Ilka had said to Carter that evening, "is she will not *go out*."

"Have a drink," Carter had said.

"Thank you, no. All she does is sit in Fishgoppel's apartment and have bad dreams."

Carter had brought a glass for Ilka along with his own, and said, "I'll teach you to drink good whiskey."

Ilka obediently sipped and said, "She won't go on the subway. She won't go shopping without me."

"She's frightened," Carter said.

'Why? What *of*? We're in America! I'm not frightened."

"I am," Carter said.

"You!" Ilka said.

"Didn't you know?" said Carter. Ilka had the sensation of falling in love all over again and, wanting to diminish the distance between them, came and sat on the carpet next to his feet. She rubbed her cheek against his knee.

"Drink your drink," Carter said.

Ilka sipped.

Carter said, "I'm going to come up and see your mother."

"What shall we offer him?" her mother asked.

"Nothing, *Mutti*. He's just coming in for a few minutes to meet you. *Muttilein*," Ilka began, too loudly and suddenly. All day she had been practicing in her head how to say what she had to say without offending her mother. "*Mutti*. Don't tell Carter about your burglars."

"Me? I tell him?" Her mother was offended.

"It's just that people don't want to hear other people's nightmares. Don't tell him your Hitler stories."

"I tell? Whom do I tell anything? How am I supposed to tell? He understands German?"

"Fishgoppel doesn't understand German, and you told her your Oberpest story *twice*."

"Because you would not help me how to say 'leaflets' in English."

"I don't *know* how to say 'leaflets.' *Mutti*, all I'm saying is everybody *knows* all these stories. They've been in the papers, they've been in the newsreels at the movies, on the radio."

"It's been on the radio that I left your father ill on the road before Oberpest? Did Fishgoppel know the Red Cross dropped leaflets?"

"The point is, Carter is a Negro and they have their own stories."

"I will not tell him anything. I won't even speak to him," her mother said, and the bell rang.

Ilka's father had been a small, portly man. Carter Bayoux was an unusually large portly—a weighty—man. Ilka's mother began to speak in English.

"Ilka, take the mister the coat away, isn't it?"

"We're leaving in a minute," Ilka said.

Carter took off his coat.

"Coffee for the mister, Ilka."

"You want coffee?" Ilka asked Carter.

"Please," Carter said.

"Ilka has told, isn't it, that that are not our furnitures."

"*Mutti*," Ilka whispered in order not to shout.

"That all here is belonging to a cousin which has not—how one says *auf englisch 'Geschmack'*?"

"Has no taste?" suggested Carter. "I have met Fishgoppel, and I'd guess her mind works at such a white heat it would shrivel any thoughts of furniture."

Flora Weissnix, who did not understand what Carter Bayoux was saying, understood that he was talking to her. His face, shoulders, his chair were fully turned toward her, and she said, "We have everything lost and not only furnitures. I have Ilka's father lost on the street before Oberpest. How says one in English, Ilka, the '*Nazis*'?"

Ilka had left the room, not because she mourned her father but because she thought that she did not, and her mother's frequent, easy invocation of his name seemed, maliciously, to accuse Ilka's unnatural heart. But knowing how soon and how intolerably Carter's patience could be racked, she threw water into a kettle and ran back into the room where Carter sat, his quiet hands folded on his considerable stomach, his face serious but without the gravity of the listener anxious to be perceived to be listening.

Ilka's mother was saying, "How names one in English such many little papers falling?"

"Leaflets?" offered Carter.

"On where written stood, 'It comes one only *Ambulanz* for the which cannot farther go.' Funny is," she said, "otherwise were it I which have not well gone. Ever were it, every Sunday, something with my foots, my shoe, never the daddy, Ilka, isn't it? But before Oberpest has he already fevered. How comes it I have farther gone?"

Carter offered his handkerchief. Not only were her eyes red and streaming, her nose ran, her face was a devastation. "We have nothing to offer, not cake, not fruit," Ilka's mother howled. "Ilka, the coffee! Is not as it was by us at home," she told Carter.

Ilka ran out into the kitchen and threw cups onto a tray and ran back in, and her mother was doing charades, telling Carter about the burglars. She avoided Ilka's eye.

"Is a . . . ," she made a cutting motion.

"A knife?" asked Carter.

"Exact here," and Ilka's mother pointed to a place on her back a little right of center and out of the reach of her hand.

"You come again, isn't it?" Ilka's mother said to Carter when she saw them off in the foyer. "I will make you a goulash, but not like by us! In America knows nobody how cuts one properly up a chicken."

"How do you know what one does and does not know in America?!" Ilka shouted.

* * *

"She didn't have a choice except to leave my father on that road and go on," Ilka said as they walked to the subway. "That was in the last days of the war. They were moving the camps across country, and even the Germans didn't know which were their own guns, which way the front was—but my mother enjoys to convict herself. She *wants* to tell that story over and over— only I don't want to hear it over and over. Fishgoppel just *loves* to hear all my mother's Hitler stories."

Carter said, "I ever tell you about my wife Bonnie?"

"Irene, I thought you said her name was."

"Irene was my second wife. Bonnie was my first wife, a white girl—when we were just out of high school. She used to love my dad's slave stories. I tell you my dad was born a slave?"

"Ah," Ilka said with a solemn thrill.

"Bonnie just loved to sit and listen," Carter said. "I used to walk out. I'd putter around, and I'd walk back in and there was my dad telling stories and Bonnie sitting listening."

"You had two wives?" Ilka asked.

Carter walked on. "More than two," he said.

"More than two! You had three wives?"

Carter walked on.

"*More* than three? Four? Four wives? Did you have five wives? How many wives, Carter, did you have?"

But Carter would not say.

"Why won't you tell me how many wives?"

"Because I'm ashamed," he said.

"So did you invite him for dinner?" Ilka's mother asked her when she came home.

"Did you wait up for me? Don't wait for me!" Ilka shouted. "Go to bed!"

"I am afraid. I don't want to dream again," her mother said. "It is horrible."

"What's so horrible?" said Ilka. "How horrible can something be you *know* is only a dream? It's not so horrible."

"Because they are behind my back."

"So?" Ilka said.

"It's that I can't see what is happening. I can't tell what it is they are going to do to me, and I never know exactly when they are going to do it again."

"Do *what?*" Ilka shouted.

"That's what I don't *know*. It wouldn't be so horrible if I knew what they are doing, or if I knew every time exactly when they were going to start again, because I'm sitting there every moment thinking, *Now* are they going to? Now? Now are they going to do it always at the same exact spot that hurts from the time before?"

"In your *dream* you mean it hurts," Ilka said.

"Right here." Her mother pointed to the place on her back. "That's why I don't want to go to sleep."

"You don't want to sleep because you're not tired, because you don't have anything to do. *Mutti*, why don't you let me register you for Beginners' English?" Ilka said.

"Tomorrow," Ilka's mother said. "I'll go to the corner. I can explain to the *Polischen* how one cuts a chicken up for a proper goulash, if you will come with me."

"That's not the point!" Ilka yelled.

"And then you ask your friend to come to dinner."

Fishgoppel had done well—had done spectacularly—on her examinations, and arrived for the weekend frowning: she could not afford these trips into town.

"You look wonderful!" she said, her neck and back inclined tenderly toward Ilka's mother.

"I have dreams," Ilka's mother said. "What I can't understand is why burglars wash their hands so thoroughly."

"It's a dream," Ilka said, and she experienced a release, not into her mouth but just below her chest, it seemed to Ilka, of a taste like bile. She looked across at Fishgoppel with a sort of horror, but Fishgoppel was looking from Ilka to her mother and back, trying to understand what they were saying.

Before she caught the train back to New Haven, Fishgoppel ran down and brought her aunt the *Aufbau*, a German-language weekly. Henceforward,

Ilka's mother could document her fears. "It says here an elderly woman was robbed on the subway last Sunday. Name of Rosenstein. From Vienna. Are you going out tonight again?"

"Yes," Ilka said.

"Why don't you invite him here?"

Ilka said nothing.

"I wish you would stay," said her mother.

"How can I stay at home all the time?" shouted Ilka. "I have to get a proper job. I want to meet people, I want to see America . . ."

"I don't want to dream," Ilka's mother said.

Carter said to Ilka, "Don't leave me."

"I have my English class, and my mother sits alone in Fishgoppel's apartment."

"It is terrible to be alone," Carter said, and he put his thumb on one eye and his forefinger on the other. Ilka saw the tears seeping through. She embraced Carter, who fell back on the bed, drawing her after. Ilka said passionately, "Don't be unhappy!"

"*Am* I unhappy?" Carter stopped weeping to ask in a voice of interest. "Don't let me snow you!" he said.

"Excuse me?" Ilka said.

"I'm a terrible ham," Carter said.

"Pardon me?" Ilka said.

"I can't tell anymore where the whiskey stops and the tears start," Carter said, weeping.

"You are, you are very unhappy!" Ilka cried enthusiastically.

"Well well well well well," Carter said. He allowed Ilka to help him sit up. He sat very still until she relaxed her embrace. Then he reached for his glass. He sipped. "Friend of mine," Carter said, "he said he had the 'Negro Problem' solved. Said, 'Get it disseminated to all white folk: We don't do it so good either.' "

"Excuse me?" Ilka said.

"When did I last fuck you?"

"You do! You did!"

Carter raised his huge, immensely slow head till he was looking full into Ilka's face, and said, "You love me."

"I told you," Ilka said.

"You're crazy"—and he still looked into Ilka's face. "Women in love are crazy people. Don't even *notice* they're not getting it. You think all this is terrific," he said. He covered his eyes with his thumb and forefinger and wept.

"I think they have moved in," Ilka's mother told Ilka.

"Who has moved in where?"

"The burglars. I think they live in our kitchen."

Ilka had the impression that some little self inside her was looking rapidly to the right, the left, the right. Ilka's mother said, "I can't even remember if anything was said about their father coming back."

"Come in your dream, you mean," Ilka said, while the little self not only looked but frantically ran from one side to the other in her head, where there *are* no exits.

Ilka's mother said, "He doesn't know what is going on here. Are you going out?"

"Just going to make a phone call."

Ilka put a call through to New Haven. She was going to tell Fishgoppel, "I think there's something wrong with my mother." Fishgoppel was out, and Ilka called Carter. There was no answer. Ilka took the Manhattan telephone directory, and with a hectic hand riffled through the *A*'s to the *F*'s.

"Whom do you call?" her mother asked.

"Nobody. I don't know anybody *to* call," Ilka said.

All next day, and the next, Carter did not answer his phone.

Ilka's mother said, "What I'm going to do is turn around and ask them, 'What are you going to do to me?' Where are you going?" she asked Ilka.

"I'll just hop on the subway, see if Carter is all right."

"Ask him to dinner," her mother said. "I'll teach the *Polischen* how to cut the chicken."

Carter's door stood ajar. He slept with his face to the wall. Ilka had a notion of cleaning the place up, but there was something ferocious about this litter of soiled clothing, bottles, papers, moneys, wires; it struck Ilka once again that she must disentangle herself from this useless mess. She took the subway home.

* * *

Ilka's mother said, "I keep wondering if there is a way I could get word to the police and let them know what is going on here."

Ilka yearned to lay her head down on her mother's lap and say, "Help me. If you are going crazy, I won't know what to do." But her mother's lap was out of sight, under Fishgoppel's kitchen table.

Ilka's mother sipped her coffee with an air of reluctance and said, "I have no way of knowing when either or both of them are looking at me. I wouldn't know when to make my move. Did you see," she said to Ilka, "where they held a girl at knife point from the Bronx to the Battery? What *is* the Bronx? Where is the Battery? A nice-looking girl. They have her picture here. Look."

"*Mutti*," Ilka said, "I think Carter may really be ill. I'm going down to see."

Her mother followed her out into the foyer and said, "Why don't you marry him?"

"What are you talking about?" shouted Ilka. "You don't understand anything about it!"

"I understand that you like him," her mother said. "I understand it is not good for a man like that to live alone."

Carter's door was locked and taped with a police seal. Ilka went back down in the elevator. The desk clerk leveled his eyes at Ilka's collarbone.

"Where have they taken him?" Ilka asked.

"To the nuthouse," said the desk clerk.

Ilka's mother meant to turn around. She listened to them quarreling behind her.

"Let *me*," the boy said.

The other one said, "You hold it and I will. Hold it here, by this."

"*I will*! I can!" the boy kept saying. "Why can't *I* do it?"

The knife was introduced at a shallow angle with a slicing motion; she imagined a knife with teeth—a saw, perhaps, for which the boy must be grappling, because it was violently agitated. She shouted out.

"My mistake," she told Ilka, "has been to keep hoping that the father was coming back to stop them. In other words, I've been wishing to not have the pain, which is not one of the choices. What I *can* choose is *how* to have it, and what I'm going to do is concentrate on having it. Perhaps that's a way to bear it, by fixing what exactly the pain *is*."

"You do that," Ilka said. She had gotten used to knowing that her mother was unbalanced, and she had gotten used to doing nothing about it, there being nothing, it turned out, *to* do. She had called Fishgoppel. Fishgoppel had not understood what it was that Ilka was telling her. Ilka felt relieved.

Ilka was surprised that around this central abyss their lives continued to revolve—had even eased up some. Ilka had a job as a file clerk that must do, for now. Her mother had learned to go to the corner every Thursday for her German paper. She quarreled with the Polish butcher; she sat on a bench in the sun. Spring had come. A strong white sun sparkled the garbage of upper Broadway when Ilka walked to the early bus to spend Sunday with Carter at the state hospital.

Carter was quiet. He looked good and seemed optimistic. "I could pull myself together over the summer if we could find a house in the country. I don't drink when I get out of that bitch of a city."

"Without me," Ilka said.

Carter looked frightened.

"It's just this is not *useful*, is it? Shouldn't I put my mind on getting a better job, on getting on with—everything, Carter, don't you think?"

"That is not something on which I can advise you," Carter said.

It's not when you decide to get out of bed that you get out of it. "Now I will get up. *Now*," you say to yourself, lying in bed. Then you are up. You have gotten out of bed in a moment that is already past, in the absence of your decision or attention. It was in such a moment that Ilka's mother had turned around. She said, "Why do you hate me?"

"What I had forgotten," she said to Fishgoppel, "is that you can't look them in the eye. They don't have their eyes where we have our eyes. They don't have faces. I mean, they have faces—everybody has a face—but not what *we* mean by a face, so maybe they don't recognize that my face is a face. Maybe they don't *know* my flesh feels like flesh, because they are made out of something completely different, not like black beads so much—and nothing *like* patent leather, as I thought at first," she turned to say to Ilka. "Different—more like the shiny black parts of a motorcycle."

"I don't understand a word she is saying," Fishgoppel said sadly.

Fishgoppel's term was over. She slept on the couch in the room with Ilka.

Ilka's mother was sure it was Carter who had called.

"Impossible," Ilka said, but she rang the hotel. Carter picked up the receiver. A summer house had materialized in Connecticut.

Ilka had never heard a grownup's voice so hilarious. She regretted the cautious sound of her own.

"I can't leave my mother with Fishgoppel."

"Bring your mother. Bring Fishgoppel. Come weekends."

He fetched her from the station on late Friday afternoon. "This is it?" cried Ilka when he turned up the drive toward the exact little wooden house with fence, window with curtain, roof with chimney, sky with cloud that Ilka used to draw on pieces of white paper on the dining table in Vienna.

Inside, the walls were raw wood. "I don't believe this," Ilka said. The floor was a collage of rich, faded odds and ends of antique Oriental rugs. "This is silly. I don't believe it." Ilka meant the condition of happiness. At night the air was a flawless black. In a bed like a cavern hewn out of some aboriginal wood, immovable as ship's furniture, Carter Bayoux taught Ilka Weissnix how to sleep spoon fashion. Ilka was moved by the delicacy of the big man's sleep; her slightest motion—hardly more than an incipient impatience of the flesh—could turn him. His bulk fitted into her angles.

Telephone for Ilka.

Fishgoppel said there was no need for Ilka to come home. She could take Aunt Flora to the hospital.

"What is it?" Ilka's gut somersaulted and short-circuited the common light.

"She's not in pain now. She says she's all right. She doesn't want to see a doctor. She doesn't want to go on the subway."

The hour on the train so harrowed Ilka that she was surprised to find her mother looking just like her mother.

"I must have lain badly." Her mother pointed to her back. "I'm fine now."

"Of course you're going to be fine. We're both coming to the doctor with you."

"Why don't you wait in the waiting room with Fishgoppel?" Ilka's mother said.

"Don't be silly. I'm coming inside with you."

"Don't look at me," Ilka's mother said when she lay waiting on the table.

"Why shouldn't I look at you?!"

"Don't shout," Ilka's mother said and folded her arms over her thin breasts. Her legs were thin.

"What's wrong with being naked?!"

"Go wait outside with Fishgoppel," Ilka's mother said.

Ilka said, "You're afraid of being naked! You're afraid of the subway! You won't learn English . . ."

"Not now, Ilka."

"You're not an old woman! Do you know you're born the same year as Carter?"

"The father has come back," Ilka's mother said.

"Terrific," Ilka said, breathing hard, grateful to have her tirade stopped.

"It is terrible," her mother said.

"What is terrible now?" Ilka said.

"He is not going to stop them. He has known all along . . . it was his idea from the beginning. Ilka, he *is* the police. The black is their uniform! They are three policemen. That is the real horror."

"Why is that the real horror?"

"Because they are permitted. It is the law, Ilka. They are supposed to do it, Ilka."

"What are they supposed to do?"

"Cut me," said her mother. "Here's the doctor."

The doctor came out to talk to the three women in the waiting room. He said, "Why don't we keep her here, do a couple of tests?"

"Now?" Ilka asked.

"What does he say?" Ilka's mother asked.

"Why not now? We have her here; we happen to have a bed . . ."

"Is something wrong?" Fishgoppel asked.

"That's what we're going to find out, isn't it?"

"I don't understand what he says," Ilka's mother kept saying in German. "What are they going to do to me? *Now* are they going to do it?"

THE DAUGHTER OF
SURVIVORS

HILARY THAM

She is screaming again.
You stand at your bedroom door.
Her dream claws her sleep to shreds.
Shivering, you will her to stop, will it
to go away. You father's voice
rises and falls with the burden of her name.

She is awake. You hear her voice cling
to his, as a shipwrecked cat
digs its claws into a floating spar.
You hear the creak of bedsprings as they rise.

Soon, the kettle whistles in the kitchen.
When you peer in, they are huddled together
over the kitchen table. Her pale hands clenched
around the teacup, she whispers her dream.
He has heard it six million times,
but he listens, his arm clamped around her
to contain her shudders.
He, too, has bad dreams, different faces,
the same sequence of events.

You are afraid of this trembling woman
who replaces your mother each night.
You want the daylight woman
who bakes honeycake, and brushes your hair
smiling, as if you are her good dream.

Your father does not change at night.
He, too, fears the knock on the door.

He makes you learn street maps
by heart, sends you out alone
on the New York subway so that
if you should come home from school
and find them missing, you would
know how and where to run.

PANTOUM FOR THE CHILDREN, SO THEY WILL KNOW YIDDISH

JUDY GOLDMAN

The language of parents, their Pig Latin,
when conversation must be kept secret
from children, as in *shh, the kinder* . . .
consonants hard as a cough, a stutter.

When conversation must be kept secret
from the rest of the world,
consonants hard as a cough, a stutter,
mitn-der-rinen, in the middle of everything, a *shandeh*, a shame.

From the rest of the world
they hide their hopes, despair—sometimes the same,
mitn-der-rinen, in the middle of everything, a *shandeh*, a shame,
though nothing to *kvetch* about, to nag or complain.

They hide their hopes, despair—sometimes the same,
wishing the sweet wine sweeter, the salty no more,
though nothing to *kvetch* about, to nag or complain.
Kine-ahora, they intone,

wishing the sweet wine sweeter, the salty no more,
afraid to let the juice run down the chin.
Kine-ahora, they intone,
words to ward off the evil eye.

Afraid to let the juice run down the chin,
they spit on fortune, whisper *pu pu*,
words to ward off the evil eye.
People who know loss like a member of the family,

they spit on fortune, whisper *pu pu*,
know that nothing really matters in this *meshuggeneh* world.
People who know loss like a member of the family
know that everything matters, everything,

know that nothing really matters in this *meshuggeneh* world.
Crazy. Crazy the way suffering is all they can afford. They
know that everything matters, everything
God will allow His children.

Crazy. Crazy the way suffering is all they can afford. They
know the words that sound like bodies falling, the only words
God will allow His children
to whisper in His ear.

Now the words that sound like bodies falling are words
for the children, those *shayneh kinder*
who whisper in His ear
the language of parents, their Pig Latin.

PART FOUR

ॐ

TALKING BACK

*Now that I'm in my forties, she tells me I'm beautiful; now
that I'm in my forties, she sends me presents and we have the
long, personal, and even remarkably honest phone calls I
always wanted so intensely I forbade myself to imagine them.
How strange. Perhaps Shaw was correct and if we lived to be
several hundred years old, we would finally work it all out. I
am deeply grateful. With my poems, I finally won even my
mother. The longest wooing of my life.*

Marge Piercy
Braided Lives

THE FISH

LILA ZEIGER

"Without fish, there is no Sabbath."
(AN OLD YIDDISH SAYING)

I had about as much chance, Mother,
as the carp who thrashed
in your bathtub on Friday,
swimming helplessly back and forth
in the small hard pool you made for me,
unaware of how soon you would
pull me from my element
sever my head just below the gills
scrape away the iridescence
chop me into bits and pieces and
reshape me with your strong hands
to simmer in your special broth.
You bustled about the house
confident in your design,
while I waited at the edge
imploring you with glossy eyes
to keep me and love me
just as I was.

BIRTHING

KATE SIMON

*H*e looked so much like a story character—the gentled Scrooge of a *St. Nicholas Magazine* Christmas issue, a not-too-skeletal Ichabod Crane— that it is difficult to say how he really looked. And he was ephemeral, his visits timed for the hours we were in school so that we caught only occasional glimpses of him as he strode around a corner, immensely tall (something we were not accustomed to in our Mediterranean street) and thin, wearing a long, skinny black coat and a shapeless black hat, carrying a black doctor's satchel. We knew Dr. James had visited when we found our mothers in bed "resting," an odd word, an odd event. When we left for school they had no symptoms of cold or cough or pain; preoccupied perhaps, but that was common among women who worried about getting the rent paid on time, about shoes for the children, about husbands who habitually came home late from work. There was never an explanation for Dr. James's visit, what he did, what he said; only the mother on the bed, a peculiar worrisome thing, like finding the library or school suddenly, without warning, closed. By suppertime the mothers would be chopping, cutting, cooking, sometimes more quiet than usual, sometimes more irritable, nothing more.

When I became a member of a medical family that had practiced in the Bronx for decades, I once mentioned Dr. James and his unexplained short visits to mothers only, and never to deliver babies. A spate of enthusiastic information poured over the dinner table. Dr. James was, even when I knew him as a child, quite an old man, retired from a prestigious and lucrative practice in Boston, they thought. His was a prosperous intellectual family, the famous New England Jameses that produced William and Henry, but to the older Bronx doctors, *the* James was the magnificent old driven scarecrow. Having educated his children and seen their arrival into respected professions, he dedicated himself to poor immigrant women for whom there was no sex information, no birth-control clinics, nothing but knitting needles, hatpins, lengths of wire, the drinking of noxious mixtures while they sat in scalding baths to prevent the birth of yet another child. At times one woman would inflict these well-meant injuries on a sister, a neighbor; sometimes they were solitary acts of desperation. Some women died of septicemia; some of those who could not kill the fetus had to wait out the nine months and the delivery to let the infant die of exposure or suffocation.

To prevent such suicides and murders, Dr. James went from one immigrant neighborhood to another, performing abortions. (How he was informed where he was needed no one seemed to know; there must have been one woman in each area who transmitted messages.) He lived to be quite old and, according to my informants, worked vigorously at his self-appointed job until he died, having performed thousands of abortions, the fee a dollar or two or nothing, depending on the degree of poverty he met. Every adult in his neighborhoods knew him and his function, including cops and Board of Health people, who usually let him be. It was during the periodic sweeps of new brooms in office that he was arrested and imprisoned. He succumbed to it all very calmly, didn't call lawyers or his family, nor offer bail. Apparently he got in touch with one or two colleagues who called others, who in turn called others, and together they stormed the court where he was being tried. They pleaded, the argued, they shouted; they accused the police and the court of ignorance and inhumanity, and had him released. This drama was repeated several times, memorable times for the doctors who could thus demonstrate their admiration for the old man with the courage and independence to act as they might, if they but could.

Dr. James was a careful gynecologist as well as a skilled abortionist. There were women he would not abort. My little sister was much more gently handled, more eagerly cosseted, than my brother and I were because, my mother told me when we had become close adult friends, the baby was unwanted and was allowed to be born only because Dr. James refused to perform another abortion; she had had too many and another could be hazardous. How many she had I found out when I checked her into a hospital a few years before she died. Thirteen. I asked her again when we were alone in her hospital room whether I had heard correctly. Thirteen? And three children besides? Yes, and that was by no means the neighborhood record, she said. How could I account for the fact that a number of our Italian neighbors, urged by the Catholic Church to produce large families, had no more than two or three children? Certainly it wasn't the abstinence of Italian husbands, no more controlled than Jewish husbands. It was the work of the blessed hands of that wonderful old *goy*.

When school started in September before I was quite eight, the walks with my swollen mother—watching her skirt so that she didn't stumble on the stairs, pacing my steps, skipping in place to her lumbering, rocking walk, like the elephant in the zoo—stopped. When we came home from school there was a quiet in the house that seemed to tremble against the walls, no lilting greeting, no apples and crackers on the table, in the sink a cold half-cup of tea with milk. She was resting, and resting meant sick, like the times when Dr. James had come and gone. It also meant trouble. I kept glancing surreptitiously at her ankles to see if they were swollen. In scraps of eavesdropping I had accumulated something about women swelling and having convulsions before babies were born. My mother had swelled but didn't have convulsions when I was born, a difficult delivery, "with instruments" that dented my forehead. (Tracing the dent in my forehead, I wondered if it would squeeze my brains and someday make me crazy, like Mrs. Silverberg or my father's sister Surrele, whose name was thrown at me when I threw shoes and slammed doors.) "Instruments" were enormous black pincers, like those the iceman used to pull blocks of ice from his wagon, stuck in my mother's belly, ripping through the flesh and searching among her bleeding bowels until they hit my forehead and grabbed me, pulling up and out again through the red, messed flesh into the air, and dropped me, a doll covered with pee and shit, into hands that slapped to make me breathe. And now, in our house, a few paces from the kitchen, fewer from the dining room, it was probably all going to happen again; tonight, tomorrow night, the next night. It always happened late at night, a shameful, secret thing, too dark and terrible for open day.

One afternoon in early October we came home to find Mrs. Nagy and Mrs. Kaplan bustling around the kitchen and Fannie Herman standing in the hallway wringing her hands. Mrs. Nagy gave us a piece of strudel and told us brusquely to go down and stay in the street until our father came home. We hung around the stoop feeling uncomfortable, lost. We had to go to the toilet, we were getting cold in the falling light, we didn't feel like playing. Something was happening to our mother and why couldn't we see her? It had to do with her belly and the baby. I wanted to watch and at the same time wanted to be far, far away; to be someone else in another place, a girl who lived in a book.

When our father arrived and asked us what we were doing in the street so late, my brother mumbled something about the baby and we ran upstairs. We could hear Mrs. Kaplan's voice in the far big bedroom as my father walked into it and closed the door. Mrs. Nagy was in the kitchen putting stuffed cabbage and pieces of cornbread on the table. Our father called to us to eat and do our homework in the kitchen, he would eat later. We were to be quick and quiet and go to bed—and close the door—as soon as we were through. We didn't talk, as we often did, in bed; there was no point at which to start a discussion of something so large and forbidding, and words might betray our fear.

During the night we were awakened by a shriek and then another. Our door was pushed shut and we knew we were not to open it, not to get out of bed, not to see what was happening. People bustled in the hallway, to and from the kitchen, to and from the bathroom. Someone rang the doorbell and was admitted, probably the doctor. Through the sound of feet and the hushed voices, another scream and more, louder, more piercing, like ambulances. This I, too, had done to my mother, distorted her goodnatured, singing person into a howling animal. I imagined her hair wild and swept across her staring green eyes, her pretty mouth torn by the screams, the doctor pushing the immense pincers into her belly and searching, searching for the baby, ripping her to pieces as my birth had done. My brother was asleep or pretended to be. I was alone in a guilt that made me want to disappear, to die.

Not knowing how to die, I separated myself from myself, one girl not there, one girl going through familiar actions in a dumbness and deafness like a thick rubber Halloween mask. I don't know who gave us breakfast; I ate it. I don't know what happened in school; I was there and managed to perform whatever was asked of me. I did my homework; it was correct. They told me I had a little sister; I didn't say anything. The women on the street asked me how my mother was; I said all right. This went on, the living in a cold, flat country, for several days, the guilt pushed down, out, away, and kept away. When my mother called to me from her bedroom to come and see the new baby, it was pretty, I called back, "Tomorrow," and ran to the street.

One of the days when my mother was still in her bed and we still fed by the neighbors, a monitor came into my classroom and handed a note to the teacher. We all sat up, eager for whatever news it might bring, an injunction from the principal about noise in the auditorium, an announcement of a shortened school day, possibly. My teacher called me to her and told me that I was wanted by my brother's teacher. All the kids stared as I walked awkwardly (was my skirt hitched up in back? my socks falling?) out of the room. When I reached his classroom, my brother was standing at her desk, looking shamefaced but not especially stricken. His teacher, Miss Sullivan, one of the smiling young ones, said she knew my mother had just had a baby but a big girl like myself could take care of a little brother almost as well as his mother could. But maybe I was too busy to notice that he didn't wash too well. Pulling his collar away from his neck, she showed me a broad band of dirt that began at a sharp edge just below his clean jaws. I had said every morning, "Wash your face," but forgot to mention his neck. Everything became hard and clear, as if it were cut out of metal, in that room, as deeply indelible as the painting of the boys listening to Sir Walter Raleigh's adventures in the auditorium: Miss Sullivan's blond lashes, her left eye a little bigger than the right, the spot of spit at the corner of her dry lips, the gray clouds of old chalk marks on the blackboard, the word cards, SENT, WENT, BENT, on the wall, the gluey tan wood of the windowsill, the pale afternoon sun streaking the floor, a red sweater and a brown sweater hanging crooked in the half-open wardrobe, the brown desks on iron legs, on each desk hands folded as for a somber occasion like a visit from the nurse, above each desk eyes staring at me.

I stood there leaden with shame until Miss Sullivan dismissed me with, "See that he washes better," and sent me back to my classroom. It was difficult to open the door and walk into those eyes that were going to stare at me and later, at three o'clock, come closer to ask what happened. I answered, "Oh, nothing. Miss Sullivan wanted me to check my brother's homework; he's careless, she said." I wanted to vomit, to stamp, to scream, to break, to kill: him, me, them, my mother, my father, everything, the whole world. But I had to walk him home. He searched my face as he ran across the playground toward me, hesitated, and attached himself to Jimmy, walking near me, as he had to, but a safe distance away, on the far side of Jimmy. As soon as he dropped his books on the floor of our bedroom he ran into my mother's room, where I heard them giggling together. She called to me, "Don't you want to come and see the baby?" I yelled back, "Tomorrow," still afraid of what I might see, a baby with a ditch in its head, a mother all rags of flesh, an exploded, splashed cartoon animal. All my fault. My brother came back into the kitchen where I was trying to peel an apple in one long coil, an especially delicate operation because I was using a big breadknife. He pushed my arm, breaking the coil, and ran toward the hallway, laughing. I threw the knife at him and saw it quivering in the wall where his head had been a second before. It fell from the wall. I picked it up and continued cutting the apple as I listened to him screaming to my mother, "She tried to kill me! She threw the knife, the big knife, at me! She's crazy! Send her away! Please, Mama, send her away! I'm afraid of her!" I heard her slippers patter down the hall, closed my eyes tight shut, and waited. She shook me. "Open your eyes. Look at me." I looked, I would have to sometime, and saw her as she was most mornings, in her thick brown bathrobe, her short hair not yet combed, her lips pale. "What's the matter with you? Do you know you could have killed him? Do you know he would be dead, forever dead? Never talk again, never walk, never see, never hear? Do you know that you would be locked away in an asylum for crazy people? And spend the rest of your life, many, many years, with other crazies?" I said nothing, tried not to be there. "I've got to go back to bed now and attend to the baby. This your father will hear about and I won't get in his way. Whatever punishment you get you'll deserve."

It rained that evening and my brother was granted the privilege, usually mine, of carrying the umbrella to the El station. It was a special pleasure, a special ceremony, to go out into the wet night as if on an emergency mission—a nurse, a doctor—to rescue our fathers. We clustered at the bottom of the steep El stairs, admiring the dark shine of the trolley tracks, the rain bubbling the puddles like boiling black cereal, holding the handles tight as the wind fought our umbrellas, listening to the rumble and roar of the train, the screeching stop, the rush of feet down the stairs. For many of us, the big smile as we yelled, "Pa, here I am, here," and were recognized and patted on the arm or head was the only overt affection we knew from our fathers. The umbrellas, now taller and single, separated to walk on their two long legs and their two short up Tremont Avenue, down to Bathgate, or shadowed themselves under the struts and tracks of Third Avenue.

By the time my brother and father got home and the wet umbrella placed in the bathtub, the story of the knife had been told, so serious a matter that it came before supper. Asked why I had thrown the knife, I answered—and it seemed a feeble reason—"Because his neck was dirty and he made me ashamed in front of his whole class." I couldn't say, "Because I hate mothers and babies and screaming in the night and people being pulled out of bellies with instruments and brothers who jump around and play while I have to take care of them." I couldn't find the words or shape the sentence because they were truly crazy things to say, worse than throwing knives. There was no preliminary lecture, cause and effect clear and simple. With a few words to my mother about the *gilgul*, the restless, evil spirit I must have in me—although he didn't really believe in such superstitious things—my father pushed me into the bathroom and, while he carefully pulled his belt out of the trouser loops, told me to lie across the covered toilet, pick up my skirt, and pull down my bloomers.

I had been slapped, on the face, on the behind, punched by boys and pinched by girls; my knees were often scraped, my fingers blistered and cut, but there was no preparation for the pain beyond pain of this first beating, the swish of the strap becoming a burning scream through my whole body, my arms shaking as they clung to the edge of the bathtub, my fingers scratching at the squealing porcelain, my ribs crushed against the toilet lid. I shrieked and begged, "Papa, don't. Stop, please. Please stop. Please, Papa." He stopped when he was out of breath, his face red, his brown eyes bulging. Replacing his belt, he walked out of the bathroom, closing the door. I stood there for a long while, then splashed cold water on my behind, fixed my clothing, and stood some more, not knowing where to go. In time I heard fumbling at the doorknob and my mother's voice telling my brother to get away, to let me be. A few minutes later she opened the door to tell me it was time to eat. I slipped out of the bathroom and into my bedroom, pushed the big chair against the door that had no lock, piled my books, my brother's books, the wooden sewing machine cover, and the heavy coats that were in the closet on the chair, and got into bed, pushing myself way, way down under the featherbed, stroking and rubbing myself until I fell asleep.

The next morning my brother banged on the door for his books. As I pulled the heavy chair away so he could get in, I noticed his neck was clean. My mother was back in bed with the baby I had no intention of seeing. I grabbed a roll from the breadbox in the kitchen and ate it as I dressed, then left the house quickly, passing my brother, who stood on the third floor waiting at Jimmy's door. We avoided each other for the next day or two, he hanging on to Jimmy, I watching that they looked each way down the street before they crossed broad, busy 180th.

After my mother had spent her traditional ten days in bed, she put on the clothing she wore before the big belly and fixed us nice lunches: noodles, pot cheese, and raisins with cinnamon and sugar, radishes and cucumbers in sour cream, salami sandwiches. Ordinariness washed, day by day, over our lives except for the baby lying in my mother's lap in the kitchen. She looked unfinished and wandering, making strange faces, her eyes a milky blue and bobbling in her head, the tiny fingers reaching and curling toward everything, nothing. When her eyes turned to gold and steady, and some of the grimaces became smiles, I began to like her a little and let her pull at my fingers and hair.

GIFTS

IRENA KLEPFISZ

$\mathcal{M}$y mother is about to wrap a present—two white cotton handkerchiefs or a green glass vase. I'm very young—ten, maybe twelve.

"Ma, take off the price," I beg. "You're not supposed to show how much you spent." Where did I learn this?

"It doesn't matter. There's no reason to take it off." The price sticks, the tag dangles.

"Ma, *proszę cię*!" I plead, reverting to my primal Polish. "Please!"

"What's the big secret? Let them see! Why shouldn't they see?"

Indeed, why shouldn't they? Why should they think it was nothing? What rules of etiquette require my mother to give silently without anyone having a clue as to her feelings, which, I suspect now, must have been a knot of pride and rage each vying to dominate her public persona:

—See how much I'm willing to spend!

—See how much you're costing me!

—See how generous I am!

—See how much you're making me sacrifice!

A gift from my mother, I would eventually realize, was as much a complex statement about herself and about her place in the world as the note she attached to it. During my childhood I didn't always understand it. But I did grasp this: the gift's price had meaning.

Of course, the nature of the price varied. During our first years in the States, I unconsciously deciphered and tried to obey my mother's coded lessons, which taught that a generous gesture possible only at one's own expense and trouble was the most prized. So as a teenager it seemed natural to secretly embroider a pillowcase with two blue swans floating amid yellow and brown reeds, present it to my mother on her birthday, and then proudly relate how for weeks I had backstitched late at night, using my reading flashlight under the covers. My mother appreciated struggle and hardship, the discipline required to make room in an overburdened life for someone else's need. The greater the sacrifice, the greater the value of the gift, the greater the love of the giver. For years, my Jewish immigrant mother tried to let me and others know that her gifts were the gifts of the Magi. Only rarely did she feel she received such gifts in return. But when she did, she boasted. "See, *Irka* sewed this *herself*! I never knew! In the dark. With a flashlight. *After* I'd gone to bed—late at night. She must have lost a lot of sleep."

My mother expected presents from me twice a year: on Mother's Day and on her birthday. This was not easy. When we came to the States I was eight and had no adult to remind me of dates, to consult with on gifts, or to provide me with money to pay for them. I am an only child. My father had been killed during the war. In those early years, if I wanted to do something without my mother's help or knowledge, I was on my own. Looking back, I don't remember how I managed to get money, nor (except for the pillowcase) the presents I gave her. Perhaps they were drawings from school or repackaged gifts I'd received. But they must have been a success, for, as someone once pointed out, our memory is selective: what we remember most clearly is the pain.

It was the early fifties. I was deeply unhappy. It wasn't that complicated. My immigrant status was no longer exotic or protective ("We have a new girl in class. She came to America on a big boat. She crossed the ocean.") but a source of shame ("Look at those stupid braids! What's she got on her legs? Ugly stockings her big-eyed mother made!"). American children bewildered me. Their unpredictable shifting loyalties—I was Dawn's best friend one day, her archenemy the next—were totally incomprehensible. I had no one to hold onto except my mother and I held on tight, fierce in trying to draw her away from her world of sewing and dress fittings into my world of sidewalk potsy and bicycle rides around the reservoir. She, of course, was trying to earn a living, and most of the time her world won. Most of the time I was lonely.

Summer brought solace. The heat and light gave me strength, made me believe that I could survive—even alone. While my mother sewed, I'd roller-skate at top speed along the colored slate paths of the courtyard and around the blocks of our building, the skate key heavy and solid against my heart. If the layers of scabs on my knees made skating too painful, I'd lie and dream in the Grove—a grassy, ragged field between our building and Mosholu Parkway. Other times I'd climb the boulder on Sedgwick Avenue and gaze at Van Cortlandt Park and the street below like an explorer annexing a new continent. I'd fantasize power and space and place myself at the center.

But the true gift of the summer was John, the Good Humor man, whom I adored. Making contact with him was as important to me as eating the ice cream he sold. John was constant: always ready to talk, always fully supplied. His truck, with bells sounding as natural as the birds of Van Cortlandt, would wind its way through our neighborhood, making predesignated stops at park benches and on street corners. If I missed him at one, I'd run or skate to the next. On the few occasions when my mother forgot to replenish my funds, John provided credit. I was good for it. My mother had instilled in me an honesty which would never have allowed me to cheat him—or anyone else for that matter.

In those days, ice cream was uncomplicated: orange-and-white creamcicles for seven cents, vanilla sundae cups or chocolate pops for ten. My mother always gave me dimes (ice in creamcicles was a waste of money) and I, in turn, gave them to John. He'd open a small door at the back of the truck, immediately releasing jittery clouds of white smoke from the "hot" ice which kept the ice cream solid. ("How can something be so cold that it can burn you?" I asked my mother over and over.) Though I yearned for the forbidden creamcicles, I was quite content with the thick sweetness of the sundaes. I'd lick the gooey chocolate syrup off the cover of the Dixie cup, then carefully peel off the wax paper protecting a blue photograph of Susan Hayward or Victor Mature. American custom required me to collect these. Dutifully I stacked them in my desk drawer, though I never really understood why.

At some point I realized I had a choice and I stopped spending the dimes and began saving them. I derived enormous pleasure from my secret thrift. First, saving demanded long-term Discipline and Diligence and Order, all three of which my mother had fully mastered, but which I, already at ten, was finding elusive. Second, and more important, it demanded I give up John and the sundaes, in other words, make a sacrifice, the sole element in gift-giving which guaranteed total success.

Since my mother's birthday is at the end of July, I had plenty of time to exercise self-denial. But let's face it—my sacrifice was probably not as enormous as I chose to believe. (Is this true? Or is this my mother's voice: "So you didn't have ice cream so often? So what?" Have I finally come to accept the fact that *her* sacrifice of leaving my father and the ghetto in order to pass on the Aryan side—"After all *someone* had to be responsible for you, at least one of us had to try to stay alive"—*her* sacrifice of surviving into poverty and lonely widowhood will never be matched by anything I do? She'd given up eternal oblivion for lifelong memory and regret to guarantee me natural mothering. How can I judge today any of my sacrifices, especially ones so trivial as ice cream Dixie cups on hot Bronx afternoons?)

That summer I'd been saving for my mother's birthday for a long time. The final sum: twelve dollars. (Eight dollars? Five? Any of these were enormous amounts for those days.) I wanted to buy something "big," something different. It had to be very expensive. Its price had to reflect how much I loved her, how much I was willing to spend on her rather than on myself, how much I was willing to give up to make her happy. I thought about it incessantly as I walked up and down Jerome Avenue, our main shopping strip. I looked in clothing stores, the five and dime. I was stumped. What could I buy her that would wow her, bowl her over? I searched for weeks. Finally, I spotted it in a hardware store window: a lazy Susan.

My mother needed this, as we say in Yiddish, *vi a lokh in kop*, like a hole in the head. She was an overworked seamstress, ill with a goiter condition, a woman alone. She barely had time to cook. She certainly never "entertained," nor did her friends. Entertaining was for Americans, for the rich. We were neither. Instead, on Saturday and Sunday evenings my mother and her friends would gather around each others' kitchen tables to sip tea from tall glasses and eat slices of golden pound cake. There was genuine pleasure in this coming together, but inevitably the true purpose would emerge: to confirm once again the existence of the glasses, the food, the table; to review yet again the accounts.

"Shimon Vaysberg? *Er lebt?* He's alive? In Paris?"

"I heard he'd disappeared in Lodz."

"He's married? Bronka? His brother's wife?"

"What happened to his sister? Patti? *Zi lebt?* She's alive?"

"Also in Paris?"

"Didn't she marry very young? *Far der milkhome?* Before the war?"

"Yankl. A gangster and a pimp. The mother was beside herself."

"Joined the Jewish police."

"*Zhob hot im derharget.* The ŻOB* had him shot."

As the evening progressed I'd watch the glasses being refilled, the tea bags redipped, and another loaf of pound cake sliced and distributed. (*"Nem nokh a shtikl! Nem! Nem!* Take another piece! Take it! Take it!" they'd urge each other breathlessly.) Even on the few occasions when we'd share a meal, it was always simple, direct. No hors d'oeuvres (except for the oil-drenched *schmaltz* herring), no fancy desserts. To us food was never mystical. It was a pressing need. We did not savor, we ate. Our one-pot dinners of Polish *krupnik*—a thick, nearly solid stew of boiled chicken, beans, barley, and potatoes, served in large bowls—were intended to fill us up, not to satisfy our senses. If by chance they provided more than nutrition, that was an extra.

So the moment I saw the lazy Susan, I was in love. I remember the blond wood, the delicately carved trays which rotated at different levels around the central golden bar. It may even have been collapsible—the trays folding inward. Among other characteristics, I have inherited my mother's passion for *tchotchkes*, knickknacks and gadgets. At the age of ten the gene was already manifest.

I went into the store, had the salesman bring it out. I touched the polished trays, pushed them with one finger—round and round.

"Yes," I told the salesman quietly and watched as he lowered it into a box and wrapped it with festive red paper. I gave him the money, picked up the box and carried it home. I even managed to hide it.

Then it was time. I gave it to her.

At first she seemed just puzzled. *"Na co mogę to użyć?* What's it for?" she asked.

I shrugged. *"Może na owoce."* I suggested fruit.

I suspect she accepted it with some forced enthusiasm. I don't remember the thanks, only the disaster.

Did she insist on knowing how much it cost because she always had to know *everything?* Did I broach the subject because I was proud of how expensive it was and wanted to tell her how much I thought she was worth or

*ŻOB—Polish acronym for Jewish Fighters Organization

how grown up I was to have so much money to spend? I have no idea. I only know that by then the price was important—to both of us. The point is, I told her.

"*Twelve dollars?* [Five? Eight?]," she whispered. "*Twelve dollars?*" she repeated more loudly. "What's the matter with you? *Bist meshige?* Are you crazy?"

Now she was furious. "You can't waste money like that! This is not what money is for." She was putting it back in the box. "I work and work—and you go out and spend it on *this*? What do I need a thing like this for?"

She closed the box. The lazy Susan was gone.

"I don't want it. *I don't want it!*" She was folding the red paper in half, then again in half. "Give it back! Give it right back. Buy me something I can use. An apron. I need an apron. Buy me an apron," she ordered. She put the red paper in the bottom desk drawer.

I froze. My throat locked, then opened. I began to cry—shock, disappointment, but above all, fear. I'd never returned anything before. The prospect of having to face the salesman and to ask for my money was mortifying. It seemed ugly, demeaning—maybe even immoral, like stealing. After all, there was nothing wrong with the lazy Susan. My mother simply didn't want it, didn't think it was worth the price. How could I ever tell the salesman that?

But I obeyed her. Did I have a choice?

It was getting dark. My mother, usually overly protective, did not seem to notice. I left and, crying the whole way, took the fifteen-minute walk to Jerome Avenue. At the store the salesman was kind. Perhaps it was my obvious misery. Perhaps he figured out the script. In any case, he was merciful and returned the money instantly. No questions asked.

The lingerie shop next door was still open. It was dimly lit, a deep, narrow cave lined with grey cardboard boxes. Behind the counter stood a tiny, stooped Jewish woman waiting to close up and go home. She seemed part substance, part shadow as she stared at the white nylon slips and cotton nightgowns hanging in the window. I told her what I needed. Barely moving, the old woman brought out three aprons from under the counter and spread them out in front of me. I pointed to a green one with white trimming. It had a little pocket on the right side. It cost—who knows? The right amount. The woman folded it and put it in a brown paper bag.

I walked home in the dark. As I entered our courtyard I could see the light in the room we shared—where we both slept, where I did my homework and she fitted her customers. Unlike other nights when I'd come home late, she was not at the window watching for me.

I walked up the two flights, unlocked the door. She was sitting at her sewing machine, but stitching a hem by hand. She looked up at me. I handed her the bag and she pulled out the apron.

"Now *this* is nice," she said, getting up. She slipped it over her head and tied it in the back. She put her hand in the pocket to feel out its size. She smiled as she looked at her reflection in the full-length mirror which hung on the back of the door to our room. "I like this. I like this *very much*. What a wonderful color! What a wonderful gift! Oh, thank you, Irka! Thank you!"

Then she kissed me.

THE THOUSAND ISLANDS

LYNNE SHARON SCHWARTZ

$\mathcal{S}$omewhere in the drift between sleep and waking, night and light, I heard a man call my name from far away, in a voice that meant I should come join him. It couldn't be my husband—he was lying beside me. I thought it sounded like my father, long dead. And I was afraid, because I can rarely resist the lure of a trip.

My mother used to tell me it was not good to ride the down escalator. She kept the reason mysterious—whether a superstition, or maybe a bizarre moral stricture, or a past disaster, I could never quite make out. In any event, we shouldn't take the risk. So in department stores we rode the escalator up and walked or took the elevator down. Later I learned it was something very personal she drew me into: simply that the down escalator made her dizzy and sick to her stomach. I never felt leery of escalators, nor of elevators in any ordinary, claustrophobic sense, but when I lived alone on the top floor of a tall building I feared, while going down to the basement, that the elevator would not stop there but continue down, down to a subterranean region of eerie, phantasmagoric happenings, just as when Don Quixote is lowered into the Cave of Montesinos and falls asleep, to meet long-dead creatures dwelling in "enchanted solitudes" and enacting floridly romantic adventures. Even going back up, in the instant's pause between pushing the button and the elevator's ascent, my heart and breath again hung suspended as I waited to be transported to the earth's secret, exotic core, from which I too might wish never to return and might chide friends who hauled me up with ropes, for "robbing me of the sweetest existence and most delightful vision any human being ever enjoyed or beheld." The car always went up. Gasping in relief, I would shift my visions accordingly, and imagine that instead of stopping at the top floor it would continue on through the roof and sail aloft like a balloon, past this world in which every single thing was a boundary, to a region of open, dazzling spaces without logic or limits.

My mother never wearied of telling the story of her trip to Watertown, New York, before I was born. She had a seductive way of telling a story, a way that ensnared me in the filaments of her emotions and made me impatient for the time when such worldly adventures would happen to me. It was towards the end of the Depression, on the eve of war in Europe. My father had been fortunate enough to find a government job in Watertown, something to do with taxes. She stayed behind with my sister in her parents' house in Brooklyn, a brownstone with each floor given over to a daughter and her family. She seems to have considered it perfectly natural to stay behind with her parents, which is odd since in another part of her mind she believes a woman should go wherever her husband goes. Except, perhaps, to Watertown. My father would come into town every second or third weekend, and on one of these visits he persuaded my mother to ride back part of the way with him, half an hour or so, no great risk, then he would drop her at a bus stop where she could catch a ride home. She gets into the car, leaving my sister in the care of the extended family, and after a time notices that they are out of the city, speeding along a highway. When she remarks on this my father says he'll let her out in a while. Pretty soon she realizes they are far from the safety of Brooklyn, headed for Watertown.

"He kidnapped me," she would declare with pride and delight.

On the way to his rooming house my father waved from the car window to a couple of his office mates passing on the street, and called out happily that his wife was paying him a visit. My mother found his landlady courteous enough, though a type she was not accustomed to—tight-lipped, chalky-faced, austere in a particular small-town fashion. While my father was off at work they chatted. Towards the close of the chat the landlady told my mother that she seemed to be a nice woman but that in Watertown nice women, though they might wear rouge and powder, did not wear lipstick. This amused my mother as a lesson in provinciality. Especially since, as everyone in Brooklyn knew, lipstick was the most modest form of makeup, powder next, rouge next, mascara next, and eye shadow the ultimate. Eyeliner was not yet used.

On the second day in Watertown it was arranged that my mother would go downtown to meet my father for lunch. She started walking along the road he had indicated. Soon a car slowed alongside her; the driver honked and called to her to get in. She ignored him. For quite a while he tracked her, occasionally blowing the horn, but, a city girl, she steadfastly ignored him.

When she got to the office she told my father about the man who had tried to pick her up, then they went to lunch. In the restaurant my father greeted some people and introduced her. Imagine her surprise when one, looking puzzled, said, "I saw your wife walking to town. I figured she was coming to meet you and I wanted to give her a lift, but she wouldn't turn around." One of the very men they had passed on the street the day before!

Of course my mother was embarrassed. He had meant well, but how was she to have known? How to explain that in New York City a sensible woman never gets into a passing car with a stranger?

I was conceived, legend has it, on the Watertown trip. Then my father brought her home to her parents' house.

There was another trip my parents made early in their married life, before I was born, that my mother liked to tell about. The Thousand Islands, in Canada. Even though my mother described the Thousand Islands in vague terms—peaceful, small old-fashioned houses, lots of water—she managed, with her talent for narrative and her candid face and expressive voice, to make them sound highly exotic, and thus they remain, the very name thrilling in its magnificent profusion. There too she met a landlady, who told her—my mother is sociable with strangers—that she had never seen Jews before and always believed, as she had been taught, that Jews had horns. My mother informed her, no doubt in the winning, candid manner I know well, that Jews assuredly did not have horns. From my mother's stories I sometimes confuse the two landladies, the horns and the lipstick, and the two trips—if indeed they were separate experiences: Watertown is very near the Thousand Islands, I have since learned. She talked about her travels so often, I imagine, because they were so infrequent. I don't count the Catskill Mountains and Florida: those were not trips but transfers of the corporeal self in a car or an airplane in order to arrive at the same place but with better weather.

Before she was born her parents traveled halfway round the world at great peril, and whether or not they told her about their travels, she, along with many in her generation, desired nothing more than to stay put where it was safe.

But I always yearned to go on exotic trips and nagged about it till at last, I must have been nine or ten, my mother said, all right, we would go to the Thousand Islands. My outlook on life was transformed—I had something to live for beyond the asphyxiating routine of school—and I began making lists, secret lists that I kept hidden in a night-table drawer, of what I would take to the Thousand Islands: 2 pr. shorts, 2 bathing suits, 3 skirts (white w. belt, red print, pleated) . . . Every night I revised the secret lists—for, unlike my mother, I thrived on secrecy—and copied them over, picturing myself in the various combinations of outfits, doing things on my secret agenda: ambling down foreign streets lined with picturesque cottages, or standing on a pier in the salt breeze, gazing over the rippling water dotted with hundreds of tiny gleaming islands. Sometimes I would ask my mother about the impending trip and she would retell her story about going there as a young woman, the landlady, the horns, and get a nostalgic look on her face which I interpreted as sweet longing and anticipation. But as weeks passed, her responses grew vaguer and then dismissive, till it dawned on me that there would be no Thousand Islands trip and I would never be packing the clothes on the lists. At first I thought the plans had fallen through for some adult reason, then with a kind of gradual shock I understood that there had never been any trip planned, she had said it only to placate me, to shut me up, as she did with five-minute spaghetti. When I was impatient for dinner she would sometimes tell me she was cooking a special type of spaghetti, five-minute spaghetti, and in fact those spaghetti meals did seem to materialize more quickly than most. Only when I was a teenager and be-gan to go to supermarkets alone—for from as far back as I can remember, my mother shopped, pulling me along, in a tiny grocery with barely room to stand, where she had to ask the waddling grocer to fetch each item, one by one, which revelation of our family's intimate tastes and needs seemed a violation of privacy—did I learn there was no such thing as five-minute spa-ghetti. I was mortified, not so much on account of having been duped, but to think that my hunger—evidently an urgent, abandoned, exposed, un-seemly lust—required such strategies.

I forgot about my secret lists and when I found them a few years later, under a pile of new secret lists and agendas in the night-table drawer, I studied them with contempt—7 pr. socks, sneakers, white sndls—and tore them up. There would come a time, I thought vengefully, when I could go to the Thousand Islands by myself, and not need to beg anyone to take me.

One summer afternoon I went on an excursion with a man I knew. I was going away soon on a long trip, and we wanted to spend one unfettered, leisurely afternoon together. He said he knew a place in the country, an old friend's house on a lake; the friend was away. He picked me up on a street corner in his car—I knew him well, so it was all right to get in. But when we arrived we found the friend's brother there. We were all very civilized and pretended this was not a tryst, and as we sat on the porch overlooking the lake, eating sandwiches and drinking iced tea, we discussed the troubled politics of the Middle East, where none of us had ever been. After a while the friend's brother excused himself to do some paperwork inside and urged us to enjoy the lake and the house, to make ourselves at home. We swam and lay on the wooden dock in the hot sun, where he caressed my back, and just from that simple motion and from the absurdity of the situation we reached such a pitch of excitement that he wanted to make love then and there, but I couldn't do that right in the middle of a lake with cottages around it, so we went inside to a downstairs bedroom, tearing off our wet suits recklessly and barely in time to fit ourselves together in some frenzied slapdash fashion. Later we told the friend's brother, all of us with composed faces, that we had had a nice swim and a nap, thanked him, and drove back to the city to resume our workaday lives.

Some time later my husband went on a weekend camping trip that wasn't really that, a trip he said he needed for solitude and an imprecise sort of spiritual refreshment which I, of all people, would not dream of challenging—nor of joining him on, not being a camper. He carefully, almost ostentatiously, unearthed supplies like hiking boots and a canteen. Months after, when I found out that the trip had not really been a camping trip, what could I, of all people, say? I would not have been altogether devastated except for one thing. He had borrowed my knapsack for the trip. "Do you mind if I take your blue knapsack?" he asked the night before he left, and I shrugged and said, "Sure." That still rankles, that my knapsack was a witness, kidnapped, and on top of that he really didn't need a knapsack (or a canteen) in the city. I don't like to think of why he did that, even less than I like to think of how mortified and disillusioned I was when I learned, after so many years, that there was no such thing as five-minute spaghetti. But these are earnest, candid people. It was probably nothing despicably complicated, just for verisimilitude, and again to placate me and any (nonexistent) anxiety or suspicion.

So I became a well-traveled person (though never to the Thousand Islands— I have lost that urge), but unlike my mother I rarely entertain or lure with travel stories. Nor do I tell about the lists of things to take along the next time and the agendas of things to accomplish. I would never have done a thing like that, taking the knapsack. Not simply because I would not run such risks, fully as mysterious as the risk of the down escalator. But because secrecy has its own proprieties, utterly unknown to those earnest candid people who have to snare others in their travels, who cannot travel alone.

TALKING BACK

for my mother

CHANA BLOCH

You don't tell it right, either. And you were
there with your clever fingers from
the beginning. When you printed
my mouth on your cheek, and crooned: *She's
kissing me.* When you made your voice small
as a sparrow's, and sang: *How I love*

my Mommy. O master
ventriloquist, yes.
Yes, it was good. Very good. It was horrid.

The deadbolt of evening.

But when I tell it, I always leave out
the soft-boiled egg you set
on the bedside table, the satin
talcum powder, the little fringed terry-cloth robe
after the bath.

Your rhinestone earrings, your hatpins, the red-knobbed
radio laughing
on Sunday afternoons as the sun
coasted down the sky—

Yes, mother, I saved them. I braided the good past
into the bad till it grew
long, lustrous, tough. And let it down
hand over hand through the dormer window,
slow, down the slippery wall.

FIERCE ATTACHMENTS
(EXCERPT)

VIVIAN GORNICK

$\mathcal{I}$t's a cloudy afternoon in April, warm and gray, the air sweet with new spring. The kind of weather that induces nameless stirrings in unidentifiable parts. As it happens, it is also the anniversary of the Warsaw Ghetto Uprising. My mother wants to attend the annual memorial meeting at Hunter College. She has asked me to come with her. I've refused, but I've agreed to walk her up Lexington Avenue to the school. Now, as we walk, she recounts an adventure she had yesterday on the street.

"I was standing on the avenue," she tells me, "waiting for the light to change, and a little girl, maybe seven years old, was standing next to me. All of a sudden, before the light changed, she stepped out into the street. I pulled her back onto the sidewalk and I said to her, 'Darling, never never cross on the red. Cross only on the green.' The kid looks at me with real pity in her face and she says, 'Lady, you've got it all upside down.'"

"That kid's not gonna make it to eight," I say.

"Just what I was thinking." My mother laughs.

We're on Lexington in the lower Forties. It's a Sunday. The street is deserted, its shops and restaurants closed, very few people out walking.

"I must have a cup of coffee," my mother announces.

My mother's wishes are simple but they are not negotiable. She experiences them as necessities. Right now she must have a cup of coffee. There will be no sidetracking of this desire she calls a need until the cup of steaming liquid is in her hand being raised to her lips.

"Let's walk over to Third Avenue," I say. "There should be something open there." We cross the street and head east.

"I was talking to Bella this morning," my mother says on the other side of the avenue, shaking her head from side to side. "People are so cruel! I don't understand it. She has a son, a doctor, you should pardon me, he is so mean to her. I just don't understand. What would it hurt him, he'd invite his mother out for a Sunday to the country?"

"The country? I thought Bella's son works in Manhattan."

"He lives in Long Island."

"Is that the country?"

"It isn't West End Avenue!"

"Okay, okay—so what did he do now?"

"It isn't what he did now, it's what he does always. She was talking to her grandchild this morning and the kid told her they had a lot of people over yesterday afternoon, what a nice time they all had eating on the porch. You can imagine how Bella felt. She hasn't been invited there in months. Neither the son nor his wife have any feeling for her."

"Ma, how that son managed to survive having Bella for a mother, much less made it through medical school, is something for Ripley, and you know it."

"She's his mother."

"Oh, God."

"Don't 'oh, God' me. That's right. She's his mother. Plain and simple. She went without so that he could have."

"Have what? Her madness? Her anxiety?"

"Have life. Plain and simple. She gave him his life."

"That was all a long time ago, Ma. He can't remember that far back."

"It's uncivilized he shouldn't remember!"

"Be that as it may. It cannot make him want to ask her to sit down with his friends on a lovely Saturday afternoon in early spring."

"He should do it whether he wants to or not. Don't look at me like that. I know what I'm talking about."

We find a coffee shop on Third Avenue, an upwardly mobile greasy spoon, all plastic wood, vinyl leather, tin-plated chandeliers with candle-shaped bulbs burning in the pretentiously darkened afternoon.

"All right?" my mother says brightly to me.

If I said, "Ma, this place is awful," she'd say, "My fancy daughter. I was raised in a cold-water flat with the toilet in the hall but this isn't good enough for you. So okay, you pick the place," and we'd go trudging on up Third Avenue. But I nod yes, sit down with her in a booth by the window, and prepare to drink a cup of dreadful coffee while we go on with our weighty conversation about children and parents.

"Hot," my mother says to the heavy-lidded, black-haired waiter approaching our table very slowly. "I want my coffee hot."

He stares at her with so little expression on his face that each of us is sure he has not understood. Then he turns toward me, only his eyebrows inquiring. My mother puts her hand on his arm and cocking her head to one side smiles extravagantly at him. "Where are you from?" she asks.

"Ma," I say.

Holding the waiter fast between her fingers, she repeats, "Where?"

The waiter smiles. "Greek," he says to her. "I Greek."

"Greek," she says, as though assessing the value of the nationality he has offered her. "Good. I like Greeks. Remember. Hot. I want my coffee hot." He bursts out laughing. She's right. She knows what she's talking about. It's I who am confused in the world, not she.

Business over, she settles back into the argument. "It's no use. Say what you will, children don't love their parents as they did when I was young."

"Ma, do you really believe that?"

"I certainly do! My mother died in my sister's arms, with all her children around her. How will I die, will you please tell me? They probably won't find me for a week. Days pass I don't hear from you. Your brother I see three times a year. The neighbors? Who? Who's there to check on me? Manhattan is not the Bronx, you know."

"Exactly. That's what this is all about. Manhattan is not the Bronx. Your mother didn't die in her daughter's arms because your sister loved her more than we love you. Your sister hated your mother, and you know it. She was there because it was her duty to be there, and because she lived around the corner all her married life. It had nothing to do with love. It wasn't a better life, it was an immigrant life, a working-class life, a life from another century."

"Call it what you want," she replies angrily, "it was a more human way to live."

We are silent. The waiter comes with the coffee. She has the cup in her hands before he has fully turned away. She sips, looks scornfully after his retreating back. "You think it's hot?" she says. "It's not hot."

"Call him back."

She pushes the air away with her hand. "Forget it. I'll drink it as it is, the devil won't take me." Clearly the conversation is depressing her.

"Well, all I can say is, if he wasn't her son Bella would never lay eyes on him again."

"That makes two of them, doesn't it? He certainly wouldn't lay eyes on her again if she wasn't his mother, would he?"

My mother gazes steadily at me across the table. "So what are you saying, my brilliant daughter?"

"I'm saying that nowadays love has to be earned. Even by mothers and sons."

Her mouth falls open and her eyes deepen with pity. What I have just said is so retarded she may not recover the power of speech. Then, shaking her head back and forth, she says, "I'll tell you like the kid told me, 'Lady, you've got the whole thing upside down.' "

At this moment the waiter passes by carrying a pot of steaming coffee. My mother's hand shoots out, nearly unbalancing him. "Is that hot?" she demands. "This wasn't hot." He shrugs, stops, pours coffee into her cup. She drinks greedily and nods grudgingly. "It's hot." Satisfaction at last.

"Let's go," she says, standing up, "it's getting late."

We retrace our steps and continue on up Lexington Avenue. The air is sweeter than before, warmer, fuller, with a hint of rain now at its bright gray edge. Delicious! A surge of expectation rises without warning in me but, as usual, does not get very far. Instead of coming up straight and clear it twists about, turns inward, and quickly stifles itself to death; a progress with which I am depressingly familiar. I glance sideways at my mother. I must be imagining this, but it seems to me her face reflects the same crazy journey of detoured emotion. There is color in her cheek, but her eye is startled and her mouth pulled downward. What, I wonder, does she see when she looks at me? The mood of the day begins to shift dangerously.

We're in the Fifties. Huge plate-glass windows filled with color and design line the avenue. What a relief it's Sunday, the stores are closed, no decisions to make. We share an appreciation of clothes, my mother and I, of looking nice in clothes, but we cannot bear to shop, either of us. We're always wearing the same few articles of clothing we have each picked hastily from the nearest rack. When we stand as we do now, before a store window, forced to realize there are women who dress with deliberation, we are aware of mutual disability, and we become what we often are: two women of remarkably similar inhibitions bonded together by virtue of having lived within each other's orbit nearly all their lives. In such moments the fact that we are mother and daughter strikes an alien note. I know it is precisely because we *are* mother and daughter that our responses are mirror images, yet the word "filial" does not seem appropriate. On the contrary, the idea of family, of our being family, of family *life* seems altogether puzzling: an uncertainty in her as well as in myself. We are so used to thinking of ourselves as a pair of women, ill-starred and incompetent (she widowed, me divorced), endlessly unable to get family life for themselves. Yet, as we stand before the store window, "family life" seems as much a piece of untested fantasy in her as it is in me. The clothes in the window make me feel we have both been confused the whole of our lives about who we are, and how to get there.

Suddenly I am miserable. Acutely miserable. A surge of defeat passes through me. I feel desolated, without direction or focus, all my daily struggles small and disoriented. I become speechless. Not merely silent, but speechless. My mother sees that my spirits have plunged. She says nothing. We walk on, neither of us speaking.

We arrive at Sixty-ninth Street, turn the corner, and walk toward the entrance to the Hunter auditorium. The doors are open. Inside, two or three hundred Jews sit listening to the testimonials that commemorate their unspeakable history. These testimonials are the glue that binds. They remind and persuade. They heal and connect. Let people make sense of themselves. The speeches drone on. My mother and I stand there on the sidewalk, alone together, against the sound of culture-making that floats out to us. "We are a cursed people," the speaker announces. "Periodically we are destroyed, we struggle up again, we are reborn. That is our destiny."

The words act like adrenaline on my mother. Her cheeks begin to glow. Tears brighten her eyes. Her jawline grows firm. Her skin achieves muscle tone. "Come inside," she says softly to me, thinking to do me a good turn. "Come. You'll feel better."

I shake my head no. "Being Jewish can't help me anymore," I tell her.

She holds tightly to my arm. She neither confirms nor denies my words, only looks directly into my face. "Remember," she says. "You are my daughter. Strong. You must be strong."

"Oh Ma!" I cry, and my frightened greedy freedom-loving life wells up in me and spills down my soft-skinned face, the one she has given me.

WHAT GOOD
IS A SMART GIRL?

MEREDITH TAX

*J*married twice.

The first time was to show my mother I could. Hadn't she always said I would never get married? I was doomed, like her sister Ruthie. Who could live with such a temper, such a mouth?

Now I can understand why she said these things. But in childhood I understood only this: no one would ever want me. They might put up with me for a while, or pretend, but in the end, they would push me away.

She did, when I ran to her. She didn't want to be touched. Her skin hurt. Her stomach hurt. She had a bleeding ulcer. I aggravated it. I drove her crazy. I almost killed her. She held my baby brother on her lap, but wouldn't touch me.

Of course she loved me. She said she loved me. She was my mother. She had to.

But she didn't know much about love. I could tell that from reading *Little Women*.

Where would she have learned? Who had ever hugged her as a child?

"Never a kind word," she says, "not for any of us."

Even now, when she tries to speak of love, you can hardly hear her. Her voice tightens as if she will choke. The words crack coming out. Praise her, she almost faints. She's used to insults or nothing, she who was called "Schmaltz" growing up because she was the only one in her family who didn't look like a starving horse. In that little country town where they were the only Jews.

She passed down what she had learned of family life: it was a trap, full of bitterness, not joy. Still, it was woman's fate, all there was. You didn't have to waste time hoping. She had learned the rules in childhood: "Expect the worst, then you won't be disappointed."

Childhood! She might as well have been raised by wolves in the forest. They groomed her with snarls and bites, taught her to howl at the moon. Those who survived were the lucky ones. It was the State of Nature according to Hobbes, "No arts, no letters, no society, and . . . the life of man solitary, poor, nasty, brutish, and short."

How did they get that way?

What made them so like wolves?

The brutality of rural life? Peasant savagery? In *The Childhood of Maxim Gorky*, in *The Woman Warrior*, I recognize my mother's family, born so far from the city that they knew no shame. Brought from somewhere way out in the country. *Oysfersheint*, as they used to say, in that peculiar brand of Yiddish I can find in no dictionary.

My grandfather's father was a blind shoelace peddler in Latvia.

Nothing romantic about that kind of poverty. Frenzied with anxiety, desperate with hunger, they pecked at each other like crazed birds. Flinging themselves against the walls of culture and economics, beating out their own brains and each other's, throwing words like knives, covering their children with wounds. Who says acquired characteristics can't be transmitted?

"You're just like Ruthie," she said year after year. "You don't care about anybody but yourself! You do what you goddamn please no matter who gets hurt!"

Why did she yell at me all the time?

What had I done wrong?

I was just a little girl.

What was she so afraid of?

Did my murderous thoughts, my sulks and tantrums, really hurt her? Was it true I'd made her ulcer bleed? Had I really ruined her life?

She loved me when I was little. What made her change?

I was too smart. What good were brains to a girl? A girl should be pretty, practical, hard-working. Other qualities were superfluous.

Sentiments bred in centuries of exile, from Babylon to the Russian Pale. Men did the studying and women did the marketing. Brains were for men; what else did they have in Galus? They couldn't own land. Couldn't be doctors, lawyers, tavern-keepers. They became specialized for brains, a Jewish

secondary sex characteristic. Hypertrophic brains, like a peacock's tail—
the bigger and more extravagantly useless, the better.

Not necessarily a survival trait, these florid, ornamental brains. But who
ever expected Jews to survive?

Female poaching was fiercely resented and counter to the will of God.
Oh, the resentment of Jewish men against smart Jewish women, with us
still! Along with an intellectual arrogance nurtured in the bosom of the
family, in boys taught to despise their mothers and sisters, taught to say a
morning prayer thanking God they were not born a woman.

They had to be better than somebody.

"Shon iz sie nicht, ober dumm." A proverbial saying frequently quoted by
my mother. "She ain't pretty but she's dumb." To be said in tones of
recommendation.

What good were A's to a girl? What good were brilliant papers, stories,
poems? Drawings and paintings were all right, decorative objects hardly
more threatening than embroidery. But nothing written.

If I had been a boy I could have been a doctor like my father. He said I
would have made a good doctor. Since that was impossible, I should use my
talent for art to become a medical illustrator. They made good money.

"Why can't I be a doctor?"

"They don't let girls into medical school."

They. Meaning the AMA, protector of his own privilege, an organization for which he would have laid down his life.

My mother's reactions were more complex. When I showed her a piece
of work, a story, a poem, a report card, she would say, "That's very good,
dear," or even, "We're proud of you."

But her voice wouldn't sound proud. It would sound strained.

At other times she would sneer, "I suppose you think you're so smart."

Or cry out, "What difference do you think it makes?!"

She was torn. Maybe broken.

Broken in two, like a dropped plate.

You can glue a dropped plate so it looks almost whole. But it is never as
strong as it was.

Only now that I've had children and felt the draining exhaustion, the hysterical need for privacy and quiet that cannot be had, can I see how it might

have been with her. She was so fragile she couldn't survive unless she could control everything in her environment. And she couldn't control me. I was too alive. I had too many strange ideas. I looked at everything, wondered about everything, asked a million questions, wrote poems and stories, drew pictures that the teachers thought amazing. How that must have terrified her, she who believed with her mother that to compliment a child was to bring down the evil eye.

Bad enough if I had been a boy. But I was a girl. People took one look and said, "It's a shame."

They said, "She's so smart, who will ever marry her?"

She had to protect me from myself.

She had to protect herself from me.

What good was independence to a girl? I would be doomed like her sister Ruthie—impossible to live with, impossible to love.

She had to break my spirit.

When I reached adolescence, our home became a battlefield, with my father absent and my brothers watching, appalled, developing their own strategies to avoid such conflict, never being too independent, never wanting to go too far away. One became her good boy, her right hand; the other stayed a baby as long as he could and hid the rest of the time. I remember him asking me, in a terrified whisper, "What did you *do* to make her hate you so much?"

I hated her back, for she made me fear my own powers. Her weapons were ridicule, scorn, and rage. She used words with great force; she might have been a writer had she been stronger or more fortunately born. I too use words with great force. Like a curse, I pass this heritage on to my daughter, tempered a little by America and the passage of time.

And education.

My mother's father owned two books, the Bible and Spinoza—Spinoza, one of the few Jews ever excommunicated. *Eppes* in the seventeenth century—Grandpa may have been a freethinker but he was not exactly up to date. He did triage on his children, helping the ones with brains, throwing the rest aside, placing his best hopes on his second son, Joe, who was so smart he got through law school before he was old enough to vote.

When Joe's education was paid for, Grandpa turned his attention to his middle daughter, my mother. He sent her to college at a time when nobody wasted that kind of money on a girl. Not just the Normal School, either; he sent her to Madison, where she could be an English major, get a B.A. instead of a teaching certificate, and live at Langdon Hall, not in a boarding house.

Everybody said, "What's the point? She's only going to get married anyway."

They said, "The only degree a girl needs is her M.R.S."

She graduated and got a job in the classified section of the *Milwaukee Journal*, no easy task in the depths of the Depression. But she paid for her good fortune, paid with anxiety attacks that grew worse every year. In her early twenties she developed an ulcer so severe she fell down the *Journal* stairs, weak from the loss of blood. She never held another job.

So much for female education.

Still, it was not wasted. There were riches stored up in her mind. She gave me her fierce love of language, reciting soliloquies from *Hamlet* while mopping the kitchen floor.

"To be or not to be, that is the question."

That is always the question. But her answer was not mine.

TROPICAL AUNTS

ENID SHOMER

$\mathcal{A}$unt Debs and Aunt Ava. They were my father's sisters. Dramatic, glamorous women who, my mother said, had "been around." I saw them every July when we traded the humidity of Washington, D.C., for the even more oppressive heat of Miami, where my father's people lived amid piña coladas, guava jelly, and floral print clothing. I still have a picture of them mounted in one of those plastic telescopes that were popular keychain trinkets in the 1950s. They look tan and healthy and non-Jewish standing arm-in-arm in front of the cardboard palm trees.

Debs was the older, a stormy, rich blond who had been widowed. She lived a reclusive life in a houseboat on the Miami River. Without a phone, she could only be contacted through her attorney, like a movie star. Ava was a redhead with a reputation for borrowing money. Everyone knew she'd had to get married to her first husband. This was the biggest scandal so far in our family. After she had the baby she got divorced, lost custody, and married an osteopath who worked nights as a stand-up comic in the hotels of Miami Beach.

My Florida aunts came north to visit us only twice. The first time was for my sister Fran's wedding. They drove up together in a big white Chrysler sedan. "My teeth started to chatter as soon as we hit North Carolina," Aunt Debs said, hugging herself as she closed the car door. She regarded our snow-covered lawn as if it were the surface of the moon. Then she picked her way slowly up the front walk. Ava followed, relatively surefooted in doeskin loafers and thick white socks. She leaned down to touch the snow shoveled into a heap alongside the front stoop and put a drop of it on her tongue. "Sometimes we put Hershey's syrup on it and make snowcones," I told her. I knew they'd be exclaiming and complaining about the weather but that the cold fascinated them. Also, when I saw my aunt Ava eating snow, just like that, I understood how she could have gotten pregnant.

As soon as they had hung up their clothes, they unveiled the presents: chocolate-covered coconut patties (my favorite candy), sea-grape jelly, and fresh papayas. For my mother, a white lace bathing-suit coverup, for my father, a book called *Fish of the Southern Waters*. My gift was a pearly-pink comb and brush set with tiny shells and seahorses embedded in the handles. For Fran they'd chosen salmon-colored lingerie that made my father blush as my sister eagerly held it up for us to admire. "Baby-dolls," Aunt Ava explained to Fran. "I hope your Herb will like them."

The night before the Florida aunts arrived my mother had given my sister and me a briefing. "Don't mention Uncle Teddy," she cautioned. Teddy was Aunt Debs's dead husband.

My father, within earshot in his lounger, pitched in. "Did you put away the liquor?" Fran and I looked at each other. The only time my parents drank was at Passover, when they sipped reluctantly at four glasses of Manischewitz Concord wine. Beer had never crossed our threshold. Once at a restaurant I had seen my mother drink a Brandy Alexander, but afterward someone told her mixed drinks were fattening and she never had another one.

"All I have is the bottle of schnapps," my mother said. I knew exactly which bottle she was talking about. It belonged to my grandfather, Velvel. My mother kept it on hand for him the way you'd keep emergency medicine for an asthma attack.

"Are we supposed to pretend Uncle Teddy never existed or what?" Fran asked.

"She took his death so hard," my mother said. "Just avoid the subject if you can."

I remembered when Great Uncle Benny had died. The whole family mourned for a week at my aunt Florence's house, where the gilt mirrors were covered with black cloth and the satin loveseats crowded out by low, uncomfortable wooden folding chairs.

"Aunt Debs must have really been in love," I said, looking at my sister and remembering an old movie about a girl whose fiancé was killed on the way to the wedding. Would Fran turn to drink if Herb were tragically killed after the final head count had been given to the caterer?

"Teddy was a real charmer," my mother said. "Could charm the birds out of the trees."

My father lit a Lucky Strike. "That girl really suffered when he went. I even had to hide the scissors. No hospital could have handled it."

This explained, at last, my father's prolonged visit to Florida the autumn before. My parents had flown down for the funeral, but my father had stayed an extra three weeks. At the time he had said he was helping Aunt Debs settle Uncle Teddy's estate. Now my imagination ran wild with passionate scenes in which my aunt Debs, her large blue eyes reddened by grief and alcohol, was saved from self-destruction by *my father*, who in my experience had not been up to dealing with bloody knees or temper tantrums.

Later that evening I persuaded Fran to let me into her room. She was setting her hair. I eyed the birch bedroom set and pink clock-radio, the wallpaper with its soothing dusky primroses being visited by small yellow birds. As soon as Fran was married I'd be moving in. I smeared some of her Dippity-Do on my hair.

"Your bangs will look like sheet metal if you use that much," she said through a mouthful of bobby pins.

"Who do you like best, Aunt Ava, Aunt Debs, or Aunt Florence?"

"You must be joking. Ava and Debs treat us like their own kids."

"Mom says they spoil us rotten."

"That's because they don't get to see us very often," Fran said.

"I wish Aunt Florence would move to Alaska," I said. Aunt Florence was our mother's brother's wife. She was a stout woman, later diagnosed as diabetic, whose bleached-blond hair was done up in a zillion curls like a telephone cord on top of her head. She referred to her kids as "my Maury" and "my Melissa," even if they were standing right next to her. I was jealous of and hated both these cousins.

"I'm glad you're getting married before Melissa," I said.

"Melissa's a bit young to be thinking of marriage," Fran said, from her great tower of eighteen years. Melissa was sixteen.

"Aunt Ava eloped when she was sixteen." "Eloped" was the word everybody in our family used for her shotgun wedding.

"Aunt Ava's different," Fran said as she opened the door and gestured me through it. "You can't talk about her and Melissa in the same breath."

Fran was right. The Florida aunts were different. Aunt Ava was a model, but not the kind who strolls down runways or appears on the cover of *Vogue*. Her portfolio was full of magazine ads for shoes, gloves, detergent, and jewelry. She had supplied the hands and feet for the photos. "A perfect size 7B," she'd say, pointing her toe. "And feet don't show age like a face does."

Aunt Debs had kept her husband's accounts. "They weren't ordinary books," my father had told my mother last fall after Uncle Teddy died. "Well, when he had the dry-goods stores, all right, pretty regular. But after the deal in Las Vegas?" His voice had trailed off to a low, knowing snicker.

At the wedding the two sides of our family would have a chance to get to know one another better, my mother said at breakfast the next day. The Florida aunts were still upstairs asleep.

The Northern half of my family—my mother's side—had always acted superior to the Florida half. It had nothing to do with pedigrees—they were all immigrant Jews from Russia, Poland, Hungary, and Rumania. I think now it was envy, for the Northern relatives vacationed in Florida for two weeks each winter and talked of retiring there to a life of golf, sunshine, and shrimp cocktails. For them, Florida meant relaxation; anyone who lived there year-round had chosen good weather over hard work. My father had told me at least a thousand times that I wasn't a Yankee like "them." This was confusing coming on the heels of my mother's pleas that I attend Hebrew school and join the Young Judea group at my junior high. Would they need to know if I was a Northern or Southern Jew?

My father's family—fifteen of them—had left Baltimore's harbor district in the early twenties, part of the Florida land boom. My father spoke of this period with such reverence that as a very young child I pictured them in covered wagons, carrying rifles and beef jerky. My grandmother Minerva opened a beauty shop in Lemon City, claimed to have invented the permanent wave before Nestlé, and dropped dead of heart failure at the parimutuel window when I was four. She and her children took to the tropical landscape without a hitch. They ate hearts of palm, gambled on dogs, horses, and jai alai, and carried fishing tackle at all times in the trunks of their cars. Though my father claimed that the aunts spoke Yiddish just like my mother's side of the family, I'd never heard a word of it pass their lips in eleven summers in Miami. They had picked up *un poquito español*, which, Ava said, came in handy on weekends in Havana.

"I want to sit with the aunts at the wedding," I told my mother, handing her my empty cereal bowl.

"Out of the question. We've already discussed it."

"It's *my* sister getting married," I argued. No good. I looked at the wall calendar where the large red circle that represented Fran's wedding loomed at me like an angry eye. The entire month of December was full of arrows and asterisks and my mother's notes to herself. If I ever got married, I'd run away to Elkton, Maryland, just for spite.

On the day of the wedding, Debs and Ava included me in all their beauty rituals: eyebrow tweezing, oatmeal facials, shampooing, hair setting, leg waxing, manicuring, and eyelash curling. Much of this was new to me because my mother, a size 20 most of her life, spent her cosmetic energy experimenting with the silhouettes various corsets and girdles provided. She paid little attention to her face. I'd watched her countless times after her morning bath. She used no foundation but blotted her shiny freckled face with a puff dipped in light rachel powder. The lipstick was applied the way you'd put a dash in a sentence.

Finally, after six hours of primping, we got dressed. Debs wore a green satin sheath that showed off how slim she was—without dieting, my mother said. Ava was startling in a silver sequined dress that fell from her body like enchanted water. I stepped out the door in my red French-heel pumps as if I were wearing someone else's body, one that was fragile, required stiff posture, and allowed no contact with anything that might smudge my makeup.

The wedding went exactly as rehearsed. I had to eat with Maury and Melissa, but after dessert Debs and Ava made room for me at their table. Debs was a little drunk. She leaned on her elbow, her chin in her hand, and spoke slowly, drawling and cooing like a pigeon. Ava spent much of the night on the dance floor, sometimes dancing alone. The light bounced off her silver dress as she twirled and dipped. At eleven o'clock Fran tossed her bouquet—right through Aunt Debs's arms and onto the floor. Debs stumbled trying to pick it up but managed not to fall.

After the wedding my mother relaxed, went off her diet, and spent a week with her feet up playing card games with the aunts while a record snowstorm buried the capital city. She set aside the donor luncheon she was organizing for the synagogue, where she was president of the sisterhood and where the rest of us set foot only for the High Holidays.

Looking back now, I think she didn't quite approve of the Florida aunts. If they had been men, she'd have had no trouble appreciating their guts and eccentricities. But as women they must have frightened her. They had survived hurricanes. They had moved alone through nightclubs, funeral parlors, divorce courts, and casinos.

Under their influence my mother recollected her girlhood. "When I was fourteen I had a blue silk matching coat and dress that cost two hundred dollars," she told Aunt Debs. She turned to me to explain. "That was when you could buy a dress for six ninety-five."

"Hen," Aunt Debs said, taking the pack in a canasta game, "you wouldn't believe some of the getups I've seen in Vegas."

"Not in your wildest dreams," Ava added. She had visited Debs and Teddy while the casino was being built. "It's hard to tell the hookers from the rest of the crowd."

"Hookers?" I asked.

"Whores," Debs explained.

"Please watch what you say," my mother whispered, glancing at me.

"I'm old enough to hear," I protested.

"I'll decide that," my mother said.

"Teddy knew everybody," Debs said, without a hint of wistfulness in her voice. This remark was met with silence by my mother and Ava.

"Even Frank Sinatra?" I asked.

"Sure," Debs said. "You want to know something about Frank Sinatra?" I nodded. "He still calls his mother every day. Just to check in."

They talked, too, about people who were long dead, people out of the family mythology. They ran through a slew of names and infamies, recalled favorite foods, recited the names of my grandmother Minerva's eight brothers and sisters, listed every set of twins on both sides of the family, and praised the spirit which had brought all our relatives out of the hopeless bondage of Eastern Europe and onto the shores of America.

"You know you're part Gypsy, don't you?" Aunt Ava asked me at the end of one of these recitations.

We were playing rummy in teams. My mother and I against the aunts. "Gypsies?" my mother and I repeated.

"Our grandfather's father was a Gypsy who became a stable boy for a branch of the Rumanian royal family," Ava explained.

"Really?" I asked, my mind already full of campfires, gold hoop earrings, and wide, colorful skirts.

"Absolutely," Debs said, stubbing out a cigarette and lighting another.

"I never heard that one," my mother said.

Aunt Debs cupped my chin in her free hand. "That's why you're so dark. Like your great-great-grandfather."

"Come on," my mother said. "There are no Jewish Gypsies." Her laughter was met with silence.

"Hen, we wouldn't kid about a family thing," Debs said. "He worked in the stables, taking care of the horses. And the riding boots."

"Riding boots?" My mother's voice sounded for a second, just like Eleanor Roosevelt's, it was so shaky and high-pitched.

Ava elbowed me and smiled. "If you ever get the urge to roam, you'll know where it comes from."

I knew it had to be true. I could already feel the Gypsy blood in my veins. It had always been there. It was the reason I didn't want to join Young Judea. I couldn't belong to any group.

"He must have converted," my mother said, still puzzling out loud.

After the aunts left I moved into Fran's room. The wallpaper with its profusion of birds and flowers reminded me of the house we had rented the year before in Miami, with its hibiscus bushes and iridescent hummingbirds. But we didn't go to Florida the following summer. My parents sent me, instead, to a Jewish camp in the Poconos, where I stumbled through transliterations of blessings and songs and sneaked out at night to smoke with the boys. I didn't see the aunts again for eleven years. They stayed in touch, though—chatty letters on pastel stationery arrived several times a year.

Debs continued to live in seclusion on her houseboat. She became involved with the Humane Society, gave up meat, and adopted a variety of dogs and cats. Ava gave up Judaism, a faith she claimed only barely to have embraced, for the teachings of an Indian avatar named Meher Baba. When I was about fifteen she sent us a photograph of him with his finger to his lips. Her letter said he'd taken a vow of silence more than twenty years before and that she was going to India to live in an ashram with his followers.

I wasn't too surprised to learn in the midsixties that Ava and her husband were living in a religious commune near Orlando and that Debs, who'd been hitting the bottle again, had been persuaded to join them.

I like to tell my friends that I was the poster child for my family—the one with something wrong that no one could fix. After Fran married she moved into a split-level home ten minutes away from my parents and had four children in quick succession. I tried not to hold it against her that my parents never complained about her, that she was my mother's idea of a model daughter. My own interactions with my father and mother over the following years went something like this:

"Have you met any nice boys lately? What about that boy Maury introduced you to? What does his father do? Is he going to college?

"*What* boy?"

"Maury's friend."

"Maury *who?*"

"Your Aunt Florence thinks you should go to college here in town. What's wrong with George Washington University?"

"It's here in town."

"She hates me. My own daughter hates me."

My brilliant report cards failed to impress them. In my mother's eyes I was valuable cargo waiting to be unloaded. Then her marriage mode would set in: invitations, napkins and matchbook covers with a red embossed heart and my name intertwined with the name of someone nice, someone they approved of, someone Jewish. Caterer. Photographer. Bridesmaids' gowns. Ushers' handkerchiefs. Dyed silk pumps. And me, dressed up in white, an offering to the same God my mother served at her donor luncheons.

At last I graduated from high school and won a scholarship to a college in New England, a Yankee after all, my father complained. I didn't come home for the summers. After college I went to Europe for a year. I threaded my way across the Continent on a Eurail pass, picked grapes in Italy, and worked as a secretary in London. I pictured my relatives speaking of me the way they used to speak of the Florida branch—with the slightly disapproving nonchalance reserved for the inexplicable. My parents sent me a couple hundred dollars every month, an emotional blackmail I gladly extorted knowing they felt helpless—except financially—to influence my life.

It was a beautiful fall day when I picked up my mother's letter from general delivery in Edinburgh, where I was visiting friends from college. General delivery was the only address I used that whole year; it gave me the illusion that I never had to settle down, that I was beyond the reach of family. The letter was marked URGENT and explained that Fran was very sick. It ended with a plea for me to telephone as soon as possible.

"She had a tumor on her spine," my mother said when I finally reached her. "We think it came from a bad fall when she took the kids roller-skating. They removed it," she whispered. "It was malignant."

The word "cancer" filled my mind, hordes of fiddler crabs with their pincers upraised like the ones I'd chased every summer as a child along Biscayne Bay. I tried to imagine Fran with a life-threatening disease but could only produce the image of her with baby after baby in the maternity ward of the hospital. "Will she be all right?" I asked.

"I waited to write you, hoping to have good news."

"When—?"

"Two months ago. She's had radiation and all her hair fell out. She weighs eighty-six pounds."

I remember looking through the window of my friends' house at the heather that purpled the September fields and wondering if heather grew anywhere else in the world. Everybody was pitching in, my mother said. Herb, though, was falling apart. Could I come home and take care of the kids? I could sleep in the guest room in the basement. I agreed and made arrangements for the next plane back to the States. In my mother's voice there had been a music, a music that caught me up in its melody, its refrain. We can save her, it said, if the sacrifice is big enough.

But we couldn't save Fran, and my mother, who lived all her life conservatively as a kind of white magic against such a tragedy, was beyond consolation. My father called in the Florida aunts toward the end of Fran's illness. They flew to Washington and stayed at Fran's house with me, sleeping on cots in the rec room. They took on cooking and cleaning and babysitting with a fervor I wouldn't have expected of them. But even they, with their perpetual Florida tans and tropical radiance, were lost in the larger crowd of family, in that swaying throng of mourners dressed in black.

The funeral was held in the poshly appointed Zimmerman's Star of David, the largest Jewish establishment in town. I had never experienced grief before, and now I used it as an excuse to avoid Melissa, Maury, and the rest of the Washington clan. Everyone overlooked my aloofness, impressed, I knew, with my devotion to Fran, with my selflessness. I held onto my sacrifice like a shield and refused to cry through the rabbi's long eulogy. All the time I kept waiting for the grief to hit me like a tidal wave, for it to grab me like a claw.

At the cemetery, a beautiful snow-covered hillside in Virginia, both my parents fainted and were helped back to their feet by the Florida aunts. Those two were everywhere, consoling the family, lending a hand when the awning threatened to blow down at the graveside, helping mourners into and out of cars. They wept unashamedly, not so much for themselves, as Debs confided to me in the limousine, but on my parents' behalf. Ava was more silent than I had remembered her. She had a silver streak through her hair—whether natural or peroxided—like Indira Gandhi. It gave her an otherworldly look, as if it were the badge of some wisdom obtained at great expense. All she said to me that afternoon was "There are no rewards for us here." Her green eyes swept the horizon and arced into the clouds and back.

After the burial, there was the shiva, the period of ritual mourning. Zimmerman's had delivered to Fran's house a dozen wooden chairs small enough to be elementary school furniture. When we returned from the grave, my aunts dutifully unfolded them and set about serving the platters of food that friends of the family had sent. Only the immediate family had to sit in the little chairs, terribly uncomfortable on purpose to keep the mourners' attention on pain and grief. The aunts brought us food and encouraged us to eat. During all of this service they were as humble and quiet as geishas.

The eating and crying continued all evening until the last guest left and my sister's husband, Herb, collapsed into sleep. Finally only my parents, the aunts, and I remained. Ava suggested my mother switch from her mourner's chair to the sofa. My mother, mute as she had been all day, obeyed, moving in a daze. She took off her shoes and stretched out the length of the couch. "God," she suddenly said. "I helped Frannie pick out this fabric." She felt the nubby tweed of it and sobbed. "What's the point?" she asked us all.

"Oh, Hen, I'm so sorry," Ava said.

"I know," my mother said.

"But Hen," Ava went on, "there's something I want to tell you. Something you have to know."

All of us looked at her.

"She isn't really dead," Ava announced. I could hear the sound of genuine jubilation in her voice, of conviction. "No one really dies. We all come back. I knew it when I was in India. You mustn't think of her as lost forever."

My mother looked to Aunt Debs.

"Yes," Debs agreed. "It's a comfort. Somewhere your Fran and my Teddy go on. Transformed." She exhaled, and we watched her cigarette smoke hang in the air for a moment like a magician's rope trick.

Then my mother bolted upright on the couch. "You're crazy!" she shouted. "Both of you."

"No, Hen, you don't understand—"

"You've always been crazy. Only now you call it religion. We're leaving. Get our coats," she ordered my father.

"Please," Aunt Debs begged, tears streaming from her eyes.

"Wait, Ma," I called to her as she punched her fists through her coat sleeves.

"Wait for what?" my mother said, turning on me the same venom she felt for the aunts. "My Frannie's dead. Who cares if she comes back as something else? She isn't coming back to those four children. Or," she socked her chest, "to me."

That was the last time she ever saw the aunts, though she and my father eventually retired to Florida. The aunts tried to contact her repeatedly, but she dismissed all apologies and offers of reconciliation and returned their letters unopened. And I think, mild as she was, that she took pride in having taken so absolute a stand against them. Years afterward she refused to speak their names. She tended her anger like a rock garden, nourishing it once a year on the anniversary of Fran's death. Fifteen years later, when I came home for a visit, I saw her light the *yahrzeit* candle and heard her say bitterly, "Back as a flame? Only a little flame?"

The aunts left the day after the funeral, hugging thin coats around their print dresses at the airport as we waited for their call to board the plane. I knew I'd want to defend them if their names ever came up, if I ever found myself sorting through the family mythology. And I knew I'd never change my parents' minds about the incident. They needed that anger too much. I could imagine myself far into the future, living perhaps in Taos or San Francisco, someplace I'd never been, talking to a child with a face I couldn't picture clearly, a dark face like mine. I'd tell her about the wedding—not my own, but Fran's.

When their plane taxied down the runway I wished I were on it with them, our faces leaning together in a threesome toward the small window, the city spreading out below us like a game board. The trip south would have felt like walking under a very large shade tree, a tree so large that the coolness under its branches went on and on into nightfall.

THE DIFFERENT LANDSCAPE

MARGARET KLEE

*D*yke, dyke, dyke!" they called as my daughter Susanna and I strolled across the town parking lot, our arms around each others' shoulders, in a small fishing village in Maine.

Susanna was working on an organic farm for the summer—planting, weeding, haying, selling the produce—and I was visiting her. Susanna was nineteen; she was about to enter her third year at a small, progressive Midwestern college in September.

The town kids were clustered in the parking lot in Chevys, Jeeps, Hondas, a station wagon. There were a couple of kids on bikes, roaring shiny Japanese models. They wore black and had an Addams family aura. This was their five o'clock Saturday evening prowl. The sun was slipping away and the night was young.

Horns honked. "Dyke, dyke!" The riffraff kept up a chorus. Suddenly we were the main event.

Susanna and I kept walking, arm in arm, smiling, talking. Instinctively we skirted the pack of cars. But we did cast supercilious glances in their direction. Beneath our commanding prowess we were uncomfortable. All of a sudden Susanna broke down.

"My God. So pathetic! Some of my best friends are gay."

We proceeded through the parking lot. We cut out the other end to the main street in search of an appealing restaurant. We peered into a pub window. We asked for a menu at another establishment. I could see Susanna was blue. We sat down on a village bench facing a not inconsiderable number of town pigeons.

"It makes me so sad the way people are," she said. "It bums me out."

"I know, I know. It's ridiculous."

"It's more than ridiculous. It's cruel. It's not fair. I mean, here you are, my mom. Sure, they don't know that. What *is* it they're so afraid of?"

"I don't know, really. I don't know why the idea is so threatening, but they're so young, too. Don't you think they're about fifteen? And that's a hip way to act. Peer pressure's part of it."

"It's more than that." Susanna sat there, dejected. I was impressed with how mournful she looked. I tried to raise her spirits, brush the incident off, because my discomfort was on the rise, too.

We kept talking until finally Susanna was arguing the politics of it with *me*, with noticeable intensity.

"Look," I said, "why don't we go back, and we'll walk up to them, tell them who we are. You might feel better if we talk to them."

She lit up.

"Let's do it," I said.

"But let me do the talking, okay?" Susanna searched my eyes for agreement.

Back down to the parking lot we marched. Once the kids saw us again they began jeering, honking horns, and yelling "Dyke, dyke!" They kept up the hounding as we approached. "Dyke, dyke, dyke, dyke!" And then the chorus muted as Susanna picked out two parked cars to approach. A pair of teenage women sat slumped in the station wagon to the left, stony and silent. A skinny boy at the driver's seat of an old Pinto gulped his beer next to his girlfriend (presumably), as he stared sheepishly from the right. Susanna, hands tucked in her back jeans pockets, advanced on the youngsters slowly. She smiled.

"I'm really sorry," she began gently, "that you're so uptight about homosexuality. It really hurts me. This is my mom, and we happen to be heterosexual, but there's nothing so terrible about being gay." She paused. "Homosexuality is just about love." She said this with quiet confidence. "And I'm really sorry you feel the way you do."

She gave me a signal and slowly, deliberately, we walked away.

I spent time again with Susanna in the fall. It was Parents' Weekend. She didn't want us to do all the scheduled things, the lectures on U.S. foreign policy, brunch with the college president, the main concert event. She wanted me to meet her friends. She wanted me to meet "the terrific women in her life," women who were strong and independent and coming into their own.

So we went to one of the all-women's houses for a special evening of spontaneous performances. The comfortable rumpled living room was packed with women of all cultures and bents, squeezed next to each other on couches and on the floor. One by one each performer stood to recite an autobiographical poem, to play guitar behind her personal lyric, to perform a Hebrew song, to direct a traditional sing-along.

As a woman I was moved by these young women, by their directedness and intensity, by their open friendship, by the lengthy warm welcome each gave the other. I had never known anything like this, I said to myself. I too had been in a special dorm in college, for women with either unusual artistic or scholarly talents. My house was making an anti-sorority statement. We revelled in our own interests. But we kept, now that I think of it, emotional confrontation out of our interactions. We brought home our study dates, for example, to watch the Kennedy-Nixon debates on television, rather than get involved too intimately with each other.

I was exhilarated for Susanna to see her drawn to so many substantial, self-assured women. She seemed bonded to many of them: Bridget, a poet from Norway; Stephanie, back from a year in Ecuador teaching modern farming and English; Meredith, a music major, separated from her parents by adoption, race, and now, Susanna confided, sexual orientation. Suddenly I understood that Susanna would leave college with the kinds of ties I had never made, and I could see that these ties would last a lifetime.

Susanna was sure of only two things as she headed toward graduation: that she didn't want to live in the city and that she wanted to be able to hike in the mountains. She had the courage to stick to this as others planned for graduate school or chalked up interviews. She got a much coveted summer job working as a forest ranger at Yosemite National Park—a volunteer position which included a meager food allowance and "room" in a tent. On her days off she spent long periods by herself hiking in the Tuolumne Meadows wilderness. There she determined she was far from wanting graduate school, and after Labor Day she set out on a crisscrossing Greyhound bus journey of the Northeast to visit friends. All the friends were women.

As a teenager, I was boy crazy. I was always falling in love. I didn't have much of a sexual impulse until I was a twelfth-grader, but I got high on the

Everly Brothers and ensnared an incessant supply of boyfriends. This was not the case with Susanna. Susanna didn't have boyfriends. I knew of one romance she'd had with a fifteen-year-old that ended badly, and between that and a difficult relationship with her father, from whom I was divorced, I decided she was put off by men for the time being. Besides, she had friends in college who had steady ties, and just as many who did not. This was, after all, the nineties.

So I never thought much about the absence of men in Susanna's life. Occasionally (once, really) she made a point of telling me about a crush on a male housemate—a relationship she dropped quickly because, she said, it could interfere with "house harmony." However, when she began traveling—clearly visiting only women, often traveling with women—I allowed myself to notice gradually, for the first time, that I was worried she might be gay.

Recently, I admitted to myself, Susanna had been dropping hints. Did she know she was doing this? She had snapped at me when I groaned about the *gay* couple next door whose music was always too loud. Once when I wasn't there she stayed overnight in the apartment with a Betsy and somehow it had sounded like a tryst. At one point in her three-week journey, she was driving on to Connecticut, to Provincetown, to Baltimore, to D.C., with this same friend, with Betsy. Like a slowly penetrating rain, I was aware of a stubborn sinking feeling—that Susanna must be romantically involved with this woman. I confided my heart to my best friend. She was not alarmed. "It would be wonderful if she could talk to you about it" was her quite genuine response. Clearly this didn't involve *her* daughter.

I knew the truth was coming when Susanna sat me down. It was after we had gone out to dinner to celebrate my birthday. Here it comes, I thought, I am really going to have to deal with this, I remember thinking. As she told me—calmly, simply, sweetly, with preparedness—I had the sensation of blanking out while she said the words *For about a year and a half now I've been wanting to tell you that I'm gay.* Then I snapped back into the room: *I'm actually excited about it, and proud.*

Moments before, I had shared some strong poems I had published when both she and I were younger, when I had been joylessly married to her father. The poems were about breaking loose, breaking away, fleeing finally back into the shoes of the person I actually was, away forever from the brittle demoralized wife that in ten years of troubled marriage I had become. Now it was Susanna's turn to free herself. Her timing was perfect.

Susanna had come equipped with books. She was intent on smoothing the way. *"Really?"* I kept saying, hoping there was some mistake. "Yes, *really*," she answered, smiling broadly and exuding considerable confidence.

We talked for hours. We hugged a lot. I hugged her because I wanted everything to be okay between us, to be as before. But a gloomy fog was settling around me. The message was: once upon a time there was Before. Now, suddenly, there's After. It was a done deal. She *is* a lesbian.

Susanna had never displayed any of the stereotypical behavior that I associated with lesbians. She is feminine, she is pretty. Lesbians in my mind were always makeupless, panted women. Hardened furrows lined their faces. They were never pretty. I knew nothing of the inner life of these people, and I never bothered to probe why being around lesbians made me uncomfortable. I had no use for such mental inquiries. During a trip just five years ago to Italy, an elderly lesbian couple was staying at our *hostelaria* in the foothills of Sienna. I remember first feeling sorry for them, then I banned additional thoughts. Never did I comprehend until this moment that I was simply being irreproachable about who I was, that I was holding myself up as a model for the best woman one could be—and that *they* had to be lesser beings. I'm unnerved now by my self-limited vision—this from me, the broad-minded and correct one about every issue—every issue, it turns out, until it has to do with my own flesh and blood.

Where on my path did I internalize these disparaging views? When I was growing up, I remember, my parents had friends who were gay and others who were Communist. Communist was okay but lesbianism was "naughty." My mother said easily of their Swiss friend Emo, "He was always in love with your father." But Claudia was "a naughty girl" to carry on with Alexander's wife.

The evening of Susanna's disclosure I was, in fact, in shock. My true feelings emerged only in stages. I had soared up to my mind's imaginary perch at the corner of the ceiling (a mental trick of mine, I segue into observer position) and I looked down on us as we talked. Most of all, that night, I was afraid of losing her to an unknown and frightening realm. I wanted my daughter, this daughter whom I adored, created, identified with, this daughter who as a bare wet gooey newborn was propped on my chest, on my heart, just after birth—I longed for this daughter to remain close to me. She is me, I have often felt. Now suddenly she is she.

Suddenly she is *different*. How could she do this? Why *Susanna*? She explains that being straight or gay is not a choice.

We expect the generations to detour in some way, but if we've loved and nurtured, we presuppose something not too far afield. Open-minded as I think I am, a dream dies. I am suffering unfathomed loss, loss of a landscape I took for granted.

How tender and exposed I discover I feel. I can tell no one about this development except my truest allies. I flap about like a frightened scarecrow, guarding an invisible garden in the wind. Two weeks later I am on a train devouring one of the books Susanna purchased for me—it had *parents* and *gays* and *lesbians* written all over the cover—and an acquaintance spotted me from across the aisle. How are you? What are you reading? she chirped. I couldn't get the words out to pronounce the title! Instead, speechless, I held up the book and smiled my exterior public smile. Oh, she grinned. And that was that. But my heart was racing, and I was rattled. What would she think of *me*? Though I'd been living with Susanna's news for two weeks now, I learned that I wasn't capable of having a conversation with anyone but the closest of friends. It was I who was in the closet now, and there I was to linger for weeks.

So where had we gone awry? Did this occur because I smoked pot during my first trimester of pregnancy? Because her father had a violent temper and I wasn't able to provide a role model for controlling him? Because I put her in daycare before she was two so I could work, even though my non-working mother told me not to?

Three weeks later—every day now—I find I am just plain blue. The reality has fully hit me. This isn't going to go away. I hurt, I ache, I walk through the park to work in the morning and everything makes me sad: the half-clouded sky, the few ducks, the drooping trees in January, the fact that hardly anyone's there but me, insistently walking to work to get her exercise. A few tears come, not many. It's grief. I'm actually grieving as though someone very dear to me has died, like when my mother died overnight four years ago and I was inconsolable. It feels like that, like loss. And it is loss of course. The old Susanna, or the Susanna from where I was coming from, the Susanna as only I, her adoring mother, could perceive her, is gone forever. So I conclude on my wintry walks in the early morning, yes, someone—who existed in one reliable way in my mind for twenty-two years—has died. I feel the future shutter.

Susanna did tell me, as part of her announcement, that she was just the same person she always was, except that her sexual orientation was to women—that, quite simply, she loved women. *But she was still Susanna*, she repeated. I agreed with her then (intellectually I will agree to anything on the "right" side of the argument) but it's taken me months to see and feel this clearly. It's in her warm smile, in the melodic tone of her voice, in the clothing combinations she chooses for herself—all this has been the same for years. I've just never observed her through the lens of her being a lesbian.

By the two-month point it comes to me consciously that I am a lunatic raging with anger. I have held this in so long. Of course I tell no one how bad it is. I tell only my journal. Susanna and I have a bad spell after the initial motions of kindness we breezed through. I seemed so good at first, so accepting, that when I tried to share the emerging negativity she backed away. She didn't want to hear it. She preferred the model parent I first showed her.

In this period I am very angry and very miserable. I admit to myself I cannot fully accept her. I haven't gotten there yet. Her lesbianism is *not* fine with me. It smashes my dreams for her, my identity with her. There won't be grandchildren from one of my two children—or not in the usual way. This is a rejection I have taken personally. I hurt from the distance this places between my daughter and me. Now Susanna declares she can't fully embrace *me* because of my homophobia.

Finally, finally, I allow my anger to be there without the battle. I allow the monumental disappointment, the just plain good old fashioned one-hundred-percent disappointment that my daughter—through no fault of hers or mine—has turned out a lesbian. I have crossed some boundary, finally, and can allow myself to lumber on through the process. How could I have faulted the boys and girls in the Maine parking lot, I now wonder, and missed myself in their rearview mirrors?

* * *

Finally, too, I've persuaded myself that it's her life after all. As with my jumbled feelings of motherhood at twenty-five, nothing in my ample experience prepared me for this awakening. Yet I have to say there is a curious excitement here, a shiny new express-train opportunity, an enlivening adventure to be realized by all in the family. Most of all I want Susanna to live a full and expressive life, a life in dignity. This is a tall order. Because if *I* am this emotional and predisposed, won't the rest of the world out there continue to be . . . more so?

LOOKING FOR TAMERLANE

JODI DAYNARD

J've written all kinds of stories in the past few years. Horror stories and love stories, family stories and experimental stories. I have written about my mother-in-law and the five dead Davidoff uncles on my father's side. But there is one person I have never written about, and that's my mother. I'd given her up for dead, literarily speaking, until now. For me to write about something, I've got to tap into love, and my relationship with my mother has always been far too mixed up with feelings other than love—which isn't necessarily the same thing as respect, or even fondness.

It's funny how the memory of one small event can rekindle buried, small-child feelings. At the moment, one particular memory outweighs all the times I've hated my mother and fills me only with the image of her bent down on hands and knees with a flashlight, looking under the floorboards of her bedroom closet in search of Edgar Allan Poe's *Tamerlane and Other Poems*, the most valuable book in the English language.

My mother spent the first years of her children's lives breaking light bulbs. We never ate well enough, it seemed; to get our mouths open she would crush these light bulbs and the sound of splintering glass was shock enough to make us gasp, at which point she would shove the food in.

Shoving in or purging out—that's mostly how I remember my mother. There was a time in 1963 when she made me vomit my lunch of tuna fish, having heard on the radio that a can out west somewhere had been found to have botulism.

We humans were less than a speck of nothing, that was the message all of us—my brother, my sister, and I—heard loud and clear. The world could kill you in a flash, like a giant crushing a nut with one knuckle. I always thought it had to do with being Jewish, since my grandmother had (apparently) seen the giant in person back in Russia, during the pogroms. But when at the age of nearly eighty, senile and widowed and poor, my grandmother lost her little boarding house to upstate city planners with ideas for an airport, this seemed to confirm that hostile forces had little to do with time, place, or religion, but were intrinsic to the very state of being alive.

Which is how, I guessed, these same bugaboos made their way to Hartsdale, New York. And which explains, at least partially, why as a small child I would not eat my sandwiches at nursery school and why I did not like the blood-red eyes of the white rabbit that all the other children found cute. And it explains, too, why by the age of five I had a definite tic in one eye, as if to blind myself to the world's terrors.

But this isn't the whole story. What made us endeavor to get away from home just as fast as we could was her belief that she, and she alone, could protect us from this hostile world. Long after we had grown up and moved away she would still, walking across the street with us, crush our hands in a viselike grip. Long afterwards her phone calls would rouse us from our beds to whisper premonitions and warnings, because if only we would listen to them we would be protected. Our mother could read the future and steer us clear of its hazards all the way to our deaths. According to mother, you probably didn't even have to die at all if only you were careful enough.

Five years ago my sister's older daughter was killed in a car accident down in New Orleans, where she was going to school. According to the coroner, it was a split second's somnolence behind the wheel that did her in. Flew right out of the convertible and hit her head on a street lamp. Six months earlier she had been in another, minor, traffic incident. This second time, though, she didn't live to tell us about it. She died, right there by the side of a lonely road.

"I saw it coming," was the first thing my mother said. Or maybe not the first thing. The day the news arrived she pulled at her hair until it fell out in whole clumps. It was at the funeral, or the day after, that she said, "I saw it coming, but I kept my mouth shut. I'll never keep my mouth shut again."

It's a promise she's done her best to keep.

Sometimes I think it must be a heavy burden to have the fate of all your children in your hands. But of course the alternative, the worse thought by far, is to understand that you don't. That you can predict nothing, control even less. That you have outlived even your small usefulness and, for everything you have done, were scarcely even loved.

I say "scarcely" because I think my mother is, for all of it, loved. I can't speak for my siblings, but I know that love is in a tiny way coming out here, in the only circuitous route it knows how to take. It is in her, too, in that small place where she loves, as opposed to fears or controls, which I know for her are all pretty hopelessly mixed up. And this place, where love and loathing are not hopelessly mixed up, is so odd that one would never think of looking there.

My mother began collecting antiques when I was a small child. She had been a mother for what seemed like forever, and at a certain point she decided to become something else. She went back to school for her decorating license, and my earliest memory of this time is of her sitting up late at our dining-room table, putting together an enormous book of pictures for her final project. For months we had to eat in the kitchen; she guarded that table as if her whole life were spread out upon it.

As is turned out, this Jewish farm girl had the eyes of a connoisseur. She could tell American Chippendale from English, an original Ming plate from a fake. She acquired a taste for originals that would never, after that, go away.

My father, on the other hand, who grew up in a Bronx apartment building and, unlike my mother, had only acquired a lusty appetite for kitsch, looked with suspicion, if not downright hostility, upon my mother's sudden yen for antiques. He was comfortable with things that had no ambiguity to them: clean Formica, sofas covered in plastic, solid acrylic carpets. My mother's dusty Shaker boxes, chipped china plates—such things threatened his world almost as much as the unseen world threatened my mother.

"What now, Fran? What have you got there this time?" he would shout at her as she pulled her little green Volvo into the driveway after another early-morning expedition to the local garage sales. "Don't you bring that into this house!"

In she'd stride, green eyes shining, happier than any of us had ever seen her. She got things, too. Some of it was junk, to be sure. But for the most part our little suburban house gradually filled up with lost treasures. I was a tiny seven-year-old with a budding collection of my own, not of antiques but of stamps and coins and first day covers. Sometimes I would get up early and go along with her to the sales. Like a miniature of her, I would run through the doors in search of priceless envelopes as, in another room, she filed through the artwork.

Looking back now, I see that my mother had distinct ages. There was her Pewter Age, which I think was her earliest. Pewter spoons, pitchers, pewter mugs and teakettles. After that there was Iron. Iron fire-stokers and andirons, an age that was quickly supplanted by the more precious Bronze. Along the edges of our bookshelves there grew whole civilizations of bronze statuettes from Africa, China, and even Early America. My mother has a silver pitcher that was made by Paul Revere, picked up at a garage sale for twenty dollars.

Then came the Shaker boxes—her Paper and Straw Age. *Tchotchkes*, my father called them.

"We don't need more tchotchkes," he'd utter nervously.

"Harold, you're just a *boor*," she'd retort, angling her way past him with her arms full.

Straw baskets, jewelry boxes. By this time my mother was going to several sales a day, getting up at the crack of dawn to be there before they opened. The dealers got to know her. They all lined up on the darkened street of the sale as dawn broke, waiting patiently like cops on a stakeout.

As soon as the front door opened my mother, a small, short-legged woman, would propel herself from the car and shoot across the manicured lawns like a bullet. Once in, it was everyone for themselves—she would swoop down on the junk and fish out the little Renoir etching or Daumier lithograph before the dealers' eyes even had a chance to focus in the artificial light.

After a while, my mother settled into a few specialties. Paintings, silver, Oriental carpets. Our house got so full that my father reluctantly agreed to build a shed out back to house things. They fought about what would go in the shed and what would stay in the house. My father seemed quite happy to throw everything into that shed helter-skelter.

"Look at him," she told me. "Look how he treats them. He won't be happy until he's broken every last thing."

And indeed my father did seem particularly clumsy with Mom's treasures, always chipping a vase or denting a painted lamp. Then, aghast, we'd find him in the garage with the wounded item, just as clumsily trying to fix his mistake with heavy-handed paint, glue, or Scotch tape.

I could not have known then how their whole sad romantic life was played out in this removed way, expressing the love that they'd misplaced somewhere between his extramarital affair and her passion for collecting. All I knew at the time was that somehow my father had become the antagonist in my mother's private drama. She was saving the world, saving everything that was being trampled upon and destroyed in modernity's blind march forward, and it was in this capacity that I found myself in strange, passionate alliance with her. To me it was magic how these things traveled across thousands of miles and centuries to find their way to a safe haven in our little split-level house. And to me, in this small way my mother was nothing less than a sorceress.

"This is Bonnard," she would say, placing some giant painting in my small arms. "This is a real lithograph. Do you see how the paint is raised? Feel, feel it." She would open the glass and press my fingers hard against the picture. "This is not a print" I heard at least a hundred times. "Don't let anyone tell you these are worthless prints. You've got to know the difference so that when I'm gone your brother and sister won't give them away."

My parents were always on the verge of dying. According to my mother they were just a step away from the grave. She always had "a lump" and my father's heart was perpetually out of beat. For nearly seventy-five years now they have had these lumps and skips, but as a child you believe what you're told. And so my mother's collecting became infused almost from the very beginning with an elegiac quality. By safeguarding my mother's trust I was, in a sense, securing her destiny as well.

So this is how I became a collector too, the self-appointed executor of my mother's artistic estate. But while I could probably tell you the value of each of her artifacts in dollars and cents, I cannot recount their stories. All that will be lost when my mother is gone. Because, as it turned out, my mother had a feel not just for art but for its creators, a compassion for them that seems almost inexplicable in a little farm girl who spent most of her fatherless childhood running from drunk and vulgar workmen. How, I have always wondered, did she come by her tears for Van Gogh's later years? How did she come to understand George Innes's dark canvases, those careless strokes in the trees' leaves made during a particularly onerous time of depression?

Later, when I was already a teenager and a goner for collecting myself (not stamps and coins anymore, but books), my mother began to take her possessions into New York City to get them appraised. Museum of Modern Art, Park Bernet, the Metropolitan—in she would walk, a tiny speck of a woman, tidily dressed, with makeup a shade too dark for her complexion and hastily applied rouge. She'd be holding a small figurine in the nest of her hands. Or sometimes she carried a black leather portfolio, bigger than she was by half.

And she would sit down and become very quiet before these grand directors, these experts, and await their verdict. Sometimes my mother would return to our house a little sad but not daunted. She would shrug and get this humorous look on her face, not embarrassed exactly, but knowing she'd been duped and knowing that the world was like that sometimes. Sometimes it fooled you.

But then there were the times these same formidable men would begin to scurry around, call in their curators, scrape at the edges of my mother's canvas and peer through tiny monocles, and after these trips my mother would gloat for months afterward.

"Pierre Matisse offered me five hundred," she'd say, referring to the painter's son, "and if he's offering me five hundred, it's worth fifteen."

My mother never sold to the museums, not once that I can remember anyway. When she did sell it was usually out of pity. Once she sold a rug to an old dealer, straight off our living room floor. Apparently the man's wife had just died.

"He looked so down in the mouth," she told me. "He needed that rug." To my mother, selling was an act of generosity, not of barter.

So then how do we get from here to my story, which I haven't even begun to tell yet, about the time I nearly tore the house down in search of *Tamerlane*? It's a difficult transition to make, because I have the feeling that the real story is neither in my mother's collecting nor in my own—the story about the priceless book—but somewhere lost between the two.

It began one day long after I had moved out. I was sitting in her kitchen having my morning coffee, and I was reading through a new *Antiques Price List* when something caught my eye.

"Look at this, Mom," I said. "There's a book in here that's worth nearly two hundred thousand dollars."

"What book is that?" she said without much interest, going about her business by the sink.

My mother didn't care about books. She would occasionally drag home a nineteenth-century edition of Van Dyck or the yearly almanacs from the Good Fellows Club, because of their gilt covers. Sometimes, if the price was right, she would buy a whole box of "throwaways" for me.

"It's a collection of poems by Edgar Allan Poe. *Tamerlane and Other Poems.* Now *that's* a book I'd like to have."

I was lost in my imaginings and it took a while for me to perceive that my mother was leaning down over the counter with a puzzled look on her face.

"*Tamerlane?*" she asked. "Well, that rings a bell somehow."

"Oh, Mom."

"No, really, I think I've got that one. I remember there was an inscription. To a Bostonian, from a Bostonian. Now where did I put it?—*that's* the question."

I forget when exactly the heat of my book collecting passion came upon me in full force, but I think it was sometime after I met my husband and before we married several years later. It's probably no accident that the frenzy took me when I was leaving girlhood once and for all, as if I were endeavoring to bring to married life some hastily sketched portrait of who I thought I was.

I was, I decided, the unrecognized progeny of stern-faced forebears. I was not spawned from the murky waters of a Russian shtetl but from the crystalline New England streams of the Early Americans. Gabled houses, spires and sailboats, and Martha's Vineyard. Poe and Hawthorne and Melville. I loved these things in the way people can only love things that are unlike themselves: with a tenderness, a wistfulness untainted by familiarity. The New Englanders of my imagining did not pay morbid heed to their own illnesses and the inevitable decay of the body. For them, life lay beyond all that. It was in the grass, or the sky. And it was especially in the mysterious light that surrounded their gabled houses.

Of course, to read Edgar Allan Poe is to know at once that my picture is false. Crypts and crumbling turrets of the soul, priests whispering behind closed doors—looking back now I can see that it was precisely their morbidity, their dark vision, that captivated me. But it was not the monochromatic Jewish vision I had always known. It was even darker and more despairing, but set off against a blinding twilight that throws every detail of a landscape into agonizing relief.

For years I could read only the Early Americans, and dreamed of owning those original editions. I wanted Melville. I wanted Hawthorne. But most of all, it was that tiny alcoholic sufferer, Edgar Allan, whom I wanted, motivated perhaps by the belief that if only I could hold him in my hands, it could somehow complete my adoption once and for all.

"Now where *did* I hide it? It must be here somewhere." Her rear end was sticking up out of the crawl space behind her bed. This was no Puritan rear end. This was my mother's. In a moment her head emerged, glowing with fiberglass insulation. "If only I could remember *where*."

My mother remembered everything. She remembered her farm in Swan Lake, winter of 1925. She remembered Clarkie, the hired hand who chased her lustfully through the snow that winter, and many other things as well. And her two older sisters, Molly and Gertrude. She remembered the time her mother unearthed a pouch of gold doubloons from the yard and sold them for a cow—a story that galls me each time I hear it. And she remembered the hospital ward where rats scurried along the walls and where, at twelve, she watched her father slowly die. He was a tall, handsome man, she told me. He'd been a traveling troubador, had left his true love behind in Europe to die of some romantic disease. Only much later did he send for my grandmother to help him out on the farm.

His heart just gave out, like a sigh. My mother was always bitter about that crowded ward with its other gaunt, dirty faces surrounding her beloved father. He held her tiny hand and closed his eyes. The next time she came to see him the bed was empty. She remembered things like that.

But she did not remember where she put my book. I call it *my* book—

why? Is it what she owed me? Had I, like some petty miser, kept count of all my losses? I don't know.

But clearly my mother thought it was my book, too—if only we could find it. We tried the attic, the basement. We tore up the wall-to-wall carpeting in the living room. My father nearly had a nervous breakdown watching us; he finally peeled out the driveway in his big old Thunderbird, warning us that the place "had better be fixed up" by the time he returned. That afternoon my mother turned up more than fifty floorboards, stuck her bare hands in the fiberglass insulation until they bled.

But we didn't find it that day, or the next. Once, though, a few years ago, we had a scare. We were up in the attic again when my mother uncovered an ancient-looking brown book. It was hardly bigger than a deck of cards.

"What's this?" she said, handing it to me; she didn't have her glasses on and couldn't read the words. It was a second edition of Webster's dictionary, dated 1814. Inside it, a few pale green four-leaf clovers were all that remained of its original owner.

My mother took it from my hands and eyed it suspiciously.

"I wonder if this is what I was thinking of," she asked quietly.

"Oh, Mom, all that for nothing?"

"No, wait," she suddenly thrust out her arm. "The inscription."

She removed her glasses from her breast pocket and peered closely at the book's inside cover.

"This has no inscription," she confirmed. From the glare of the single light bulb above her head I suddenly noticed how old my mother's face had become. Her cheek and chin hung down all in a piece, like folded drapery. But I don't think she felt old just then at all. She had not found *Tamerlane*. And this juxtaposition—joy and death in one face—worked upon me a familiar feeling. It was the feeling of my adopted ancestors, the feeling you get when the dying sun comes up over the horizon and for one brief moment illuminates life with an absolute clarity.

"Thank God," I thought I heard her say.

After that dark day we went about our business just as if that little dictionary had never come into our lives at all. For nearly a decade now we have been looking for *Tamerlane*. We look every time I come home, which, now that I have a family of my own, is less and less. Usually we look when things begin to get tense, as they inevitably do. She will begin to blame me for some failure and I will shout like a teenager and not a thirty-four-year-old woman with a child of my own.

And then I will say, "Let's look for *Tamerlane*," and all of a sudden her old owl-like eyes will change. They will get that green gleam in them that makes her look young and pretty again. She will get a flashlight from the basement and we'll go hunting. And for just a while I can, in this way we've invented, be my mother's daughter.

PART FIVE

LEAVING HOME

My mother was dead for five years before I knew that I loved
her very much.

Lillian Hellman
An Unfinished Woman

TO A DAUGHTER
LEAVING HOME

LINDA PASTAN

When I taught you
at eight to ride
a bicycle, loping along
beside you
as you wobbled away
on two round wheels,
my own mouth rounding
in surprise when you pulled
ahead down the curved
path of the park,
I kept waiting
for the thud
of your crash as I
sprinted to catch up,
while you grew
smaller, more breakable
with distance,
pumping, pumping
for your life, screaming
with laughter,
the hair flapping
behind you like a
handkerchief waving
goodbye.

L'DOR V DOR:
FROM GENERATION
TO GENERATION

JYL LYNN FELMAN

*W*hen I think about my mother, Edith, I automatically touch my head with my right hand, not because it aches but because on top of my head is my hair, or what's left of my hair; and hair is where I feel—all at once—equally close and equally disconnected to my mother. For hair, from the top of my head to the top of my toes, is where this Jewish daughter and her Jewish mother mapped out the permanent geography of our very different female lives. Hair is where our identities as Jews and women converged and ultimately diverged. One look from my mother at the top of my head could defeat me for days. We never resolved this crisis of hair before she died three months ago. So I am left to wrestle with the unsettling notion that my mother never saw my beauty as a Jewish woman. I am left to complete my own image not in my mother's eyes but in spite of her eyes, and that does not please me, but I accept it.

My mother was caught between two worlds. From the moment she kissed her father good-bye, unlinked her right arm from his, and walked toward the *chuppah* to meet my father, to link her arm with his for the rest of her life, my mother's allegiance to her future daughters was put in jeopardy. She did not know it, or plan it; she could never have imagined what lay ahead of her. She was an unwitting participant in a generation of Jews that had barely survived the Holocaust; she was convinced that her commitment to the Jewish people and to family was the most important role a Jewish woman could have. She did not understand her historical location, that her generation of women was uniquely positioned between the old and the new, between Judaism and feminism, her one husband and her three daughters. And neither of my parents understood the personal consequences upon their children of the birth of the State of Israel twelve months before the birth of my older sister Judy, my mother's first child. For my mother was almost as proud of the birth of Israel as she was of the birth of her own daughter. It was as if Israel stole my sister's birthright and became the firstborn in the eyes of my mother. My sister was next in line, after the desert bloomed. Smiling with satisfaction, my mother used to say, "Your sister Judy will always be one year younger than the State of Israel." It was Israel, then, that became the older sister with whom I would forever compete and that I would strive to be just like. And when feminism threatened to tear us apart, it was my mother's love of Zion and my own zeal for the Holy Land that kept us connected. As I grew up, in the back of my mind, no matter how difficult my relationship with my mother became, I thought that I could always make *alyiah l'eretz*, return to the Land of Israel, where, to work in the fields I could legitimately cut my hair short—be a feminist and have my mother, too. Only it didn't work that way; like my mother I could never have imagined what lay ahead of me.

For my mother, appearances mattered. She was the daughter of French Jews who sold men's hats and fancy women's apparel that they could never afford themselves; and she was the wife of a hard-working parking lot attendant whose parents fled the pogroms in their native Russia. So, out of necessity, she turned the act of appearance into a finely tuned, highly precise daily ritual in the lives of her three daughters. Before leaving the house we stood in front of my father well coiffed and well dressed, beautiful but modest, aesthetically pleasing but not ostentatious. Appearance—for the Felman girls—had been elevated to high moral ground. We were, after all, the first generation of grandchildren to be born in America. My mother took great pride in her ability to dress us for participation in the gentile world, lest we be a *shandeh far di goyim*, but she was exuberant as she prepared us for Jewish occasions, our *b'nai mitzvot* and *yontif*. And whenever education was involved, Jewish ideals and gentility merged, so that annually my mother prepared me for the first day of school as though she had invented a new Jewish holiday.

On August first, she would say, "It's time to call Teddy." Teddy was her beautician, and although she did not usually "do" children's hair, she made an exception for Mrs. Felman, her favorite Jewish customer. I liked Teddy very much, yet I never liked what she did to my head. In addition to washing it with special, luxurious shampoo, then trimming it to suit my mother's watchful eye, Teddy rolled and curled and twisted my thick brown locks into a totally unrecognizable head of hair. Before we left the shop my mother paraded me up and down the aisles so she could receive the approving nods of all the other women patrons. I didn't know it then, but she was showing off her precious Jewish princess to the *goyim*, as if to say, my daughter *is* just like yours. In the car, as my mother gripped the steering wheel and wouldn't look at me, I cried and screamed all the way home. Until, in her spotless, kosher kitchen sink, she was forced to wash out my new, fifteen-dollar permanent and comb my shoulder-length hair back to its original pre-Teddy condition. This scene, the preparation of my head for presentation to the Jewish and non-Jewish world, repeated itself throughout my entire life. My ability to choose my own style was never in question; my fundamental right to make a choice different from my mother's was always at stake. My autonomy, the commitment to a wholly realized self versus loyalty to my Jewish mother was staked out the day I started kindergarten. Today, I feel my father's sad gaze taking up at the exact same spot on my forehead where my mother's penetrating gaze ended.

After my appearance was secured, the focus switched to my future. My mother assumed my life would be very much like hers. She was never able to acknowledge that her approach to family and career was entirely unrealistic for her daughters. She was the best, most devoted teacher Hillel Academy ever had; parents begged to have their children placed in Mrs. Felman's third-grade class. But nothing could ever interfere with her vision of herself as a Jewish wife and mother. And that meant that when she finished teaching at two each afternoon she was free to be the *balebosteh* she loved to be: for the next two hours she shopped for Empire kosher chickens, picked us up at school, got her hair done once a week, visited her parents at work, fulfilled her obligations as PTA president, then pulled into the driveway at exactly four o'clock, just in time to prepare dinner for my father. In addition to working five days a week, my mother cooked all meals herself, including Shabbat and holiday dinners for fifteen or more. I didn't know how she made it through each day without collapsing on the living room couch.

It wasn't until college that I began to understand that for my sisters and me, careers in the Felman family were more like after-dinner mints—complimentary, never meant to be the main course. This was the unstated, unacknowledged tension that flowed freely between my mother and me. For her, feminism was only as good as the fit, which had to be within the confines of her commitment to my father and to Judaism; for me, Judaism had to expand to include feminism. Neither of us could imagine any other way. We both knew that a revolution had occurred in the twenty years between when I started elementary school and graduated from college. Only my mother didn't want to talk about Gloria Steinem, birth control, or *Ms* magazine. She was afraid that I, her cherished youngest daughter, no longer approved of her life. What she did not know was that until the day she died this fear of a life unappreciated and misunderstood was completely mutual.

I am nineteen and do not yet know that I am a lesbian; my hair is very long, past my shoulders. My mother drops me off at Teddy's. Walking into the beauty shop alone for the first time in years, I am light-headed, almost giddy. "Cut it off," I tell a shocked Teddy. "Short." As she begins to cut I sit in the swivel chair motionless. "When do you want me to stop?" she asks. "The bottom of my ear. Can you style it—just a little?" I am horrified that my head will resemble an upside-down soup bowl. Teddy is nervous, too. When she's done both of us look directly in the mirror. I'm grinning at my reflection; no more heavy GE blow-dryers or giant orange juice cans, no more hours of preparation, just a quick wash and an easy towel-dry.

I sign the receipt and walk out the door just as my mother drives up to the entranceway and passes me right by. I wait for her to turn around, but she doesn't; she doesn't even recognize me. I wave my hands in the air. My mother backs up the car, looks out the window, and starts screaming. She doesn't say a word, she just screams, over and over again. I'm not sure she'll ever let me back inside the car. We never speak about that moment in the parking lot of Teddy's beauty salon. I don't know exactly what my mother saw in my face once all that thick brown hair was cleared out of the way. I knew that modesty in all things was central to my Jewish mother; so the simple act of cutting off my hair for the hot summer months was ultimately an act of immodesty and thus a permanent embarrassment to her. But at nineteen I had no idea that in cutting my hair short I was also cutting the intense female bonds between us. I had become my own woman, one who thought she could choose for herself how to wear her hair. But I was wrong.

Female autonomy, the search for a separate woman self was never a goal in my family. My mother could not assist her daughters with their—our—sexual development. For her, sexuality was an extension of being a wife and mother. Any female identity outside of this context was an aberration. So when I knew for sure that I was a lesbian, I was afraid to tell my mother. What I feared most was that I lacked courage, that I would choose a relationship with my beloved mother over a relationship with myself and the woman I had chosen to be my life partner. Twenty years ago there was little in contemporary Jewish theology to assist me in my search for a Jewish feminist lesbian self; at the same time, feminism was rejoicing in the rejection of all things patriarchal, including Judaism and the State of Israel. I felt as though I wandered in the desert alone. Like Lot's wife, I could neither look back, for fear of paralysis, nor go forward on my own sacred journey. I remained caught—as my mother herself was—between two worlds. Only the order had been reversed. While my mother was pulled between her husband and her three daughters, I was pulled between feminism and Judaism—my sisters or my parents.

In the end, my mother chose Judaism and marriage, whereas I refused to make a choice. Where my mother needed structure and tradition for safe passage, my liberation came in the ability to embrace contradictory realities, including the antifeminism in Judaism and the anti-Semitism in feminism. My mother accepted her heterosexuality without question; she flourished within the boundaries of conformity. Unlike her, I have come to rely on a flexible form. And to know that for my generation, survival as a Jew and a woman is dependent upon just this fluidity. But after the Holocaust there was little choice for the survivors, and even once the Jewish nation and her family were secured, my mother could not tolerate any deviation from the perpetuation of that vision.

I wish my mother had lived long enough for me to tell her that I had to cut my hair because the bond between us was just too tight, for her and for me. I know now what I could only intuit back then: that no one would ever love or nurture me the way my mother did. But I had to cut my hair to breathe a little, without knowing that this simple act of autonomy would haunt me for years, leaving my beauty in doubt and filling us both with a disappointment so wide that we would barely be able to meet each other's eyes, mother to daughter, daughter to mother.

MOTHER,
I HARDLY KNEW YOU

LETTY COTTIN POGREBIN

I feel about mothers the way I feel about dimples: because I do not have one myself, I notice everyone who does.

Most people who have a dimple or two take them for granted, unaware of how these endearing parentheses punctuate a smile. While I spent months of my childhood going to bed with a button taped into each cheek trying to imprint nature, my dimpled friends fell asleep unappreciative of their genetic gifts. They did not notice what they had always had.

Most people who have a mother take her for granted in much the same way. They accept or criticize her without remarking on the fact that there is a mother there at all—or how it would feel if there were none. I've never had the luxury of being so blasé. Since I lost my mother when I was quite young, I keep pressing my mother-memories into my mind, like the buttons in my cheeks, hoping to deepen an imprint that time has tried to erase.

She was fifty-three when she died; I was fifteen. I had less time with my mother than I've had with my children. Less time than I've known my closest friends, or many colleagues. The truth is, if you subtract the earliest part of my childhood and the darkest months of her illness, my mother and I really knew one another for a scant ten years. I suppose I should be grateful that so little time has left so much to remember.

I think about my mother most in the spring—not just on April 20, the anniversary of her death, but whenever ordinary events, like spring cleaning, evoke everyday images of her. I remember that I would come home from school one day to find her in the midst of the annual purification of our house. She called it "freshening up." Single-handedly, she would take down the heavy damask draperies and put up diaphanous curtains, pack away the carpets and spread out rattan rugs, bathe the venetian blinds, costume the tweed sofa with some flowered chintz that announced the end of winter more defiantly than the first crocus, rearrange the furniture, and leave the air smelling like pine needles.

Since 1955, spring has not arrived with much fanfare in the houses of my life, but one whiff of pine-scented cleaner reminds me of my mother's domestic metamorphoses, a metaphor for her belief in new beginnings.

She also liked freshening herself up at the end of the day. After cooking supper she would tidy the house so that my father could return from his law office to calm surroundings and never suspect the mess of daily childrearing—a reality so many men are spared by impeccable wives. Then, like a teenage girl preparing for a date, she would dash into the shower, powder her Rubenesque body with a puff of peach-colored down, and put on a rayon or starched cotton housedress such as those sold today in vintage clothing shops at prices that would have bought my mother three winter coats.

When I see a certain kind of dress—with a tiny plaid pattern or an overall floral print—I can conjure my mother buttoning such a dress over her slip, then sitting at a mirrored dressing table like the one I'd inherited from Betty, smiling to bring out her cheek mounds for the rouge, fastening the catch on a string of pearls, scooping her hair up on each side with a tortoiseshell comb. As she dabs Shalimar perfume behind each ear, I can hear her saying, "It's good to freshen up for your husband. Makes a man glad to come home."

My father always came home for dinner, usually at seven. But no matter how lovely my mother looked, he didn't *stay* home. It wasn't another woman that propelled him out the door, it was a lifelong affair with meetings. Almost every night of the week he went out to attend meetings—of the United Jewish Appeal or the Jewish War Veterans, or any of his other organizations devoted to the welfare of Jews or of Israel. At one time or another, he was the president, chairman, or county commander of every one of them.

My mother would beg him to stay home for my sake, to give me "a real father, a real family life." But a woman in a housedress and a noisy little girl are no match for the lure of a roomful of power and adulation.

Watching him leave the house, I lost faith in my mother's axioms for feminine success, yet she kept reciting them like a litany—not only "Freshen up for your husband," but "Don't show your brains; smart girls scare men," "Always laugh at his jokes," "Act interested in his work even if you're not." My mother lived by these bromides. She freshened up, listened, laughed, and cooked up a storm, but none of it stopped the man she loved from getting into his Dodge sedan and driving away.

Passover always reminds me of my mother. The eight-day holiday demanded attic-to-basement housecleaning to rid every surface of *chametz* (leaven products), and a complete change of dishes, and because she kept a (mostly) kosher kitchen, she had to pack away two sets of everything (meat and dairy), and unpack all their Passover equivalents right down to the can opener. I never heard her complain. Maybe the Passover makeover suited her optimistic nature, her love for fresh starts and rites of transformation. I remember how efficiently she unearthed her Passover recipe files or turned to the right section of her dog-eared copy of *Jewish Home Beautiful* to double-check the traditional recipes for gefilte fish, chopped liver, chicken soup with matzo balls, potato pudding, carrot tzimmes, macaroons—all of which she would make from scratch. There was no pressure cooker or electric mixer in her kitchen, no food processor or microwave. She used a hand-cranked meat grinder and a flat metal vegetable grater. She whipped with a fork, chopped in a wooden bowl, and beat with a wooden spoon. For years she even plucked her own chickens.

I have a sense memory of the aromas that wafted up to my bedroom just above the kitchen, but few recollections of helping my mother except when she was baking. My squeamish complaints about "yucky" raw liver and "disgusting" chicken feet must have made it preferable for her to let me stay upstairs.

To this day I can remember the look of our seder table: the damask cloth with dim pink shadows from red-wine spills of meals past; the ceremonial plate with separate compartments for the parsley, *haroset*, gnarled horseradish root, roasted shank bone, and charred hard-boiled egg; the cut-glass bowls for salt water; three matzot in their layered satin case; two pairs of candlesticks, chrome and brass; the silver goblet for the Prophet Elijah. But only in recent years have I let myself think about my mother's exhaustion. It shows on her face in our home movies of the last Passover of her life. Could she have been that exhausted every year?

On both seder nights, while she and the other women served the meal and cleared the dishes, my father reclined in an oversized chair at the head of the table, ennobled in his *kipah* (skullcap) and *kittel* (white ceremonial robe). Year after year, the Haggadah, the retelling of Israel's liberation from bondage, came to us in my father's authoritative bass voice, annotated by the symbols, songs, and rituals that he brought upstage like some great maestro conducting the solo parts of the seder symphony. It took me years to see that my father's virtuosity depended on my mother's labor and that the seders I remember with such heartwarming intensity were sanctified by her creation even more than his.

Music reminds me of my mother, especially classical music broadcast on WQXR, the station she tuned into whenever she wasn't listening to "Helen Trent," "Our Gal Sunday," and the rest of her afternoon soap operas. We never went to a live performance or bought classical records, but there was always radio music in our house.

Certain songs bring to mind my mother and me as a happy pair, with my father in the wings somewhere and my parents' fights edited out. The lullaby Mommy always sang, "Old Lady Moon," transports me back to my red-and-yellow room with her sitting at the edge of my bed, stroking my forehead. I'm even further back in childhood, curled in her lap, when I hear "Oyfin Pripitshik," the only Yiddish song she ever taught me. She believed Yiddish was the language of old people and the Old Country—the language parents used to keep secrets from their American-born children, not the vocabulary of my future—but she made an exception for this song, now the anthem of my maternal mythology. Beethoven's "Für Elise" unlocks an image of me in long braids, sitting at the piano with a straight back and my skinny legs barely reaching the pedals, practicing the opening bars with Mommy in the kitchen humming along like a metronome. "My Yiddishe Momma" reminds me of my mother's devotion to my grandmother, who outlived her. "Try a Little Tenderness" brings tears to my eyes now as it did in 1954, when I played the record over and over again within my father's hearing, praying he would take Frank Sinatra's advice.

Music is a complicated catalyst. While these songs of my childhood elicit a rush of memories of my mother, they also evoke the larger reality of those times. As a woman, I long for the past about as much as I long for boned girdles and sanitary belts. I want to visit Memory Lane, I don't want to live there. My sentimentality is selective.

And my nostalgia is bittersweet. The bitter part acknowledges existential loss, and understanding that "only yesterday" was years ago and never to be seen again. But the sweet part glories in having lived, in possessing life by remembering its sounds and textures, and claiming the right to say "I was there and that's the way it was." Old music and vintage clothes are precious to me because things evoke people. And, since people die, I am grateful when things—a housedress, a kiddush cup, a song—stay around.

Springtime also reminds me of my mother because of the burst of family birthdays—my husband's and son's in April, my daughters' birthdays in May, and mine in early June. Birthdays make me realize that the four human beings who are dearest to me in the world are people my mother never knew, and that they will never know her, except as I reveal her to them, filtering the perceptions of a fifteen-year-old through the language of a grown woman. Birthdays and holidays—events we would surely have celebrated with her had she lived—are the times above all others when I think about how much we've missed.

Then, quite honestly, another thought comes to mind. If she had lived I might not have this husband and these children. I probably would not have gone away to college at sixteen, then lived alone for five years, traveling by myself, becoming self-supporting, learning to take risks. More likely I'd have stayed close to home, gone to Queens College, and married upon graduation, as my sister Betty did. My mother's aspirations for me were entirely oriented toward marriage and childbearing.

But her death forced me to live a different life. And since that life has suited me, and I have made gratifying decisions without a mother's advice or counsel, I wonder irreverently, ironically, whether my mother mothered me best by dying. That sentence is bizarre, I know, yet it is what I keep thinking. The contradictions are obvious: to mourn this woman so deeply and at the same time feel grateful to her for leaving me alone to grow up by myself; to palpably miss her to this day, and yet simultaneously dread what might have happened between us had she lived.

Suppose I had rejected her axioms of femininity? What if she didn't approve of my beliefs, my habits, my choices? What if my feminism frightened or shamed her? Disturbing possibilities. I try to imagine our relationship whenever I see mothers and grown daughters playing out their scenarios not in my land of what *if*, but in their land of what *is*. So many mother-daughter pairs are hostile and resentful. Could Mommy and I have avoided that? Could I have wrenched free of her timidity, taking with me the person she was but rejecting her formulas? Could we have drawn energy from our differences, or would she have viewed my life as an affront to hers?

Of course I will never know.

Not long ago, a friend found an old photograph of her family taken before they left Estonia on the eve of World War II. "You were four in this picture," her mother told her, misty-eyed. "You used to spend hours at that spot overlooking the valley and you'd sing at the top of your lungs."

My friend gazed at the picture in disbelief. It showed her standing in a place that, for decades until that moment, had appeared only in her dreams.

Mothers seem able to come up with these unexpected revelations about one's child-self, or to suddenly recollect a turning-point experience that explains one's adult obsession. Mothers save precious preschool artifacts in shoe boxes at the top of the closet. Mothers remember a child's first words, and quote them in tones usually reserved for Byron. Only a mother remembers her children's landmarks as her own.

Therefore, losing a mother when you are still a child cuts short your hindsight and historiography. Without my mother's testimony, I know myself almost exclusively *through* myself. I can only reconstruct that part of the past that I can remember firsthand. Without my mother, I have no possibility of being surprised by my own history. All I have is a baby book in which she inscribed my "Cute Sayings," traced an outline of my infant foot, entered my height and weight, and described my favorite foods, toys, and books. Tucked between its pages is a lock of my baby hair secured with a limp satin ribbon, some grade-school report cards, and a homemade Mother's Day poem which would not have predicted a professional writing career by any stretch of the imagination. These are my archaeological treasures. While my mother-in-law has conducted an ongoing dig into my husband's boyhood (and finds and remembers new things every year), all record of my existence from birth to six is in that baby book. There will be no further surprises.

My father was never much help in enlightening me about my former self, either because he wasn't paying attention or because he wasn't there. Although he claimed to adore me, and I remember him as lavishly affectionate, he was better at reminiscing about *his* childhood than about mine. If he did remember something about me, it was what *he* did with me, or how I reacted to *him*. He loved to recall how I didn't recognize him after he shaved off his mustache. He was amused that I had run from him in fear, but I felt sorry for the little girl he described—a child who spent so little time with her Daddy that she didn't know him well enough to see beyond a mustache.

My father lived for more than twenty-seven years after my mother died, yet he remains a father figure rather than a father. She is the parent I remember and hers is the life I keep mining for gold, running my sieve through the same old streams, searching for precious nuggets that might connect my memories of her to the life I have lived without her. I keep hoping that the missing pieces will turn up in my mother's past.

She was called Sarah when she sailed from Hungary in steerage in 1907, a little girl wearing paper shoes, and she never overcame her sense of inferiority at being a "greenhorn" in the New World. Soon after her arrival, she changed her name to Cyral and then to Ceil, undoubtedly to glamorize and Americanize herself. It occurs to me now that the name changes may also have had something to do with two of her most distinctive traits: her love of transformations and her superstitions. According to Jewish mysticism, one changed a person's name when he or she was gravely ill. This would mislead the Devil, who was thought to keep track of vulnerable people by name. Maybe my mother believed that a name change would also divert the Devil from a weak and vulnerable greenhorn like herself.

She went to work in her father's grocery store straight after graduation from the eighth grade because her parents needed her help. Later she got a job in a garment factory, doing I don't know what. She was deliberately vague about her work life until she made something of a success of it. She married the indolent first husband, gave birth to Betty, got her divorce, and sometime in the late 1920s found work with the respected hatmaker and couturière Hattie Carnegie, where she eventually worked her way up to the position of designer. Photographs from those years show Ceil as an elegant young woman whose clothes and posture were a cut above those of the friends posing with her on the running board of some big black automobile. Despite the wonderful flapper outfits and Jazz Age look of the pictures, she told me—once I knew the truth of her life—how miserable those years were for her. No career accomplishment could overshadow the *shandeh* of divorce or the disgrace of having had to send her daughter away.

I confess now that I have trouble understanding how the fiercely maternal, overprotective woman who was my mother was the same woman who could leave Betty in a boarding school at the age of three. When my daughters were three, I used to stare fixedly at them and try to imagine depositing those angelic little toddlers in some school dormitory and leaving them there all week, only to visit on Sundays. I couldn't even wrap my brain around the image. Nor did it jibe with what I knew of my mother, the kind of person she was with me. Yet it is also true that the mother I knew was a married full-time housewife with a lawyer husband, and the mother Betty knew was a struggling single working woman. In 1928, enrolling her little girl in an upstate, upscale boarding school must have made sense. What now looks like cold-hearted rejection must have been to her way of thinking an act of loving sacrifice.

Betty says it would have been easier (and free) to let Grandma baby-sit, but Ceil was determined that her little girl become a "real American," not a second-generation greenhorn. Thinking about her frequent references to "real Americans" and "real families," I can see how obsessed my mother was with what she wasn't. She believed that her parents' Yiddish accents and immigrant ways would rub off on her daughter. Rather than let such a tragedy happen, she worked long hours to pay for the expensive boarding school until Betty was twelve and my father adopted her.

As for Ceil, she spent those years polishing her English until it was pristinely unaccented. She read voraciously and informed herself about art, politics, and music. Nevertheless, she remained so ashamed of her origins and her family's poverty that the address she gave her beaus was not the Lower East Side tenement where she lived with her parents and unmarried siblings, but the home of a "rich" cousin in the Bronx. She took the subway to the Bronx so that she could be picked up there by her date and returned there at the end of an evening. When the beau left she got back on the subway and rode home to the Lower East Side alone.

After almost ten years of single life and subterfuge (which perhaps presaged her later secrets), she married the man who would become my father. They met on Visiting Day at the boarding school where both of their daughters were enrolled. Usually Ceil visited Betty on Sundays and Jack visited Rena on Saturdays. They had never crossed paths until one weekend when Jack had to switch to a Sunday. Mirroring the French film *A Man and a Woman*, the two parents were introduced by Betty, who, almost from the start, waged a campaign for them to marry. Eventually, she got her wish and more: Jack Cottin became her father.

Ceil could not believe her good fortune. She had married a "real American" and a good provider, a lawyer who, despite the Depression, was making a living. She quit her job. Now she could have a "real family" like every other middle-class woman she admired. No more boarding school, no more crowded Lower East Side tenement—they moved to a Bronx apartment that was even finer than the "rich" cousin's digs Ceil had claimed as her own. At last, by her lights, she was a success.

The one casualty of these happy developments was Jack's daughter, Rena. Although initially she spent some weekends with Jack, Ceil, and Betty, for reasons I will explain in the next chapter, the visits stopped. Shortly after I was born, Rena dropped out of sight altogether and the new family mythology was constructed, making me and Betty my parents' only daughters.

When I was about a year old we moved to Jamaica, Queens, to a semi-detached house with a front lawn, a backyard, six rooms, and a porch. This should have been the happily-ever-after part of my mother's story, but it didn't work out that way. Ceil felt painfully inferior to her well-educated, silver-tongued spouse—and if my father did not exactly flaunt his superiority, neither did he disabuse my mother of her low self-image. She worked hard to compensate, taking courses in oil painting, Hebrew, and Jewish history. She learned to play bridge—never well enough to still his carping ridicule. She learned to drive but he would not let her have the wheel when he was in the car. He gave her the allowance from which she squirreled away that secret cache that would become my nest egg, but she never felt secure.

Though she fought a losing battle against his meetings and organizations, she never gave up trying to lure her husband home by adorning herself, improving herself, and trying to win his heart the old-fashioned way—through his stomach. Her handwritten recipe cards attest to her efforts. In the 1940s and 1950s, when most housewives thought "gourmet" meant Jell-O molds, my mother was stuffing prunes with pecans and frosting the rims of iced-tea glasses. To please me—a notoriously picky eater who was by Jewish standards emaciated—she created food art, making a pear into a bunny with clove eyes, almond ears, and a marshmallow tail, or getting me to eat fresh vegetables by presenting me with Salad Sally, whose celery body packed cream cheese up its middle and wore a lettuce skirt and parsley belt.

Some of my mother's recipe entries are artifacts in themselves—reminders of her everyday life in two separate worlds. Menus clipped from the Yiddish newspaper *The Forward* alternate with cuttings from the *Ladies Home Journal*. The recipe for huckleberry cake is scrawled on the back of a ticket for the Military Ball of the Jewish War Veterans' Ladies Auxiliary (November 25, 1942), while Beet Salad is written on the stationery of the City Patrol Corps. Both of my parents served as air raid wardens during the war. I suspect Ceil volunteered for civil defense work not just as a public service but because it was one of the few activities she and Daddy could do together.

Even more assiduously than recipes, my mother collected people. Her relatives were first in her heart, time, and devotion. After the family came her many friends in the Jewish community, the women of our temple's sisterhood, Hadassah, the National Council of Jewish Women, Women's American ORT, and the JWV Ladies Auxiliary.

She also had a group of friends who played mah-jongg as if it were the Russian chess championships but without the silence. I remember iced tea with mint in tall glasses and sandwiches without crusts—cream cheese, tomato, and olives; tuna salad with swiss—and above the clicking tiles and cacophonous cross talk, I remember hearing the women complain about demanding, helpless husbands who would be lost without them. The ladies of the mah-jongg group could forecast doomed marriages and fatal illnesses long before the principals knew they were in trouble. I learned to recognize the gravity of a person's condition from the voice level of the narrator.

Whispers meant polio and cancer. Heart attacks were discussed a little louder, the flu at full volume. When they forgot I was upstairs with my big ears, the women talked about sex—either they had too much or too little, or they suffered from physical problems that I couldn't understand and couldn't find listed in the copy of *Love Without Fear* that I kept hidden in a zippered bolster. Compared to the other women, my mother didn't say much; she listened and offered a "Really?" or "How interesting!" but she didn't dish the gossip.

Other than the peripatetic mah-jongg group, there was not much house-to-house visiting. The telephone was the preferred means of communication among my mother's friends—and it was the telephone that brought Carl into our lives, this mystery man from Cleveland who was planning to come to New York for a sex-change operation in the early 1950s, when the transsexual phenomenon was virtually unknown. At first, Mommy's side of the conversations was a complete puzzlement to me:

"Don't worry, you'll learn to sit right once you get used to wearing dresses."

"I'm sure the doctors will fix your voice, too."

"So, you won't let him touch you there until you feel comfortable."

I badgered her with questions until she finally explained what was going on. Somehow this uneducated Jewish housewife who blushed at circumcision jokes had become the telephone therapist to a stranger who was about to surrender his penis and begin life as a woman. She took his calls because he had been referred to her by one of her Cleveland cousins. For months I heard her reassuring the tormented Carl, assuaging his fears, discussing his medical plans, and responding to his questions about femininity with the sort of physiological detail that would have been off limits had she not accepted the role of the comforting confidante. One day I heard her correcting herself and calling Carl "Carol." Shortly afterward the calls ceased. When I asked what happened, Mommy simply said, "Carol doesn't need me anymore, she just wants to get on with her life."

There were seven siblings and dozens of cousins in my mother's family, but Ceil was the one you would call if you had a transsexual friend in need. She was the organizer, the family glue, the counsel of last resort. Everyone leaned on her. And because her husband, the man of her dreams, was almost never home, she filled her life with everyone else. She took in uncles who returned from the war and cousins who had survived the Holocaust, putting them up until they could get settled on their own. When I was five, one of my aunts died in childbirth and Mommy insisted that my newborn cousin, Simma, live with us until her father could find another wife. Thus, from 1944 to 1946 I had a "baby sister." In 1950, my mother invited a friend's daughter to stay in our extra bedroom so the girl could continue to attend her own school while her parents moved out of the city for her father's health. And when my grandparents were too old to maintain their own home, Mommy performed one of her domestic miracles and transformed our basement into their *pied-à-terre*.

Whether it was a family crisis, a holiday get-together, a dinner to be hosted for one of my father's clients or organizations—whatever it was, if it needed doing, my mother did it with grace.

Aishes Chayil (The Woman of Valor), from Proverbs 31, is traditionally read by Jewish husbands to their wives every Sabbath Eve. So far as I know, my father never spoke these verses to my mother, but no wife deserved them more. Our rabbi, Gershon Levi, recited them at her funeral; they might have been written just for her.

> *What a rare find is a capable wife!*
> *Her worth is far beyond that of rubies.*
> *Her husband puts his confidence in her,*
> *And lacks no good thing.*
> *She is good to him, never bad*
> *All the days of her life. . . .*
>
> *She rises while it is still night,*
> *And supplies provisions for her household. . . .*
>
> *She girds herself with strength,*
> *And performs her tasks with vigor. . . .*
>
> *She gives generously to the poor;*
> *Her hands are stretched out to the needy. . . .*
>
> *Her husband is prominent in the gates,*
> *As he sits among the elders of the land. . . .*

Her mouth is full of wisdom,
Her tongue with kindly teaching.
She oversees the activities of the household,
And never eats the bread of idleness. . . .

Ovarian cancer was the recorded cause of her death. Today, with all the
talk of cancer-prone behavior and the physiological ravages of stress, I wonder if the female body's ultimate expression of feminine suffering is to de-
velop uterine cancer. I wonder if my mother died from too many years of
self-sacrifice.

More than five hundred people came to her funeral. I heard one man say
the turnout reflected my father's prominence in the community, but most
people knew otherwise; these were *her* friends, the people who had claimed
her love in my father's absence. And they appreciated her as he never did.

I'm quite sure my mother died without understanding how remarkable
she was. Once, during the last weeks of her life, when I was sitting with
her after school, she started crying. "I'm so sorry that I will never see you
grown up," she said. "I hope I've raised you well, because I've been a failure
at everything else."

"Everything else?" I whispered.

"Yes," she explained. "Choosing a husband is the most important decision in a woman's life, and twice I chose wrong."

She never saw herself for what she was: a brave pioneer in the new world,
a female wage-earner unbowed by a grade-school education, a single parent
who supported and educated her child throughout the Depression, a gifted
artist and designer, an intrepid student, a maker of feasts and celebrations,
a relentless optimist, a nourishing mother, and a true and giving friend.

I learned what success means from this woman who considered herself a
failure. In the past I have oversimplified her lesson; I've said her life taught
me what *not* to tolerate in my own. But the older I get, the more rich and
complicated her legacy seems. Before she could become the conformist that
I might today deplore, she had to learn a language, decipher an entire social
system, make the leap from a shtetl with wooden cottages and mud paths
to a crowded city tenement—and decide that tenement life wasn't going to
be good enough. Where did she get the vision? In a time when women tolerated all kinds of abuse in order to stay married and economically secure,

she walked away from an insufferable husband. Where did she get the nerve?

From my present perspective, I can bemoan the years she wasted on undeserving men, the needless humiliation she felt on behalf of her impoverished, unassimilated family, her misguided inferiorities, the excuses she made for having had a career in the design world that struck her as unseemly. Again, that critique is simplistic. I see now that my mother's brilliance lay in her ability to create a persona as original as the dress designs she coaxed out of a few folds of fabric. In her context, for her generation, she was a miracle worker. She invented herself. Then she invented the family life she thought she and her daughters deserved. Deeply, desperately, she wanted to be like everyone else, but when the American dream didn't deliver, she made up her own.

I have the luxury of pursuing my goals unencumbered by the weighty bundles of a greenhorn. Still, to unlearn the constricted, self-sacrificial, conformist kind of womanhood that my mother bequeathed to me (just as her mother bequeathed it to her), I find myself using her survival skills and tools of invention. While she never acknowledged her strengths, I recognize them in my own idealism, willfulness, and belief in the possibility of change. In a funny way, the little girl in paper shoes became my role model after all.

Along with her optimism, I've also inherited her mysticism. My superstitions are my mother's superstitions—not black cats and rabbit's feet, but the amulets and incantations that she learned from *her* mother and I learned from her. I don't mean to suggest that she intended to school me in the occult. Quite the contrary, she tried to hide her shtetl formulas; she wanted me, like Betty, to rise above her Old World ways. But eventually, just by living with her, I came to know them all: Never take a picture of a pregnant woman. Be sure you have bread and salt in a house before you live in it. When an eyelash falls out, make a wish on it. Knock wood when speaking about good things that have happened to you. Don't leave a bride alone on her wedding day. Eat the ends of bread if you want to give birth to a boy. (Betty followed this prescription during her first pregnancy, never accepting anything but the heel ends of a loaf of bread, and she gave birth to a boy. "See, I told you so!" said Mommy. But Betty's next two were also boys, even though she'd sworn off eating bread ends. Finally, her fourth child was a girl.)

The day when I first discovered menstrual blood on my panties, I called for my mother to hurry into the bathroom. My friends had been having their periods for years. At last I had mine. I was fourteen and I was thrilled. As soon as she saw the blood, Mommy said something in Yiddish and slapped me across the cheek. Then she hugged me. I'd never been struck before by either parent. I was stunned, but as she held me firm in her embrace she whispered into my hair, "I'm sorry, darling, but Jews have to slap a girl on her first menstruation to prepare her for the pain of womanhood. Please God, that slap should be the worst pain you ever know."

Often, Mommy would tiptoe into my room after she thought I was asleep and she would kiss my forehead three times while making odd little noises that sounded like a cross between sucking and spitting: "*Thpu. Thpu. Thpu.*" One night, as she pulled her face away from mine, I opened my eyes. "Mo*ther*, what *are* you doing?" I demanded.

Embarrassed, she told me she was excising the evil eye, just in case I had attracted its attention that day by being especially wonderful. She believed her three noises could suck out any envy or ill will that those less fortunate might have directed at her daughter.

By the time I was in my teens, I was almost on speaking terms with the evil eye, a jealous spirit that kept track of people who had disproportionate amounts of happiness or good fortune, and zapped them with sickness and misery to even the score. To guard against this mischief, Ceil practiced rituals of evasion, deference, and, above all, avoidance of situations where the evil eye might feel at home.

This is why I wasn't allowed to attend funerals or visit a house where someone had recently died. This also is why my mother did not like to mend my clothes while I was wearing them. The only garment one should properly get sewn *into*, she said, is a shroud. To ensure that the evil eye did not confuse my pinafore with a burial outfit, my mother insisted that I chew a thread while she sewed, thus proving myself very much alive.

Outwitting the evil eye also accounted for her closing the window shades above my bed whenever there was a full moon. "The moon should shine on you only in your grave," she explained. "Moonshine belongs in cemeteries."

Because we were dealing with a deadly force, I also wasn't supposed to say any words associated with mortality. This was hard for a kid who punctuated every anecdote with the verb "to die"—as in "You'll die when you hear this!" "This boy is to die," or "If I don't get my math done, I'm dead." I managed to avoid using such expressions in front of my mother until the day she came home from an auction with a painting I hated and we started arguing about whether it should be displayed on our walls. Unthinking, I pressed my point with a melodramatic idiom.

"That picture will hang over my dead body," I shouted. Without a word, my mother ran into the kitchen, grabbed a carving knife and slashed the canvas to shreds. Not only wouldn't that painting go up in our house, it would never surface in anyone else's either. I might as well have invited the evil eye to tea.

I think I finally understand all this now. Just as an athlete keeps wearing the same lucky T-shirt in every game to prolong a winning streak, Ceil's superstitions gave her a means of imposing order on a chaotic system. Experience had taught her that life was unpredictable and incomprehensible. Anything that might put matters under control was worth a try. Her desire to influence the fates sprang from the same source that makes the San Francisco 49ers' defense more superstitious than the offensive team. The defensive team has less control—they don't have the ball.

Women like my mother never had the ball. She died leaving me with deep regrets for what she might have been—and a growing respect for who she was. I wish I had a million clear recollections of her, but when you don't expect someone to die, you don't store up enough memories. It hurts that I cannot remember the sound of her voice, or the shape of her hands. But her mystical practices are among the sharpest impressions she left behind. In honor of this matrilinear heritage—and to symbolize my mother's effort to control her life as I in my way try to find order in mine—I knock on wood and respect her other superstitions to the letter. My children laugh at me, but they understand that performing these harmless rituals has helped me keep my mother alive in my mind.

One night when my son, David, was seventeen, I was awakened by the realization that the window blinds in his room had been removed that day for repair. Smiling at my own compulsion, I got a bedsheet to tack up against the moonlight. When I opened his bedroom door, what I saw brought tears to my eyes. There, hopelessly askew, was a blanket David had already taped to his window like a curtain.

My mother never lived to know her grandson, but he knew she would not want the moon to shine upon him as he slept.

SECOND PERSON

YONA ZELDIS MCDONOUGH

*T*he heat is an incubus, crouching on your shoulders, arms around your neck, sucking the breath out of you. Despite your cotton skirt, sun hat, and sandals, it is relentless; heat is rising in great shimmering waves from the sidewalk, grabbing your ankles, your thighs. You think that you have never endured such heat in your life, but this is untrue: Tel Aviv is miles north of where you live in the Negev, and not a desert besides. But there is relief in the desert: the wind that moves swiftly across the cracked earth, the feel of the fruit trees—peach, pear, apricot—when you finish the picking and bury your arm, your whole face even, in the green, fragrant boughs. Here there are only the newly poured concrete sidewalks, the squat concrete buildings, and the line of people that snakes out over the steps of the Tel Aviv post office onto the street on which you have been standing for almost an hour.

You shift your weight yet again; you scratch an insect bite behind your ear, feel the perspiration trickling down your neck. The line hasn't moved in the last twenty minutes. You wonder about the crowd: how is it that so many people need to make calls overseas? You thought of sending a telegram, but there is no telegraph office in Beersheba; you would have had to come to Tel Aviv anyway, so why not phone?

You know they will be happy, your parents, to learn that finally you are getting married. The two years you have lived here with Michael have been heaven on earth for you, but hell for them. The first time you ran away they found you in a New York hotel room, reading the Gideon's Bible placed on the nightstand and waiting for the ship's departure the next day. The second time they didn't catch up with you until it was too late: you were here, yes, really here; the newly formed state was euphoric with its victory and the place itself—the desert—more barren and more beautiful than you ever would have believed possible.

You imagine the telephone conversation that will take place. Your mother will answer and the line will crackle with static and tears. She cries whether happy or sad, furious or delighted; her weeping punctuated the little events of your girlhood: your first day at school, your piano recitals and spelling bees, the day you began to menstruate. She will turn the phone over to your father; his loud voice will drown out the static, his joy will speed through the fragile current that connects you, thousands of miles away. His baby, his daughter, is getting married. You'll have the biggest, the best, the most wonderful wedding if only you and Michael will come home—

The daydream is suddenly interrupted by the angry voice of a man standing ahead of you in the line. You did not notice him before, but he is drawing attention to himself with his loud voice, his large gestures. It is not clear who or what he is angry with—his Hebrew is thickly accented and very bad. You look more closely at his black felt beret—so bizarre in this heat—and his wrinkled gray jacket. You think he may be French. And then, as if to verify the accuracy of your guess, he begins speaking in French, much more softly, but still grumbling and complaining. You know very few words of this language; in high school, where it was taught, your mind drifted and wandered throughout the conjugations and compound tenses, but you can recognize a phrase here and there. At first you think he is talking to himself—he seems strange enough—but then you realize he is talking to a small girl standing by his side. You assume she must belong to him. But why is he scolding her? As far as you can tell, she has been very quiet and well behaved, especially considering the heat. As you look at her, you are struck by the utter incongruity of her appearance in this context: the white crocheted dress, neat white anklets, maroon leather shoes. Her hair is precisely arranged in ringlets. You imagine the curling iron like a silver wand, the hiss of steam as it meets a soft brown lock. Who has arranged her hair so carefully? Surely not this grouchy man, with his angry eyes and coarse hands.

This perplexing drama is interrupted by the appearance from someone who works in the post office. He stands at the top of the stairs and announces loudly in Hebrew that the telephone lines are out. A collective groan rises from the throats of those who have been standing here all morning. Everyone who is waiting to place an overseas call should return sometime in the afternoon. No, he cannot say when. But later. Then he repeats his message in Yiddish. The man with the beret raises his voice again; he has switched back to his awful Hebrew. He grabs the child by the hand and marches off.

You are hungry and very, very thirsty. In your large bag you are carrying two hard-boiled eggs, a canteen of water, and some apricots. You could sit down right here, but the merciless heat has made you feel faint. You must find some place out of the sun.

The cafe is dark and comparatively cool. Gratefully you sink into the chair, glance at the menu that is handwritten on a soiled sheet of white paper. The boy that brings it to you is no more than twelve. He has smooth brown skin and dark eyes with long lashes. He must have come here from Syria or Iraq or Egypt. He might even have walked, since most of the Jews living in these places were too poor to travel any other way. His dark eyes hold yours for a moment; you wonder where he's been and what he's seen, and then you look down as you order something to eat. When you look up he is gone. His sudden disappearance leaves the view to the back of the cafe unobstructed, and at the far table you see the man with the beret and his beautiful child.

He is now chewing on a cigar, while the girl plays with a doll. His manner toward her doesn't seem to have changed; you can't hear what he's saying, but you can see the look on his face. At one point he reaches over to grab her arm, and you wince. Without stopping to think, you rise and go over to his table. The anger that has been boiling in you for some time finally takes shape and you say, quite calmly, "Stop that."

"Stop what?" he says, snorting his contempt like a bull. He takes the cigar out of his mouth and points it toward you menacingly. "What business do you have butting in here anyway? Whose kid is she? And how do you know what she's really like? Ever spend any time with kids?"

"Yes, I have. And I wouldn't treat one like you're treating her." You are surprised that you have said this, because in fact you have never spent any time with small children.

"Listen, lady, what do you know? You think you can do a better job with her? Good! Then you take her! I'll let you walk out of here with her if you want. But I'm warning you—don't come crawling back here when you find out what a rotten little brat she is!"

You are shaking by now, but you hear yourself say, "I'll take her. Right now. Just tell me her name and—"

"Her name's Monique, after her bitch of a mother who I hope I never see again as long as I live. Here's her ration card," he hands you a small, soiled square. "And there's her stuff." He points to two neat bags that have been placed on the floor beside the table. "Good luck and good riddance!" He rises from the table and turns to Monique, who has not said anything during this exchange.

You sit down at the table. The waiter brings your food. Carefully you cut the food into bits and gesture to Monique to eat. She has no fork, so she picks up a morsel in her fingers. *"Merci,"* she says, and you realize that although you understood the first word she has spoken to you, it is not likely that you will understand many more.

This is the most rash thing you have ever done. Running away from home, living with Michael, these things pale before the thing that has just taken place. But as you watch this small person sitting beside you eating her lunch so delicately, you are not sorry and you are not afraid. When Monique is through eating you bring her to the bathroom, such as it is. You help her wash her hands, her face, straighten her wrinkled dress. Suddenly, a French word you don't even remember learning floats into your mind, setting off a little ping of recognition and delight. *"Dentelle,"* you say to her, pointing to the dress she is wearing. "Lace." And you smile. *"Dentelle,"* Monique repeats, taking your hand.

You want to return to the post office; after coming all this way you are determined to place your call. But first you open one of Monique's bags, searching for something important. She has been fed, used the bathroom, and is clean. Now you must find a hat to protect her from the sun. If necessary you will give her your own. But your search doesn't go unrewarded: in one of the bags you find a small straw boater, encircled with a blue grosgrain ribbon. Nestled inside it are several pairs of crocheted socks which you remove and put back in the bag. You also find a tiny silver hairbrush, with soft bristles and an intricate monogram on the back. You make out the letters *M-T-R*. M for Monique, of course—then you realize that you don't even know her full name. You look up at her again; she is cheerfully playing with her doll, murmuring in French and shaking a finger in gentle admonition. You say something to her in Hebrew and she looks up but doesn't respond. You try English, but again there is no response. Finally you repeat your question in Yiddish, and she answers you in what you realize could only be German. You place the boater on her head and gather her bags together on one arm. Standing by the doorway filled with the bright white glare from the street, you are again struck by the incongruity of her appearance in this harsh place. She belongs to Europe before the war; you can see her at the Tuileries with an ice cream cone, or maybe in Vienna. You have never been to these places, but you suspect she has, and that she possesses a knowledge that is no less powerful for its being inchoate. As you leave, she once again slips her hand into yours, and you feel a sudden rush of pure and incandescent love. Her small, grave face, with its full cheeks and pointed chin, reminds you of an acorn; her wide gray eyes are trusting and clear. Altogether she is the most perfect thing you have ever seen, and you know you will never willingly let her go.

The two of you return to the post office, where the line is much shorter now. In what seems like no time you are inside and placing your call. Just as you envisioned, your mother weeps and your father laughs. But you are barely conscious of them, so intoxicated do you feel by the quiet child standing beside you. "And next year a grandson," your father is saying. You do not tell him that all your dreams for a child have been fulfilled beyond your wildest imagination.

By the time you are on the bus headed back to the kibbutz the sun has slipped down in the sky and a light wind has made the air more bearable. Monique sleeps on your lap during the long ride, her head heavy as a rock against your shoulder. You have removed the hat, and breathe in the fresh scent of her hair. As the bus heads south the sparse foliage gives way to desert. You are transfixed, as always, by the sight of the dunes far off in the distance and the setting sun that has drenched the sky in red.

When you arrive at Beersheba it is dark. Sometimes you can catch a ride with one of the wagons headed back to the kibbutz, but it is too late now. You will have to walk the last two kilometers, and because Monique is fast asleep you must carry her. Somehow you hoist her up and begin the long walk. Her weight seems to press down on you, and you don't think you will be able to make it home. But gradually even the discomfort is transformed; you have surrendered to it and it is no longer your enemy.

You arrive at the kibbutz while everyone is eating supper. By this time

Monique has awakened, and you walk into the communal dining room with her by your side. As if in slow motion, everyone stops eating and all heads swivel slowly around to watch as you make your way toward the table where Michael sits. No one says anything, but you know they are aware of something rare and precious in their midst, and they are humbled by it.

"Abby?" is all that Michael says, but his whole face, his voice, is a question. You sit down and Monique sits beside you. You begin relating the story of the day, who she is and how she came to be here with you. Michael continues to eat, but mechanically, like a sheep. You know your story sounds unbelievable, but it is true and he believes you. His eyes never leave your face as you are speaking. Finally, he turns to look at Monique.

"I wonder if there's room in the children's house," he says. You are bathed with relief that he has not offered a word of objection, for you are weary and grateful to avoid a battle tonight.

"They'll make room," you say with certainty, placing your hand on Monique's dark head.

And, indeed, they do. Monique is assigned to a room with two other children near her age: she will attend school and eat with them during the day, but she may join you and Michael for the evening meal. She will sleep, like all kibbutz children over the age of three months, in a communal dormitory.

But you are not happy with this situation, and neither is Monique. The first night, after dinner, you bring her over to the building where the children sleep. You had always supported the idea of children being separated from their parents, at least in theory. But that was before Monique. You can tell she is not comfortable in these surroundings, and after you have bathed her and tucked her into bed she clings to you, mutely begging you to stay. So you do. At least until she has fallen asleep. And you wait, to make sure she is sleeping deeply, before you guiltily slip out.

Sometime in the middle of the night the door to your room opens, as you knew deep down it would, and she appears, a small specter bathed in moonlight. You remember the nightdress you slipped over her head earlier; it is white and embroidered by hand. Now you can see her anxiously pulling on what you know to be a rosette before approaching your bed. Silently you open your arms and she slips into them. Her feet are bare and covered with the fine, powdery dust from the ground. You wrap your arms tightly around her and murmur in your broken Yiddish, learned with a vague disdain from your parents years ago, that she's all right now, that she's here with you.

In the morning you can tell Michael is displeased, but he says nothing. You bring Monique back to the children's house and help her get dressed. Her wardrobe is not suited to this life; there are no shorts, no simple dresses. You make do with a pleated skirt and a sailor's blouse. The ringlets will be impossible here, so you braid her hair neatly into two braids and hoist her up to a mirror to inspect the result.

"*Sehr schön*," she beams. When you put her down she runs to get her doll and asks you, in that voice of hers—so pretty, so polite—if you will fix her doll's hair the same way. You happily set to work, even though you know you will miss the wagon out to the fields and will have to walk. When you finally leave you see the tears poised in her pale eyes, just waiting to fall. You feel them well up in your own eyes and you hurry away.

Monique refuses to sleep in the children's house. Every night you go through the ritual of bathing her and tucking her in, and every night without fail she appears by your bed, waiting to be taken in. Michael is angry, but so far has not done anything.

More serious is what happens during the day. As soon as you deposit her back at the children's house she begins to cry, a terrible, keening sound. You can hear that sound all day long in your mind: it haunts you while you reach up to pick the voluptuous summer fruits; it will not stop while you arrange your filled baskets into large wooden boxes and load the boxes onto wagons. The sound pierces a hole inside you; the hole is burning hot and filled with tears. Nurit, the woman who cares for Monique, tells you that the child won't eat and refuses to play with the others. Something has got to change. In the evenings you visit her, and she is so relieved to see you again that she flings her arms around you and won't let go. Michael won't come with you anymore. He thinks her attachment to you is unhealthy. He does not say anything about your attachment to her.

"Abby, we have to send her away," Michael says one night when you are alone in your room. You have just put Monique to sleep and it will be a couple of hours before she appears in your room.

"You know I won't do that," you say steadily.

"It just won't work," he says, as if you have not spoken. "What about when we leave to get married? What will she do without you then?"

"We'll be back," you say, but the truth is you can't bear to leave her either. "Or we'll take her with us."

"Abby," Michael says patiently, "I hardly think we can do that."

"Why not?" you say. "Why not?"

"You're eighteen," he says quietly. "And I'm twenty. She's too much for me. And for you."

"I thought you wanted children," you say wildly. "You said you did."

"Of course I do," he says, stroking your cheek with the back of his hand. "But our children. Yours and mine. Not a stranger."

"She's not a stranger to me," you mutter, turning away from his hand before it grows more caressing, more seductive. "You're jealous. You think I love her too much. Maybe I do." You look at him then, his small amber eyes and full mouth. You are scared when you say this. Michael has been your lover since you were fourteen; you have come halfway around the world to be with him and this life you have found here has given you more happiness than you have ever known.

"That's your choice," he says finally. "But it is a choice. She doesn't belong here, and I don't want her." He gets off the bed, walks over to the wardrobe, where he takes off his shirt and begins folding it. "You decide," he says. "I've said what I had to say."

The day that Monique leaves you feel that someone has put a bullet in your heart. One of the women has a sister living in Beersheba who lost her husband and son during the War of Independence; she is eager to have Monique. With her pension from the government she can live comfortably. She'll be home all day, she can take care of a child.

"We'll visit her," Michael says. "I promise. I'll come with you if you want." But you can't be consoled. The sight of Monique's face as the bus takes her away is so wrenching that you cannot imagine seeing her again if seeing her means another parting like this one.

After she is gone you admit to a certain sense of relief. It's not that you don't miss her bitterly, but all the while you must have known this was coming; you sensed the inevitable separation like a vulture hovering in the sky senses the death that is taking place below. Once it has happened there is no longer anything to dread.

You spend weeks trying to devise a gift to bring her. Remembering her clothes, her few but beautifully made things, you know there is nothing you can think of that will be fine enough. Finally you resolve upon a handkerchief. But not one of the coarse muslin squares issued by the kibbutz. Not even a handkerchief bought in Beersheba will do. You will make it yourself, and you set about doing just that, snipping a small square from the heavy white cotton sheet on your bed. The sheet is old, and frequent washings in hot water, strong soap, and bleach have worn the fabric to a pleasant softness. Your fingers clumsily remember the stitching your mother tried to teach you years ago, and, after carefully tracing a pattern on one of the thin onionskin pages Michael uses for his letters back home, you embroider four bunches of tiny flowers in each corner of the square, and in the center, a large *M*.

The day of the visit you want to go alone, but Michael insists on coming. The street where Monique now lives with her new adopted parent is one of the older streets in the town; there are trees and flower gardens. You are shocked to see her when she finally bursts in. Her long dark hair has been closely cropped and she is wearing the shorts and sandals that all Israeli children wear. Ruth has even begun to teach her Hebrew. You see how warily she looks at you. She does not come running over, does not offer a kiss. And she is far more entranced with Michael's gift—some chocolate purchased at the bus station in Beersheba—than with your painstakingly created offering. You realize now that she won't be bought: you had your chance and you gave it away.

On the bus going back you cry and cry. Michael soothes you as best he can. "In two months we're getting married," he says. "Think of it, Abby. The wedding. You'll see your parents. We'll have a baby of our own. We can have one right away if you want."

You don't say anything, but you think, "I will never forgive him—never. We will not get married. And I will never, ever have a baby."

But things don't work out like that. You and Michael return to the States as planned. Your father is as good as his word, and makes you an enormous, splashy wedding. You wear a white satin dress sewn with seed pearls, and your bouquet is made of gardenias—smooth fat petals spilling over waxy green leaves. Your mother cries throughout the ceremony. At the reception your father gets drunk and whirls you around in his arms, then flings his glass to the floor. The flying shards of glass delight the guests.

Michael pulls you close, away from everyone for a moment, and says, "I love you, Abby. This is the happiest day of my life." When you return to Israel and the kibbutz, you get pregnant immediately. You have a baby, a bright-faced boy named Ari. Sixteen months later he is joined by his little brother Ben. Michael is thrilled; a house filled with sons. You are happy, too; you love the boys fiercely, but when the time comes to surrender them to the baby house you offer not a word of protest. Sometimes, though, when you are lying next to Michael at night and you can hear in his peaceful breathing the echo of the breaths your babies are taking a few doors away, you think of Monique and are stabbed by the memory. "My daughter," croons the voice of your silent lament. "My darling girl."

MY DAUGHTER
THE CYPRESS

RUTH WHITMAN

Sleep, little daughter, I'll plant you a tree
Even as grandmother planted for me,
One tiny sapling more for the hill
Where two little cousins are flourishing still.

Sleep, sleep, dream of the sea,
Your cradle's a caïque, your tree, your tree
Will be a mast to take you from me
Grown for the boy who fells you free.

Sleep, sleep, the tree is yet small,
An infant tree, not three years tall,
It mocks its sisters, flutters its boughs,
Hush, hush, it rains, it snows,

Summer suns lengthen your hair,
You grow tall, you move with care,
And from the sea bright blue and white,
A sailor whistles in the night.

But sleep, sleep, not yet, not yet—
The hull is carved, the mast is set—
Sleep one more night in Arcady,
My little girl, my cypress tree.

PRESERVES

for Mom

JOAN SELIGER SIDNEY

Katahdin was covered with blueberries—wild blueberries,
bushes low and thick, sprawling across the trail,
as we climbed higher. Stepping lightly from rock

to rock, across surfaces patched green with lichen, we
outstripped Dad, left him sitting on the ledge, his hand
filtering sun so his eyes could follow us to the top.

That was the first time he complained his chest felt tight.
Years still had to pass before his steps grew slower
and his breath more strained, before his heart would burst.

Superstition says, *Tragedy comes in threes.*
This is number two: always in memory you
are hiking the Carpathians, nibbling from wild vines.

You stop just long enough for the camera to catch you
and your friends. I can't remember their names, though you've
told me many times. The one who married and had children,

the one who studied medicine or mathematics. I recognize
only the survivors—you and Dad.
Today, after all your losses, how can I tell you

why I drag my feet to walk? Each week the muscles tighten more,
as I stretch and swim and lift my legs with weights, fighting
to keep them supple enough to move me through my house.

But with every step on these wobbling legs, I know
I disappoint you. I remember how carefully you brushed
and combed my curls, tying the satin ribbon in a perfect bow.

How you stood ironing, your tears on my dress
hissing like steam, as you spoke of the world you fled.
How can I tell you: *Multiple Sclerosis?*

Blueberry day. I drive us to the Agriculture School
a half-mile from my house. Pint baskets line
the salesroom shelves, as we line up to buy.

At this moment, I know you are still grieving.
In my kitchen, you watch me sit on the stepladder
stirring six pints of blueberries with sugar, bubbling

in a stainless pot. *In Zurawno, you tell me,*
poor people came to our village with their broken-down
wagon of blueberries. They cried: "Afinys! Afinys!"

We ran out with our iron pots and bought so many blueberries,
like this . . . You spread your arms as wide as they'll go,
forgetting your arthritis. *For days we made pies, pirogen,*

jam. Our hands were black from berries, our lips and teeth
from tasting. Your grandmother, Gisella, complained: "Enough!"
She was so worn out, her legs streaked from standing

over the stove. But each time the wagon came through town,
I ran out again to buy. The season was so short, the winter
so long. It was worth sacrificing a few swims in the Dniester

to be able to open the trapdoor, to climb down the wooden
ladder, and to bring up a jar of dark jam shimmering
in the kitchen light, like a field of summer stars.

HOME FOR WINTER

MARCIA FALK

Late Sabbath afternoon, remembering—
Father leaving through the snow for shul
to hear the final reading and the prayers,
mumbled cacophony in ten-part tune;
while here, Mama and I would sit and watch
the evening sky close down, unveil three stars
that marked the end to Shabbes. And between

the first three to appear and all the rest,
while Father, walking, bore the new week home
with spices in his pockets, light between
his fingers, sanctifying the mundane,
we knew a time suspended out of time,
not Shabbes, not yet week, and ours alone.

Then window turned to mirror by the night
would catch our eyes in accidental glance,
holding us there; and turning, she would ask
if I would spend the evening here at home.
Other things her eyes alone would ask:
Where would I be next winter? In whose home
and through what windows would I watch for stars?

Unspoken questions—how they echo through
the rooms of later weeks and later years,
for silence is a presence we still share,
and even under distant skies we trace

those same ascending paths of early stars.
Mama, if I knew—but you know better

where our stars gather, on what tangent curves
they bend their light, and where they congregate
in threes this Sabbath waiting, waiting for night.

PART SIX

WHEN HER MOTHER DIES, HER MOTHER'S DAUGHTER . . .

I have a last thank-you. It is to my mother, Celia Amster Bader, the bravest and strongest person I have known, who was taken from me much too soon. I pray that I may be all that she would have been had she lived in an age when women could aspire and achieve and daughters are cherished as much as sons.

Ruth Bader Ginsburg,
on the day she was sworn in
as a justice of the Supreme Court,
June 14, 1993

THE CHAIN

MAXINE KUMIN

My mother's insomnia over at last,
at dawn I enter her bureau drawers.
Under the petticoats, bedjackets, corsets,
under the unfinished knitting that crossed
continents with her, an affable animal,
I come on a hatbox of type-O any-hair,
heavy braids that have lain fifty years in this oval.
Between them, my mother's mother's calling card
engraved on brittle ivory vellum:
Mrs. Abraham Simon, Star Route 3, Radford.

Radford, Virginia, three thousand souls.
Here my mother spent her girlhood, not
without complications, playing
the Methodist church organ for weddings,
funerals, and the Sunday choir.
Here her mother, holding a lily-shaped
ear trumpet, stepped down from the surrey
Grandfather drove forty miles to Roanoke
to witness the blowing of the shofar
on Rosh Hashonah and Yom Kippur.

Affirming my past, our past in
a nation losing its memory, turning
its battlegrounds into parking lots,
slicking its regional differences over
with video games, substituting outer
space for history, I mourn
the type-O any-deaths of Mecca,

Athens, Babylon, Rome,
Radford, country towns
of middle-class hopes and tall corn.

Every year a new itinerant
piano teacher. New exercises
in the key of most-flats. 1908,
the first indoor toilet. The first
running hot water. My mother
takes weekly elocution lessons.
The radio, the telephone,
the Model T arrive. One by one
her sisters are sent north to cousins
in search of kindly Jewish husbands.

Surely having lived this long confers
a kind of aristocracy on my mother,
who kept to the end these talismans,
two dry links in the chain of daughters.
In the land of burley tobacco,
of mules in the narrow furrows,
in the land of diphtheria and strangles,
of revival meetings and stillborn angels,
in the land of eleven living siblings
I make my mother a dowager queen.

I give her back the chipped ruby goblets.
I hand over the battered Sheffield tureen
and the child I was, whose once-auburn hair
she scooped up like gems from the beauty-shop floor.

THE RIBBON

ROBIN BECKER

We earned them
by completing the course
without error,
by showing the best form
at the walk, trot, and canter.
Blue, red, yellow and white,
the ribbons fluttered
from the horses' bridles
as we trotted
proudly from the ring.

Each night before sleep
my mother removes
the piece of black
fabric from her blouse
and places it beside her glasses
on the night table.
The dark threads
have started to fray.
In the morning
she will pin it to her dress
and everyone she meets will know
she has completed one life
and entered the ring
for another.

YAHRZEIT

ENID DAME

In Jewish tradition, it is customary to light a yahrzeit, *or memory candle, on the anniversary of a family member's death.*

The *yahrzeit* flame
is beating its wings in a cup
on the edge of my kitchen sink.
Its stealthy gold shadow
breathing along the wall
suddenly terrifies me:
like finding a bird in my bedroom
still alive   pulsating   nervous,
changing the shape of the day.

No intruder is ever harmless.
And, Mother, I've got you cornered,
fierce memory pacing your glass cage,
houseguest with nowhere to go.
I'll lock myself in alongside you.
Today, we'll remind each other
of old connections, old journeys,
from muddy, sincere Indiana
to ragged-edged Brooklyn
with all its stray cats, its ecstatic
vegetable stands.

MOTHER

GRACE PALEY

*O*ne day I was listening to the AM radio. I heard a song: *Oh, I Long to See My Mother in the Doorway*. By God! I said, I understand that song. I have often longed to see my mother in the doorway. As a matter of fact, she did stand frequently in various doorways looking at me. She stood one day just so, at the front door, the darkness of the hallway behind her. It was New Year's Day. She said sadly, If you come home at 4:00 a.m. when you're seventeen, what time will you come home when you're twenty? She asked this question without humor or meanness. She had begun her worried preparations for death. She would not be present, she thought, when I was twenty. So she wondered.

Another time she stood in the doorway of my room. I had just issued a political manifesto attacking the family's position on the Soviet Union. She said, Go to sleep for godsakes, you damn fool, you and your Communist ideas. We saw them already, Papa and me, in 1905. We guessed it all.

At the door of the kitchen she said, You never finish your lunch. You run around senselessly. What will become of you?

Then she died.

Naturally for the rest of my life I longed to see her, not only in doorways, in a great number of places—in the dining room with my aunts, at the window looking up and down the block, in the country garden among zinnias and marigolds, in the living room with my father.

They sat in comfortable leather chairs. They were listening to Mozart. They looked at one another amazed. It seemed to them that they'd just come over on the boat. They'd just learned the first English words. It seemed to them that he had just proudly handed in a 100 percent correct exam to the American anatomy professor. It seemed as though she'd just quit the shop for the kitchen.

I wish I could see her in the doorway of the living room.

She stood there a minute. Then she sat beside him. They owned an expensive record player. They were listening to Bach. She said to him, Talk to me a little. We don't talk so much anymore.

I'm tired, he said. Can't you see? I saw maybe thirty people today. All sick, all talk talk talk talk. Listen to the music, he said. I believe you once had perfect pitch. I'm tired, he said.

Then she died.

A LEAK IN THE HEART

(EXCERPT)

FAYE MOSKOWITZ

*M*y mother wrote me one letter in her life. She was in California then, seeking treatment for the disease whose name she was never allowed to utter, as if in some magical way, speaking the illness would confirm it. I found the letter in a dresser drawer the other day, written in the round hand of Americanization school on tissue-thin paper banded at the top with the narrow red edge of gum rubber where it was once attached to a tablet.

March 7, 1947
Dear Faye Chaim and Roger,
 How are you kids? I am filling little better. My beck still hurts. Today I was at doctors for a light tritement and Saturday I am going again for a tritement. I hope to god I shut fill better. Please write to me. How is evrething in the house? How does daddy fill. The weather is her wondufull nice and hot. I was sitting outside today. Well I have to say good night. I have to be in bet 9 o'clock for my health. Take care of daddy.
       your mother
       Regart from evrywone.

On the back flap of the envelope she had written her name, Sophie Stollman, and the street address of the sister with whom she was staying in Los Angeles. On the last line she had lettered in *Detroit, Mich.*, her home. Now, older than she was when she died, I am shattered by that confused address. Loneliness, homesickness, and fear spill out of those laboriously penciled words, and the poignant error that was not a mistake speaks to me still.

I supposed I realized from the beginning that my mother's illness was a serious one: I had seen the fearful loss of symmetry where the breast had been, the clumsy stitching around it, like that of a child sewing a doll's dress. I had caught her one morning weeping in front of the mirror as she poked at the rubber pad that kept working its way up to the open collar of her blouse. But I was sixteen years old and worried enough about keeping my own physical balance. One false step and I might fall off the edge of the world. I was afraid to walk the outer limits of her sickness; I dealt with death the way the rest of my family did . . . by denying it.

I buried myself in books, played the "will-he, won't-he" games of adolescence, worried about the atomic bomb, tried to keep my little brothers from acting like children in a house where the sounds of childhood were no longer appropriate. My father and I clung to each other, but the veil of my mother's illness fell between us, too, and we were silent.

She got worse, and the family began to gather. Covered dishes and pots of food appeared, crammed our refrigerator, molded, were thrown out and replaced by still more food. Visitors came and went, swirling like snowflakes in the downstairs rooms, sitting around the kitchen table drinking tea from glasses, talking, talking. Still, they said nothing, and it seemed to me, sometimes, their silence would awaken the dead.

A time came when my mother's wardrobe was reduced to open-backed hospital gowns; our home was invaded twenty-four hours a day by a succession of starched uniforms and the incessant whisper of white nylon stockings. My mother was terrified by hospitals and refused to go, but still we were forced to trust her to the hands of strangers. She lay, as in a crib, imprisoned by iron bars; her own bed, where she had slept, knees in my father's back so many years, had been taken down to make room for a mattress scarcely wider than a coffin.

Alone for a moment, she called to me one day as I tiptoed past her bedroom. (Perhaps the nurse was downstairs preparing the unfamiliar food on which they kept her alive.) I stood next to her, watched her pluck at a fold in the bedclothes, smooth them, try to make the question casual by the homely gestures. "Faygeleh," she said, finally, "do you think I will ever get better?"

How could I answer her truthfully, being bound as inextricably as she was by the rules of the complicated deception we were playing out? Perhaps I understood in my heart's core that she was doomed, but I hadn't the permission of knowledge; I could only answer, "Of course, of course," and help to wrap her more tightly alone inside her fear. She never asked me that question again.

A few weeks before my mother died, when the sounds coming from her room began to move beyond speech, an older cousin was given the responsibility of articulating to me the name of her disease. I remember he took me to an Italian restaurant where we stirred the food around on our plates, and to a movie afterward.

Cordoned off by heavy velvet ropes, we stood in line under the prisms of rococo chandeliers, and there, surrounded by people I had never seen before, I was told the truth, at last. No room to cry in that glittering lobby, fire spurting from crystal lamps and mica-sparkled placards. So I sat, in the darkness of the theater, watching *Johnny Belinda* flickering on the screen, the salt of buttered popcorn swallowed with the salt of tears.

I was out late with friends the night of my mother's death. Walking alone up the darkened street, I saw my house, windows blazing as if for a party, and I knew what had happened. Word must have already spread, for on the sidewalk behind me I heard low voices and soft footsteps, stripped of purpose now, by her surrender.

In my mother's room, the mirrors, according to the old custom, had been shrouded (so the mourners would not have to confront their grief, some say), and damp, chill February fluttered curtains at the open window. My uncle, in a heavy jacket, sat next to his sister's bed. He would watch her until morning. "No, I'm not afraid," I told him. "Let me sit with her a little while."

She lay, hair bound in a white cloth, and I could feel her body, blood and bone under the sheet, pulling away from me, slipping into stone. The memories crowded around me, witnesses to my guilt: the many times I had resented caring for her, the times I had yearned to flee my house when her pain became an intimation of my own mortality.

I remembered, in the bas-relief of shame, the evening I came home from somewhere, to find her leaning on the kitchen sink, washing a stack of dishes I had left undone. "Shut up!" I had shouted when she spoke to me, angered at the robe and slippers, the cane lying on the floor, the medicine bottles, accouterments of a mother too sick to care for her own. Now we were cut off in midsentence. Now I would never be able to tell her how sorry I was for everything.

I still grieve for the words unsaid. Something terrible happens when we stop the mouths of the dying before they are dead. A silence grows up between us then, profounder than the grave. If we force the dying to go speechless, the stone dropped into the well will fall forever before the answering splash is heard.

MY MOTHER'S OBITUARY

LYN LIFSHIN

Others' parents
die. My father
falls on his
face in the snow,
stains December.
But my mother's
obit is a shot
gun, machete.
AIDS virus in
needles I clutch,
a tree crashing
thru the roof,
pulling wires
that sizzle in
light up night
like KKK flames
loud as Crystal
Night or The
Challenger I'm
the car that
she's in that
plunges into
rock and steel
as the bridge
we're on lets go

GIFTS

DEENA LINETT

*T*he night after our mother died, my brother and I slept in the same room for the first time in twenty-five years. He made an uncomfortable joke about sleeping with another woman (he's married), and then, casually, in that pure, male way, took his pants off, revealing a wildly printed nylon bikini and hairy, columnar legs.

We didn't sleep then. I had to tell my brother.

In all the years since we've grown, college years, professional schools, marriages, we'd gone such separate ways, I suppose we didn't think it possible that we still had so much in common. Our childhoods were disparate, our adult lives even more so, yet there it was: we are brother and sister. The closeness of that tie remains unexplored since, countless generations ago, Antigone risked everything to bury her brother.

I have to tell you, I said, even though you're her son, and you may suffer from my telling you.

It's okay, he said, and settled on his side to listen, both of us covered in matching brown blankets spread over yellow plaid sheets on twin beds that I had separated with a night table.

The whole day before she died, I said, the whole day she didn't move. I should have realized the end was near, but it was so unreal. On Monday, the day after you left, she talked the way she always did, and I kept thinking, How can she be dying? She is herself, she sounds like herself, her concerns are what they've always been. She can't really be dying.

But on Monday night, my hallucination came true. That was what was so terrifying. I had known it would happen, and when it did, I was transfixed, horrified. She began to throw up blood. Cups and cups of dark red blood into a green plastic basin. And after she stopped, and she lay back on the pillows, exhausted, and after I wiped her mouth with a damp cloth, I sat beside the bed, and Daddy sat on the other and he asked me for his prayer book, and she fell asleep, and I watched her chest rise and fall, and I was overcome. Before I came home, I'd had hallucinatory dreams—well, they weren't really dreams, they were visions that come in that state between sleeping and waking, hypnopompic hallucination, I think it's called—and I used to see her doing that, throwing up blood, and I knew that she would die that way.

She didn't, of course. And Tuesday she couldn't take liquid from a straw any more, I don't think she had the strength, and we poured minute quantities of water into her mouth from a little crystal cream pitcher. She was so implacably thirsty.

And on Tuesday her brother and his wife came. What had happened was, sometime while she was resting after vomiting the blood on Monday, the phone had rung, and it was Uncle, and I was nearly hysterical, and I said, I'll call you back, I can't talk now, she's throwing up blood. And when I came back into her room, she said, Did you tell him how bad I am? And so he came the next day. And he and Aunt and the housekeeper sat there with me, taking turns, mostly two of us at a time, on opposite sides of the bed, watching her. Occasionally she talked a little. And late in the afternoon Uncle said, This is what a deathwatch is, I've read about it in books. And he shook his head wonderingly, and I was in a panic of discomfort, worrying that she would hear him.

Wednesday was two days before their anniversary. Remember how Daddy sent her a rose every year? At four o'clock the sun came out, and I ran into her room, even though there were two of them there, because I had it in my head that she would die at four o'clock. But her chest was rising and falling, and she looked very still, but she hadn't changed, and just about then a truck came up with thirty-nine roses in an enormous vase, the one you threw out today, and Daddy came home then, and put the roses where she would see them if she opened her eyes, in front of the bright lamp on the dressing table. She never saw them. She was parched and couldn't drink, and she hadn't moved all day, and had said nothing. Even though she looked uncomfortable, it would have been a pity to move her, so we left her there, kind of slanted on the bed, and I said to Daddy, There'll be no room for you to sleep there. Uncle said, We'll take turns sitting with her, and you can get a good night's sleep, but Daddy said no, he had slept in the same bed with her for thirty-nine years.

The previous night I had slept in my clothes, with my light on, and that night I did, too, or at least, a robe with underwear underneath. I heard Daddy call my name, and in a flash I was standing a few feet from their bedroom doorway, and all the lights in there were on, the brightness she couldn't stand in her illness, and he said, She's gone. I couldn't bear to go in. I stood there in the living room, about halfway across the living room from our bedrooms to hers, and I could see her lying there, just as she had for the last week. And I knew I ought to go in, but I couldn't. I just stood there, wringing my hands. And he began to take off her ring, and her earrings, and he would stop, and wring his hands, too, and hesitate, and then, with a kind of sad duty, he would bend over her to arrange something. And he said he'd already called the funeral people, and I stood there, twisting my hands together. Then I asked him what time it was. And he said it was just after four. Then he moved in a way I'd imagined he would, and I said, Don't. Then I thought of his own agony, and I said, Please. Please don't cover her face. But she doesn't look pretty any more, he said. Really she had looked terrible for days, and the last two days her face had had that sheen that you read about, a kind of translucence. I didn't want to see that sheen. I had told myself that it was sweat. So I didn't look in there any more, I guess I wandered around the living room, and he stayed with her.

Then the funeral people came with a narrow cot and a navy blanket, and they folded it up to get it past that bookcase, that one that was Grandpa's. And Daddy was horrified, and he said, We'll have to move the bookcase, but it's heavy, because he was worried about how they'd get her out on that cot, if they had to fold it to get it in. So these men in their business suits moved the bookcase, and I'd awakened Aunt and Uncle, and they sat on chairs looking away from the bedroom, and then the housekeeper came, I'd called her, and when Daddy was out in the living room with Aunt and Uncle, we'd stripped the bed, and folded up the air mattress, and put new linens on, and we were working very fast, so he would have a nice, clean bed if he wanted it. And then he gave me a book.

On Tuesday, Daddy had taken me out on the porch and said, There's a tradition of our people. We wash our own dead. It's a last act of loving kindness. I plan to do that for your mother. Would you like to help me? I was stunned into silence. Then, I said, hesitantly, I want to do it, but I don't know if I'm able. He was silent. Finally I said yes. You don't have to if you don't want to, he said. I can do it alone. Mother's only preoccupation the last week had been how alone and lonely he would be, how he shouldn't be alone, how we should let him know he was not alone.

Now, how could I let him do this alone? Yes, I said. I'll help you. I'll try.

So at five o'clock in the morning he gave me a book. It was a big, fat book, maybe three hundred pages. I opened it to the pages on mourning and read, We have never felt the body to be a source of evil. Speedy burial has seen to it that our people have never felt the body of a deceased person to be a source of putrefaction. When we attend the dead we should remember that the body was the home of a spirit that laughed and sang, that made love. . . . And I thought, How can I be afraid of her body that gave me life?

I was sitting in her chair, reading the book, and it was dawn, and cold in the house. I put the heat on, and we all sat at the dining-room table and drank coffee the housekeeper had made, and ate chocolates from a box that lay there. I can't remember if we talked. I was cold beyond imagining. I put on one of her sweaters, and I thought, It's like having her arms around me.

Thursday after we ate breakfast, Daddy and I went to the funeral home. I was surprised at the quiet and efficiency there. I'd expected . . . obsequiousness, something of a servile attitude . . . I don't know what. . . . The place was decorated with antiques. I stared at them; I fixed them in my memory. I sat with Daddy and calmly planned my mother's funeral. And we had difficulty scheduling the service, because we didn't know when you would get in, and Daddy quoted the Talmud which said that it is an honor to the dead to wait their burial on a child; the child's coming to the funeral does the parent honor. So we scheduled it as late as we could, and of course you made it. Then for some reason I can't remember, we went home, and ate, and then Daddy said, It's time to go to the funeral home to wash your mother. I got a box of Kleenex and some cigarettes and we left. Uncle said something about it being too much for me, but I assured him I could handle it.

In the car, Daddy said, There are a couple of things you should know about the washing. We never uncover the entire body, and we never turn the body face down. We treat the dead with the same respect we would treat the living. I was slightly irritated, because I knew that, but I said, Of course.

All the way there, riding in Daddy's little red foreign car (such an uncharacteristic purchase!), I petitioned God. I prayed that I would be strong enough to help Daddy, that he wouldn't be alone, that I would do honor to my dead mother whom I'd loved so much. I don't think I'd ever prayed for strength with such intensity before. I kept telling myself that she loved him and did not want him to do this alone. Finally I asked him, even though he had told me this before, Why do we do it? And he said again, with his usual patience, It is the last act of loving kindness.

We went into the funeral home, and I walked quickly, not like one going to a distasteful chore. We had brought a prayer book, and Daddy found a certain page, and then he opened the double wooden doors into the room where Mother lay. I had never seen anyone who was dead before. I was stunned and terrified that I would scream, or cry; fail him, and her. I stood there, clutching the prayer book and praying for strength not to fail them, and he washed his hands and got two clean sheets from a cabinet (not one false step . . . everything he reached for was right where he expected it to be). She was covered to the neck with a sheet, and her head was elevated on a curved wooden headrest. Her hair looked like yellow straw, and her color was yellow. I thought, I'll never forget the smell of this place, which was not a bad smell, but a singular one.

I stood some distance from her head. I did not want to look down into her face. I could see only her profile, obliquely. Her face was closed, and she did not look peaceful. She had a troubled look, in fact. I said, I don't know if I can help. That's all right, he said.

He began by spreading a clean sheet over her and removing the one the funeral people had placed from underneath it. Then he took a basin and filled it with soapy water and a washcloth, and having folded two dry towels and left them near me on a table, he began first to carefully wring out the washcloth and wipe her face and neck. He washed one arm. An eternity flew by. He wiped her face with a dry towel, and I thought, I can't just stand here. I moved toward them, and holding the towel in two hands, so as not to touch her flesh, now cold, I began to dry where he had washed. Eventually, I did touch her, and it was not so bad. She felt just like she always did, only cold. And we washed her entire body that way, a little at a time, exposing only that part we were washing, and he washed her and I patted her dry. Then he picked up a little flat cardboard box, about the size of a book, only very flat, not at all thick like a book is. And I said, What is that? A shroud, he said. It was made of white cotton, and had pants, a tunic top, a belt and a little hat something like the hats on medieval women in pictures.

We put the pants on her. They had feet in them. Then the tunic, so that no part of her body was exposed except her lovely hands with their faded softly pink nail polish. Then the belt. She seemed to have a faint smile on the corners of her lips now, and when the hat was in place, she looked so peaceful and clean that my heart lifted. Right in the room, I felt my heart lift up. She'd always been fastidious, and in her last days we couldn't wipe the blood from her mouth because it was so sore. Now her face was clean, her body was clean. She looked beautiful, and like my mother. The shroud is a marvelous garment, modest and serenely humane.

Then the men came with the coffin and Daddy asked me if I wanted to leave the room, and I said no. I stood to one side while they lifted her and lowered her into the coffin. As they began to close the lid I ran out of the room. Soon Daddy came out, and gave me a cigarette, and he and I walked out of there. We were quiet most of the way home. Then I said to him, I'm happy that I had the opportunity to do this for Mother. I thank you for giving it to me. I'd forgotten my anger on the way there, when I'd been praying for the ability to help, and I'd asked myself why he'd asked me to do this, why I'd had to go, and had decided that he asked, not demanded, and that it had been my decision to help.

When we walked into the house, Uncle and Aunt were sitting in the living room. They rose, and Aunt outstretched her arms. I walked into them crying, She looked so peaceful! So beautiful and clean, just the way she would have wanted.

And then you came.

I was praying you'd come earlier, because Daddy had to teach me to give her shots, and I thought, raging, fearful, you're a doctor, it would be nothing for you to give them. I prayed that you'd hurry. But I had to learn to give her shots anyway, and after the first time, I was pretty good at it. She said, Bless you, when I gave her the injections, and, Thank you. Not a single time went by that she didn't say, Thank you, darling. And the washing. I thought again, you've handled dead people before. Why couldn't we wait for you? But of course I knew why, and I did it. And I feel a certain strength in myself that I never thought I'd be capable of, just because I helped him prepare her that way.

She gave me everything, I told him. Even in death she gave me these gifts.

YOU NEVER CAN TELL

SUSAN P. WILLENS

*L*ate in December 1991, on the first anniversary of my mother's death, I went to the synagogue to say Kaddish, the traditional prayer of grief and reconciliation. At home, I lighted a *yahrzeit* candle and watched it gutter out after its brief day of life. Then I turned to the clear plastic box of letters that had sat on the shelf of my study for months, since the last shipment of furniture, household items, photos, and papers arrived from the house where my mother had lived for forty years. For the last twenty years, since my father died, she had lived alone there, more and more isolated by depression.

I dreaded those letters. My sister and I came upon them while cleaning up our mother's house in the weeks after her death. There, at the back of one of the crowded, dusty, tumbled closets in that house that smelled of moldy food and old lady, they sat, amid unused dime-store towels and skeins of yarn that our mother had bought in a mood of *"you never can tell"* frugality.

While we were efficiently dividing tons of accumulation into "give away," "throw away," and "keep," the thirty-five letters in the plastic box stopped us. Postmarked July and August 1927, two cents postage, with return addresses of Belle Rosenthal in New York City and Hy Popkin in Detroit, they promised the voices of our parents when she was twenty-three and he was twenty-six, three years before they were married, our parents before we were born, while they were young, younger than our own children are now.

I dreaded reading them because my mother always spoke of her time in New York with derision. "I never knew anything," she would say. "I never went anywhere. I never met anyone. I was just a stupid girl, a mouse in a hole. And they never taught me anything, anyway."

"But, Ma. You'd already been teaching. You'd gone all the way from Detroit to Columbia Teachers College, a good school. Your sister Ethel was a lawyer working in the city. How can that be, that you never got out?" "Ethel," she would sneer. "She didn't help me at all. She was just selfish, and I could just as well have stayed at home."

More than that, to the young man who would be my father, I knew I would want to shout, "Don't pursue her! She'll only make you unhappy. She'll darken your days with her depression. She'll make you die before your time." In that fantasy, of course, neither my sister nor I would ever be born, but the memories of our mother's inconsolable sadness made not-living seem almost bearable, to save Hy Popkin from his future.

On New Year's Day, though, I opened the first envelope, a letter from my mother to her beau. "Hy dear. Last night we heard the loveliest concert—N.Y. Philharmonic—Lewisohn Stadium—I am looking forward to the concerts we plan to see together in the Fall. I wished so that you were here. . . ." She goes on, about plans with her sister, about traveling to visit family in Philadelphia, about having a date with an old boyfriend, Paul: "It seemed so funny talking to him and being so disinterested."

The other letters confirm the revelation: she is busy all the time, going to bridge parties, dinners, theaters (Norma Talmadge in *Camille*), movies (Emil Jannings in *The Way of All Flesh*), even to a speakeasy. She reads and comments on novels, picks out one for Hy because Heywood Broun had praised it that day in *The New York World*. She drives with friends to New Jersey, Coney Island, Brooklyn, but the friends mean less to her than her sister: "One person I never tire of is my sister Ethel. We each seem to go our own way and yet there is, under it all, an understanding, a tolerance, a desire to please and help. I know why the relationship is so fine. It is because she knows me and because she inherently has a bigger and finer character than I, that we are happy together. You are that way too. You're not petty at all . . ."

During the busy two months covered by the letters, a last visit to New York after two years at Teachers College, she is active and curious. She travels by herself to relatives in Philadelphia and Baltimore. She tolerates the family, especially an agemate named Isabelle, although they kid her about getting letters from a mysterious swain every day. From Baltimore she takes herself to Washington, where she so loses herself in admiration of the Library of Congress that she has to return another day with Isabelle to see sights she missed the first time.

Pictures of my mother from this time show a young woman of solemn beauty, with large dark eyes and waves of dark hair gathered in a knot at the nape of the neck. She is a knockout, so slender that she drinks cream instead of milk to fatten up. In her letters she flirts, she cajoles, she makes fun of herself, she mentions other men who take her out. "New York is just full of places that are havens to a romantic soul." Who is this captivating young woman?

She is certainly different from the woman I knew in later years, who resisted going anywhere and refused to surrender her imagination to stories, movies, or plays. My mother rarely mentioned Baltimore, Philadelphia, or even New York. Life had flattened to fact, except when she was doing safe things, like teaching school, cooking, seeing her own family, or shopping for bargains at thrift shops and the J.L. Hudson Company's month-end sales. Later on, when paranoia triumphed, she became hysterical in Chinese restaurants and in grocery stores because someone said something or looked somehow. She was inert, incurious even when Hy arranged for them to travel in Europe and Asia. The letters tell me, all these years later, she was not always like that. They tell me that I did not really know her.

Hy's letters speak of love and doubt. "I've fallen hard, sweetheart. I dream and dream about you. . . . I haven't known a time when I've wanted you more, Belle, you seem to be the only one that brings to me love's depths and its soaring heights. And when I think of what you require materially and what I am able to give materially it discourages me a lot. . . . You know you're so hard to satisfy." He is often "disconsolate" and "sad," sensitive to coolness in her letters.

He is working in Detroit's planning commission as an impecunious young engineer and attending law school at night. He lives with his parents and sister, plays golf and poker with friends, visits with the rest of his family and with hers, goes to parties, reads, and reads.

From his letters I learn about a prizefight—Tunney beats Sharkey—and an office half-holiday in honor of Lindbergh's transatlantic flight. Just before Labor Day he and some friends go to a fishing cottage and then on to Chicago for their summer vacation. Unlike hers, his summer's activities seem to be marking time until he can be with her. He mentions marriage; they will be engaged in a few months.

There is a playful tone in Hy's letters that stayed with him through his life. Like that love of fun, all his loves remained constant: swimming and fishing, poker with friends, studying the law, listening to music, and reading, reading. The letters show me that I knew my father; he was reliable in his personality and passions.

From my vantage point, so far down the passages of time, I am mesmerized by what the letters reveal: efficient one-day mail service and the grand fact of my parents' youth, their innocence.

The dread I felt before I read the letters continues, but in a different, more global way. In 1927 my parents do not know that the Depression is imminent, that World War II and the destruction of European Jews wait beyond that, and beyond that more horrors and wonders. All that I know about their futures, including my sister and me, their careers, their relatives and friends, and their intimate lives in later years, their sadness, illness, death—they cannot know.

I discover that these letters have been a gift from my parents, now dead. They have given me back my mother as she was before I knew her, when she was active, interested, healthy. I now recognize myself in this woman Belle, as I rarely did when I knew her. I wanted to say to her, "All those years at the end, when you insisted on staying in the house, when we came to see you from the East every month, you were so lonely and so sad, living in shadows. Ma, I am sad, too, for what I lost as the sorrow claimed you. You were a wonderful girl."

The letters make me want to tell my father, "Now I see why you devoted yourself to her, even when the devotion was thankless, maybe misguided. It was your love, and—I know you, Dad—when you put these letters together, yours to her in New York and hers to you in Detroit, and set them aside in the plastic box—that was love, too, for us who would find them later."

I can put the letters away now, with those I myself have written, received, and saved. Someone—maybe one of my four children or a grandchild—may someday want to watch time roll back to my own days of hope.

AUTUMN 1980

for Judith McDaniel

MARILYN HACKER

I spent the night after my mother died
in a farmhouse north of Saratoga Springs
belonging to a thirty-nine-year-old
professor with long, silvered wiry hair,
a lively girl's flushed cheeks and gemstone eyes.
I didn't know that she had died.
Two big bitches and a varying
heap of cats snoozed near a black woodstove
on a rag rug, while, on the spring-shot couch
we talked late over slow glasses of wine.
In the spare room near Saratoga Springs
was a high box bed. My mother died
that morning, of heart failure, finally.
Insulin shocks burned out her memory.
On the bed, a blue early-century
Texas Star, in a room white and blue
as my flannel pajamas. I'd have worn
the same, but smaller, ten years old at home.
Home was the Bronx, on Eastburn Avenue,
miles south of the hermetic not-quite-new
block where they'd sent this morning's ambulance.
Her nurse had telephoned. My coat was on,
my book-stuffed bag already on my back.
She said, "Your mother had another shock.
We'll be taking her to the hospital."
I asked if I should stay. She said, "It's all
right." I named the upstate college where
I'd speak that night. This had happened before.

I knew / I didn't know: it's not the same.
November cold was in that corner room
upstairs, with a frame window over land
the woman and another woman owned
—who was away. I thought of her alone
in her wide old bed, me in mine. I turned
the covers back. I didn't know she had died.
The tan dog chased cats; she had to be tied
in the front yard while I went along
on morning errands until, back in town,
I'd catch my bus. November hills were raw
fall after celebratory fall
foliage, reunions, festival.
I blew warmth on my hands in a dark barn
where two shaggy mares whuffled in straw,
dipped steaming velvet muzzles to the pail
of feed. We'd left the pickup's heater on.
It smelled like kapok when we climbed inside.
We both unzipped our parkas for the ride
back to the Saratoga bus station.
I blamed the wind if I felt something wrong.
A shrunken-souled old woman whom I saw
once a month lay on a hospital
slab in the Bronx. Mean or not, that soul
in its cortège of history was gone.
I didn't know that I could never know,
now, the daughtering magic to recall
across two coffee-mugs the clever Young
Socialist whose views would coincide
with mine. I didn't know that she had died.
Not talking much, while weighted sky pressed down,
we climbed the back road's bosom to the all-
night diner doubling as a bus depot.
I brushed my new friend's cool cheek with my own,
and caught the southbound bus from Montreal.
I counted boarded-up racetrack motel

after motel. I couldn't read. I tried
to sleep. I didn't know that she had died.
Hours later, outside Port Authority,
rained on, I zipped and hooded an obscure
ache from my right temple down my shoulder.
Anonymous in the midafternoon
crowds, I'd walk, to stretch, I thought, downtown.
I rode on the female wave, typically
into Macy's (where forty-five years
past, qualified by her new M.A.
in Chemistry, she'd sold Fine Lingerie),
to browse in Fall Sale bargains for my child,
aged six, size eight, hung brilliantly or piled
like autumn foliage I'd missed somehow,
and knew what I officially didn't know
and put the bright thing down, scalded with tears.

COLLECTING HERSELF

PEGGY SHINNER

$\mathcal{W}$hen Her Mother dies, Her Mother's Daughter

twists the wedding band off the dead mother's finger and slips it on the
fourth finger of her right hand. She pronounces:
You are now your Mother's Daughter;
combs the tangles from Her Mother's hair to weave into a sweater worn on
nights alone and cold;
tries on Her Mother's shoes although it is a well-known fact, from shore to
sea, over mountains, in valleys, across plains and deserts, in high-rises,
single-family dwellings, two- and six-flats, that the mother's feet are always bigger than the daughter's;
licks her finger and smooths Her Mother's eyebrows, ruffled from a lifetime
of mothering;
hears the words of Her Mother: I just want you to be happy;
files Her Mother's fingernails and cuts the cuticles and trims the toenails,
saving the clippings in a painted box lined with burgundy velvet per-
fumed with Her Mother's smell and stored with Her Mother's jewels;
wipes away Her Mother's tears;
washes and irons Her Mother's leopard nightgown;
wears Her Mother's turtleneck sweaters, Her Mother's full-cut Carter's un-
derpants, Her Mother's amber necklace, Her Mother's leather belt with
the gold buckle embossed with ballet dancers, all Her Mother's hand-
knit scarves;
becomes more like Her Mother every day;
pours twenty-four quarts of water over Her Mother's head after standing her
upright on a bed of straw;
hears the words of Her Mother: Pretend you're happy;
eats;

hates herself for it;

looks through Her Mother's drawers, the drawer where Her Mother kept nylons, and sorts through the pairs of hose, pantyhose, knee-highs, and loose stockings to be held up by garters, which are scattered at the bottom of the drawer; and looking through Her Mother's drawers, slips her hand through the leg of a pair of pantyhose, gently pulling the hose up her arm, careful to avoid snags or runs, imagining her arm is Her Mother's leg encased in the soft sheer taupe of the hosiery, feeling the stretchy nylon hugging her skin, how it felt against Her Mother's calf, hugging Her Mother's calf, taking its shape, and then tapering to the ankle, to the foot, past the heel, snuggling over the long gangly toes;

looks through the drawer where Her Mother kept gloves, several of soft fine leather, soft as a cloth, and others lined with wool or fur, which she rubs against her cheek, and then the old-fashioned ones Her Mother never wore but kept, of cotton felt, with three lines of stitching across the top, fanned out like the bones in your hand, white and black and navy-blue gloves, which you had to pull down between the fingers, finger by finger, because the stiff cotton wouldn't slide, this she had discovered when she'd tried them on when Her Mother wasn't home, carrying Her Mother's patent leather purse and wearing matching shoes; and now trying on another pair, which does not fit her short broad hands, too tight across the palm but too long in the fingers, lines up the gloves across the dresser, smoothing out the fingers, flattening the palms, like hands but not hands, phantom hands, and wishes she had Her Mother's hands, elegant and capable, and hers are so much like a child's;

looks in the nightstand, where Her Mother kept the purse that was not a purse, because she never used it as a purse, it was like a magic box, black satin with a rhinestone-studded clasp, which she's looked in before, in secret, and even now she feels like she's sneaking; empties onto the bed covered with the worn thin chenille bedspread old pennies collected by Her Mother, found in stores and restaurants and parking lots, saved because found money is lucky money Her Mother always said, and one should never spend it; costume jewelry, including a turquoise starburst pin Her Mother's Daughter doesn't remember and a tiny gold charm envelope, affixed with a coral heart on the flap and engraved with the words "Love Seal"; Her Mother's beige silk scarf, frayed from wear, which, when Her Mother's Daughter unfolds it, breathes the smell of Her Mother, strong as any perfume; a change purse with a cracked yellow tooth, perhaps Her Mother saved Her Mother's Daughter's tooth, the first tooth she lost, shot out by a BB; and keys, on rings and bank-issued key chains, never discarded because Her Mother said someone might look through their garbage and find them, front and back door keys, a set of luggage keys, a water key, the neighbor's keys, an old car key, and one key that said "Presto";

puts everything back again.

When Her Mother dies, Her Mother's Daughter

uncurls Her Mother's Toes;

washes Her Mother's head with the white of a raw egg mixed with vinegar;

reads the obits;

rends a small cut in a three-inch length of black grosgrain ribbon and pins the ribbon over her heart. Says: My very heart is split in two;

eats her heart out;

promises to eat next to nothing tomorrow;

covers the mirrors with newspapers, using the obituary page, so that each time she looks in the mirror, she reads the bare facts of Her Mother's life;

hears the words of Her Mother: Let me be your mother;

hears the words of Her Mother: You won't let me be your mother;

eats hard-boiled eggs and hard rolls;

calls Social Security;

calls the mah-jongg players;

calls everyone she hasn't talked to in years;

goes to the safety deposit box and removes all the contents;

washes her hands from a pitcher of water left outside Her Mother's door;

licks her wounds;

spends too much money;

assumes the eating habits of Her Mother, such as eating the crusts off all the bread, the cinnamon raisin bread in particular, with its cinnamon-sugar veins and raisin lodes and glazed crusts, which Her Mother tore off the slices one by one at midnight, eating them silently, secretly, while Her Mother's Daughter slept, so that in the morning before school, when Her Mother's Daughter went to toast the cinnamon raisin bread for breakfast, all the best parts were gone; sucking the marrow out of chicken bones and chewing them into a gritty pulp; eating coffee ice cream with strawberries; picking food off other people's plates; asking strangers in restaurants what it is they're eating that looks so good; wishing they'd offer her a bite;

tastes Her Mother's lipstick, kept in the medicine cabinet in Her Mother's bathroom, distinguished from her father's bathroom, distinguished by Her Mother's smells, toiletries and ablutions; walks into the bathroom, opening first the linen closet, then the medicine cabinet, where Her Mother kept hair spray, where Her Mother kept tweezers, where Her Mother kept hypo-allergenic skin formulas, where Her Mother kept sanitary napkins, where Her Mother kept deodorant, where Her Mother kept emery boards (but not nail polish or nail polish remover, kept in the kitchen, in the refrigerator); and reaches for Her Mother's makeup bag, which feels like satin and looks tropical, where Her Mother kept shadows and liner and mascara and blush-on and where Her Mother kept lipstick; rummages among the plastic tubes and cases, which sound like the clicking and clacking and smacking of tongues; hears the growling of her stomach as she looks at all the colors, all the flavors, for she thinks of them as flavors, confections, sweetmeats: Perfect Peach, Persian Melon, Persimmon Creme, Tender Berry, Coral Ice, Melonade, Honey Rose; says the names aloud, savoring them in her mouth, on her tongue; leans into the mirror, lipstick poised in her hand, like she had watched Her Mother do, sitting on the toilet seat while Her Mother put on lipstick; making of her mouth a valentine, an offering, a kiss; pursing her lips together to spread the color evenly, blotting on a Kleenex; running her tongue to the corner of her mouth, lightly to each corner, sampling, tasting; tasting Her Mother's lipstick, the taste of Her Mother's lipstick, Her Mother kissing her hello goodbye goodnight sleep tight; craving this taste, this oily, waxy substance, aching for this sweetness; sucking her lips, licking them clean, licking the tube; nibbling, biting off pieces, hewing, gnawing, whittling; devouring, digesting; digging for more.

When Her Mother dies, Her Mother's Daughter

swears she will never be like Her Mother;
stuffs straw and a handful of dirt into a linen bag;

shovels three shovelsful of earth, strews grass, and scatters stones atop Her
Mother's grave;

lights a candle;

grasps at straws;

eats poppy-seed cake;

assumes other habits, such as never throwing out unused checks or deposit
slips without tearing them into pieces so that her name and address cannot be pieced together;

never talks about money, like Her Mother told her not to, because some
things are nobody's business;

never wears a torn garment while it is being sewn; if she does, chews thread
while the repair is made, this, according to Her Mother and Her Mother's Mother, to ensure the thread of life will not be cut while on her person; never steps over someone lying on the floor because if she did, Her
Mother said, they would stop growing; refuses to pull her ear after she
sneezes even though Her Mother and Her Mother's Mother schooled her
in the necessity of this practice, to pull her ear after sneezing if at the
same time she is thinking or talking about the dead, the reason being to
confer protection against the thoughts of death; and after refusing, wonders if something bad will befall her;

hears the words of Her Mother: I love you as only a mother could;

goes to pieces;

lets herself go;

moves to another state;

cooks *kasha varnickes*;

assumes other habits, such as weighing herself first thing in the morning,
naked and only after urinating;

weighs herself several times a day;

hears the words of Her Mother: Is there anything wrong with a little
affection?;

washes her hands of everything;

cries her eyes out;

straightens her teeth;

pierces her ears because Her Mother never let her;

streaks her hair because Her Mother always wanted her to;

collects pieces of Her Mother's handwriting, as if they were pieces of Her Mother herself, as if she were picking up the pieces; roots out the scribbled notations with Mr. Kluck the plumber's phone number, directions to Romanian Kosher Sausage on Clark Street, the name of a doctor, an electrician, all in Her Mother's narrow, leaning script; scours the house like a minesweeper, digging in pockets, ransacking drawers, emptying the hospital bag with Her Mother's nightgown and slippers and glasses and at the bottom the notes Her Mother had written when she could no longer talk: Water please. Why does everyone say it's up to me? Close the shades; searches through every purse and wallet until she's sure she's gotten them all, every scrap, and then checks again, as a precaution, like checking to make sure you've turned off the gas even though you know you have, because you don't want to make a mistake; gathers up these shattered pieces, these fragments, and remembering the sliver she once had in her foot, how Her Mother picked it out with a needle, while Her Mother's Daughter, lying as still as she could, watched Miss America on TV, lays them out together on the carpet, all the bits and pieces, waiting for instructions, waiting for someone to tell her if she should keep them or throw them away;

hears the words of Her Mother: Happiness isn't everything.

THERE

MYRA SKLAREW

Under the dead surface you
surge toward me and then draw
back. What realm supports you now

and what necessity leaves me
struggling after you here
on the surface, parted
by this membranous divide.

I enfold you, what of you chooses
to come this close.
By this method you enter my body
and are lost in me.

For is it not so that I fall
asleep with my hands on my own body.
Or that my words going out can find
no suitable place for landing.

And when I stand in the company
of others, when I have gathered
my clothing about me and risen

to say good night I am surprised
by the weight of the cold
which I draw about my own shoulders.

Or when you withdrew from me
in a day not so different
from this one, your skull seemed

to shrink between my two hands. This
is the world. This is the world
with its circuitry ranging between there
and here like an animal grazing.

In the season of your death I cannot
enter the room for the saying of a thing
without encountering the danger
of fusion. Past and future support me

on either side like two crutches
while in the doorway the shadow
of my life goes on ahead
testing the unknown ground.

JOURNEY TO THE MIRROR

MYRA SKLAREW

Dead mother tendon
bundle branch little
heart eye nail and hair:

I carry you
in my small basket
of skin
up to the edge
of the welcoming glass

Who will pour you
like wine to its vessel

Who will take
you the rest of the way

PEBBLES AND STONES

ROSLYN LUND

If we can't find her, maybe she never existed.

"Pete, they close the place at five. We'll be locked in. Let's find the office."

"This is plot fifty-six. Where else could she be?"

It's spring but there's a drizzle and I'm cold. Our car is parked on the narrow path. We've walked back and forth ten, twenty times.

She always does this to me.

Approaching La Guardia I looked down from the plane and saw that other cemetery, the big one, studded with stones—the Citibank building, the World Trade Center, the Empire State—and the disquiet started in my stomach. She bought a plot of four graves and demanded that I keep them properly. I didn't come back in three years. She wanted space until her family would surround her. Someday I'll be buried in Seattle where I belong.

She left money to a male cousin, asking that he say a prayer for her every morning and evening for a year. He refused and tried to return the money. I said the prayers myself for a while, but they don't count because I'm female and irreligious. Really, I can't spend my life worrying about a grave.

"It's so long ago. Perhaps she's disappeared. Stones sink."

"That's ridiculous," Pete says. "This one is marked nineteen-twenty. She died in 'seventy, didn't she?"

I wish he would shave off that beard. It makes him look like an El Greco saint. He's no saint, neither am I.

She made me promise to pay my respects every year before the High Holy Days. I don't keep track of holy days. I couldn't travel across the country every year, never had the time or money. She was obsessive about neatness, so I paid for "perpetual" care, and they let the plot go to weeds. The big stone at her head tilted.

This country is all corruption, she'd say. Go fight City Hall.

I did. I made a row, wrote to the authorities, made them return the money. They straightened the stone and planted grass. But I haven't been back in seven years.

Pete looks exhausted but he won't give up. If he gave up easily he'd have left me like the others. We walk through Weisbergs and Rubinsons and Steins and Sterns. We walk through small iron gates with arches over them. The Lutsk Congregation. The Sons of Abraham. But we can't find the Arnolds Young Men's Association, the fraternal order that gave parties in New York hotels. I went with her once in a white voile party dress that came just above my bony knees. My cousin Eva kissed me and said I was pretty. My mother said, It's only talk. Don't let a compliment go to your head.

It did go to my head, though I knew I'd never be tall and gorgeous like Eva. I knew I'd be small and sturdy like my mother.

A crow perches on a stone and watches me while I remember Eva, married to a Kaminsky. She wore filmy sleeves to cover the numbers burned into her arm. My mother didn't want her to kiss me because she was made to do bad things. That's how she survived the camp.

"If we could find the Kaminsky plot. She's right near them."

"I know, I know. You told me a dozen times."

"I have to tell you. If you'd been here before, I wouldn't have to, would I?"

The crow caws as I speak, and Pete is trying not to smile. "Calm down, Sonya. You're getting hyped up."

My mother was luckier than Eva. She got out of Europe just in time, and on the way she visited relatives in Paris and London.

Just imagine, she said, I saw the Eiffel Tower and Stonehenge before I was fourteen. My sister Ruth was smart. She sent for me because she knew what was about to happen.

Ruth Kaminsky, the housekeeper who married the boss. Her stepchildren taught my mother dirty words for simple objects. They laughed at her and she wanted only to be like them. When she could afford it she bought graves as close to theirs as she could get.

"If we could find the office, they'd tell us where to go."

Pete says we'd get lost looking for the office. He's worried. He always thinks I'll fly apart.

"If we were lost in Hell you wouldn't ask directions at a gas station."

He shrugs and walks ahead with his usual swagger.

Where is the Kaminsky family, the ones who sang? They all played the baby grand piano, even Harry, the oldest, who never took a lesson. My mother heard him as she cleaned and cooked for her keep. He repeated three notes and a syncopated bass until he drove her crazy.

I wish the crow would be quiet.

I met Harry over coffee at Rumpelmayer's on my infrequent trips to New York. We discussed the care of the graves, his responsibility and mine.

"Did I ever tell you about my cousin Harry?"

Pete doesn't answer. He's tall enough to see over the stones. I run after him and the crow follows. "Harry had a heart attack when he was young, after his wife left him. He was eighty when I last saw him. He told me he'd been absolutely faithful to two women for forty years."

I still take them to dinner once a week, Harry said.

Both of them?

Separately, of course, he said, and looked down into his coffee. I can't stop now.

That was years ago. I wonder if Harry is still alive . . . and Eva, who kissed me.

Pete shouts triumphantly, "Here they are! The whole clan."

I look. "No, this is Kutinsky, not Kaminsky."

Pete spins around. "Why did you drag me here? We could have waited. We don't even have a place to sleep tonight."

"I offered to come here alone. I don't need you every minute."

"Okay, if you want me to leave I'll leave."

"If you want to go, then go."

A plane flies over us, scaring the crow away. Now we're the only ones alive in this place. We rented a car and came straight from La Guardia, just ten minutes away.

Pete sighs. "Let's try going this way. Keep close, this is a maze."

I hurry to keep up. The Kaminskys all played piano, so she made me take lessons. I refused to practice. "Pete?"

"I'm here, to your right."

I can't see him. "You're going too fast." I trip on a stone and fall. My knee hurts.

Clumsy, you never look where you're going, my mother would say.

You're asleep standing up, a klutz. Then came the curses that sound at home in Yiddish, the language of accumulated fury.

I was exasperating; so was she. Why have I traveled three thousand miles when she found it necessary to beat me—for my own good, she said, her round face as red as her hair? I know I provoked her. I disobeyed, lied, but I didn't send her away from her parents when she was still a child. I didn't choose the man who would leave her, the man she saw in my face.

Maybe I've come to brag because things are going well between Pete and me. I used to think, if your father leaves, what man will ever stay—yet at last I chose a man who would stay.

And there are the children. They both won scholarships, Mother. They're in college now. See how well I'm doing. Despite you.

It's bad luck to praise your children, she says.

"Wait, Pete. I can't get up. My knee—"

You know there's nothing wrong with your knee, she says, so I stand up. I can't see beyond the stones. "Pete?"

There's not even an echo. "Where are you?"

I smell weeds. No trees here. Spring has come to Seattle but I see no flowers here. A humid wind carries the stench of the city. The ex-urbanites lie as close together as they lived. I find the path but our car is gone. No, this is plot fifty, the wrong path. I go back into the stones and call but my voice is lost.

Take it easy. Try repeating your mantra.

Remember when Pete and I learned to meditate? And our friend Jerry didn't have the money to buy himself a mantra? So we gave him the Maharishi's instructions and told him to make up his own, and he burst into our loft shouting, I did it! For twenty minutes day and night I say it—mantra mantra mantra.

That's funny. I suppose I'm laughing. This is plot sixty-three. I'm going the wrong way. There's nobody here. I'm alone.

"Pete! Mother!" Where are you where were you—I never could find you.

She's shaking me, her hands on my shoulders. You slept with him. He's not our kind and you went to bed with him.

I pull away.

He's not the first, I can tell. You're like your father. She slaps me.

I look right back at her and say, I'm going away with him.

Go. You think you'll get rid of me as though I never existed. You want to wipe me out. You never had a mother.

I run through an empty square. Walk, don't run to the exit. I did get away, escaped from that single parent before the epidemic of single parents.

She said, long ago, Remember we're separated, not divorced.

True. He separated himself from us when I was seven. He came to me with his suitcase packed. Sonya, do you want me to leave?

I said no, but he went anyway—and she stayed.

Don't tell anyone our business, she said the night he left, wringing her hands. I reached out to hold them still. Her hair flamed and she rocked back and forth and I knew I was a freak because my father left and my mother was caged by day in a cashier's booth in Harry Kaminsky's movie theatre, caged by night in our small apartment.

He went away in the fall and through the long winter I was caged with her. You're my girl, she said and in her loneliness hugged me too hard and pulled back my hair from my forehead. Her hands smelled of lemon and soap. She didn't want Eva or anyone else to touch me ever, certainly not a non-Jew.

I call Pete but my throat is sore, so I sit on a rusty bench among the Goldsteins who left this earth in nineteen-thirty, 'forty-three, 'forty-five. There are more than a dozen of them, practical people, each covered with a blanket of myrtle. They must have arranged this around their dining-room table: Okay everyone? The consensus is myrtle—and let's have a nice iron bench for visitors.

I see pebbles on one grave. That means recent visitors.

She was practical, too. In the spring she opened the windows to the fire escape and piled all our bedding on the sills. The fresh air blew in and she spread her arms and breathed deep. Nobody ever loved the spring as she did. She freed herself from the apartment, returned to her synagogue, and went to night school.

Like a miracle I was free to go outdoors, to find the joy of friends. I cheated about the time out on the streets but I was as practical as she was. I knew enough to be home when she returned.

She learned the language well in school, hardly a trace of accent, but she misspelled words, so I had to win all the spelling bees. She liked to read, so we shared books spread out on the kitchen table. She leaned on her elbows and read, her freckled chest breathing. I can still smell her, the lemon and brown soap and herself. I breathed with her.

She liked Mark Twain. He's no Isaac Singer, she said, but he's funny.

I brought her to my library and she brought me to Tolstoy and Pushkin. She said, My parents read these in Russian before you were born. The Russians weren't funny but they sure could invent plots. Do you think you could ever write?

She laughed but then she touched me on the back and said, You don't have to write. Just learn to be a person, a mensch.

I am a person.

I mean a *real* person.

If you're real, then I'm real.

She looked surprised. Do you know, she said, you've got a big mouth.

Where is Pete? I'm tired. Maybe we're locked in.

Get out. I don't want to see your face ever again. Take that man and go. She pointed and her arm quivered. To the other end of the world. Go.

We went to the other end of the land. To the very brink.

But one morning I called her from a Seattle hospital. It's me, I said. I thought you'd want to know. You have a granddaughter.

A long silence . . . I suppose you're all right.

Yes.

Where are you? How do you live? Do you work?

We both teach. Pete is a professor.

Pete? He's not the one you went away with?

No. I met him in Seattle. Would you like to visit us?

No answer.

May we come to see you?

She took her own sweet time before she answered. Why couldn't you have married a nice Jewish man?

You might consider Pete a nice Jewish man.

Tell me, what's his actual religion? She spoke loud enough for Pete to hear across the continent.

He said, Tell her I'm a Druid.

I heard a grudging smile in her voice, saying to me, I get the joke but it's no joke. I guess that's better than a Nazi.

May we come?

I'll let you know.

She allowed herself to see our daughter and later our son. We almost became friends. I don't know why that makes me tremble.

We both stopped at the almost. Perhaps she had learned that I can't be held too close, that my hair, my scalp, creeps.

A far-off siren cuts through distant traffic. I can't sit here forever. Is Pete all right? I should look for him but I can't move. I'm cold.

The two sisters are dancing to a Viennese waltz, perspiring, their hair not yet turned gray. My mother says, breathless, This is called the One-Step.

Ruth laughs. This is how we danced in Baranow.

On the Wistula River.

The sisters are hopping. A crazy dance. I tell them to cut it out. That damned anti-Semitic town. A thousand horses couldn't drag you back.

Sonya's got an evil mouth, they say and they croon my name, dancing toward me. They're insane. If they dare to lay a hand on me, I'll kill them. They'll die three times over.

Their voices turn hoarse and I know that Pete is calling. I'm freezing, shivering. "Pete, I'm here."

"I can't see you. Speak louder."

I climb up on the bench. He's down among the stones, his hair and clothes disheveled. He comes and clutches my leg.

Pete, Pete, I want to say, Don't ever leave me. But talk like that makes him furious, so I speak as decisively as she would speak. "Come. We'll find the office."

I take his hand. He leads me to the car. "This place is demonic."

"But the last place was alive. I saw pebbles on a grave. That means the plot is alive."

We ride past stones. The path opens to a road. We find the main building. We came in the back entrance. The office door is locked and a sign reads, CLOSED FOR THE HOLIDAY.

What holiday?

Pete goes to a large, framed map and traces a path with his finger. "There are two sections fifty-six, one left and one right. We should have gone this way."

I see a square marked "washroom" and remember a small white building. He finds a scrap of paper and makes a sketch.

We drive up a new path and I remember suddenly—the holiday is She-vuoth. The giving of the law on Sinai. In the spring.

Where did this knowledge come from, this spring festival in my head?

The white building needs paint. There's an arched gate. The Arnolds Young Men's Association. We stop.

I go through clipped grass to the Kaminsky plot, to the graves of Ruth and her husband Maurice, head of the clan.

Husband. Father. Grandfather. Carved in stone.

I'm surrounded. I spread my arms because the cousins are all here. Harry. Died in 'eighty-three. Beneath his name I read, *A Unique Individual.* Did one of his two women suggest that? Did they meet here for the first time, standing over him?

I run, almost dance from one stone to the other. Here is Eva the beauty, the last to die. *Mother. Grandmother. Great-Grandmother.* There are three pebbles on her footstone.

Pete frowns, watching me. I know. It's not seemly to be dancing on the Kaminsky graves. I can't help it, I'm flying.

Pete points with his chin. "Sonya, look behind you."

I stop moving. I can't breathe. I turn.

Her headstone is straight, the plot clean. She is covered with ivy. In a corner a vine has wrapped itself around leaves and a small white blossom erupts.

I take a step forward. Whom, what can I embrace? I sit and touch the stone at her feet, bury my hands in the shining leaves.

Someone—who?—is taking care of this place. I'm leaning, falling forward until my head almost touches the stone. I want to embrace, but there is only air.

Pete pulls me up and puts his arms around me. We hold together.

I'm growing warm. I've stopped shivering.

I pick up two pebbles and place them at her feet.

DREAM-VISION

TILLIE OLSEN

In the winter of 1955, in her last weeks of life, my mother—so much of whose waking life had been a nightmare, that common everyday nightmare of hardship, limitation, longing; of baffling struggle to raise six children in a world hostile to human unfolding—my mother, dying of cancer, had beautiful dream-visions—in color.

Already beyond calendar time, she could not have known that the last dream she had breath to tell came to her on Christmas Eve. Nor, conscious, would she have named it so. As a girl in long-ago Czarist Russia, she had sternly broken with all observances of organized religion, associating it with pogroms and wars; "mind forg'd manacles"; a repressive state. We did not observe religious holidays in her house.

Perhaps, in her last consciousness, she *did* know that the year was drawing towards that solstice time of the shortest light, the longest dark, the cruelest cold, when—as she had explained to us as children—poorly sheltered ancient peoples in northern climes had summoned their resources to make out of song, light, and food, expressions of human love—festivals of courage, hope, warmth, belief.

It seemed to her that there was a knocking at her door. Even as she rose to open it, she guessed who would be there, for she heard the neighing of camels. (I did not say to her: "Ma, camels don't neigh.") Against the frosty lights of a far city she had never seen, "a city holy to three faiths," she said, the three wise men stood: magnificent in jewelled robes of crimson, of gold, of royal blue.

"Have you lost your way?" she asked. "Else why do you come to me? I am not religious, I am not a believer."

"To talk with *you*, we came," the wise man whose skin was black and robe crimson assured her, "to talk of whys, of wisdom."

"Come in then, come in and be warm—and welcome. I have starved all my life for such talk."

But as they began to talk, she saw that they were not men, but women;

That they were not dressed in jewelled robes, but in the coarse everyday shifts and shawls of the old country women of her childhood, their feet wrapped round and round with rags for lack of boots; snow now sifting into the room;

That their speech was not highflown, but homilies; their bodies not lordly in bearing, magnificent, but stunted, misshapen—used all their lives as beasts of burden are used;

That the camels were not camels, but farm beasts, such as were kept in the house all winter, their white cow breaths steaming into the cold.

And now it was many women, a babble.

One old woman, seamed and bent, began to sing. Swaying, the others joined her, their faces and voices transfiguring as they sang; my mother, through cracked lips, singing too—a lullaby.

For in the shining cloud of their breaths, a baby lay, breathing the universal sounds every human baby makes, sounds out of which are made all the separate languages of the world.

Singing, one by one the women cradled and sheltered the baby.

"The joy, the reason to believe," my mother said, "the hope for the world, the baby, holy with possibility, that is all of us at birth." And she began to cry, out of the dream and its telling now.

"Still I feel the baby in my arms, the human baby," crying now so I could scarcely make out the words, "the human baby before we are misshapen; crucified into a sex, a color, a walk of life, a nationality . . . and the world yet warrings and winter."

I had seen my mother but three times in my adult life, separated as we were by the continent between, by lack of means, by jobs I had to keep and by the needs of my four children. She could scarcely write English—her only education in this country a few months of night school. When at last I flew to her, it was in the last days she had language at all. Too late to talk with her of what was in our hearts; or of harms and crucifying and strengths as she had known and experienced them; or of whys and knowledge, of wisdom. She died a few weeks later.

She, who had no worldly goods to leave, yet left to me an inexhaustible legacy. Inherent in it, this heritage of summoning resources to make out of song, food, and warmth expressions of human love—courage, hope, resistance, belief; this vision of universality, before the lessenings, harms, divisions of the world are visited upon it.

She sheltered and carried that belief, that wisdom—as she sheltered and carried us, and others—throughout a lifetime lived in a world whose season was, as yet it is, a time of winter.

IN THE REARVIEW MIRROR

LINDA PASTAN

Driving all night in winter,
I watch in the rearview mirror
as the small towns disappear
behind us, ceasing
to exist the moment
we pass. Hills rise and fall
brindled with snow,
and in the fields a few
lit windows small
as night lights
remind us of a child asleep
upstairs, the blanket rising
and falling with his breath.
How the particular
loses itself. Downstairs
the dough is rising
under its cloth, and the Mother
whose hands have learned
the wisdom of kneading
touches the Father.
And one town dims
and flickers out, and another
stirs ready to rise
three hundred miles later
when the sun touches the farthest edge
of the sky in an endless
relay race of light,

at a place half resurrected
from childhood and waiting
to be unwrapped like a withheld gift
from the white ribbon
of unwinding road.

NO ANSWER

JUDITH STEINBERGH

This is the third time this week
I've tried calling you
down under the ground.
This has got to stop.
I know you don't pick up the phone
in fact, there's no number listed,
but this connection we've had for years
first umbilical
lately over the wires
is hard to break.
Who else cares
about the kids' first day of school
or my electric bill.
I phone you up in the heavens
but it's no dice.
I'm not into the afterlife
and your burial pursues me
without mercy,
I know you're down there
MA
answer me.

CONTRIBUTORS

KARREN ALENIER is the author of two collections of poetry, *Wandering on the Outside* and *The Dancer's Muse*, and editor of *Whose Woods These Are*. She is president of The Word Works, a literary organization and poetry publishing house in Washington, D.C.

ROBIN BECKER is the author of *Giacometti's Dog*, published in the Pitt Poetry Series in 1990. She serves as poetry editor for the *Women's Review of Books* and teaches in the M.F.A. program at Penn State.

RUTH BEHAR, born in Havana, Cuba, grew up in Queens. Her most recent book is *Translated Woman: Crossing the Border with Esperanza's Story*, an account of her friendship with a Mexican street peddler. She is currently at work on a memoir, *Next Year in Havana*.

SANDRA BERNHARD is an actor, singer, comedian, and author who has appeared in *The King of Comedy*, on "Roseanne," and in her own one-woman stage shows, *Without You, I'm Nothing* and *Giving Till It Hurts*. Her writing has appeared in *Playboy*, *People*, *Mademoiselle*, and *Mirabella*.

CHANA BLOCH is an award-winning poet, translator, and critic. Her poetry books are *The Secrets of the Tribe* and *The Past Keeps Changing*, both from Sheep Meadow Press. Her new translation of the biblical *Song of Songs* (with her husband, Ariel Bloch) will be published by Random House in fall 1994. She directs the creative writing program at Mills College.

JODY BOLZ teaches creative writing at George Washington University. Her poems have appeared recently in such publications as *Indiana Review*, *Sonora Review*, the *Women's Review of Books*, and *River Styx*.

BETTY BUCHSBAUM is the mother of four daughters, grand-mother of four, as well as professor of literature and academic vice president of Massachusetts College of Art in Boston. She has published her work in the *Antioch Review*, *Sojourner*, *Rhino*, *Kalliope*, and *Lilith*, among others.

KIM CHERNIN has published widely, both fiction and nonfiction. Among her nonfiction works are: *The Obsession: Reflections of the Tyranny of Slenderness* (1981), *In My Mother's House* (1983), *The Hungry Self: Women, Eating, and Identity* (1985), and *Reinventing Eve: Modern Woman in Search of Herself* (1987). She has also written a novel, *The Flame Bearers* (1986).

ENID DAME is a poet, writer, and teacher. Her books include *Anything You Don't See* (West End, 1992) and *Lilith and Her Demons* (Cross-Cultural Communications, 1986). She has recently completed a novel. Presently she is director of freshman composition at Polytechnic University in Brooklyn.

JODI DAYNARD has taught at Harvard. Currently she is teaching in the writing program at M.I.T. Her work has been published in the *New York Times Book Review*, the *Paris Review*, *Harvard Magazine*, the *Harvard Review*, the *Village Voice*, and elsewhere.

MARCIA FALK is a poet and translator of Hebrew and Yiddish. Her most recent books are *The Song of Songs: A New Translation and Interpretation*, *With Teeth in the Earth: Selected Poems of Malka Heifetz Tussman*, and *The Book of Blessings: A Feminist-Jewish Reconstruction of Prayer*.

JYL LYNN FELMAN, a short story writer, has been anthologized in such works as *The Tribe of Dina*, *Loss of the Ground Note*, *Speaking for Ourselves*, and *A Loving Voice*. *Hot Chicken Wings* is her first collection of short fiction. She is also an attorney who lectures widely on racism, anti-Semitism, and homophobia.

NADELL FISHMAN is a writer who performs her original work as part of ACME Poets, a performance ensemble based in central Vermont. Ms. Fishman was a recipient of a fellowship from the Vermont Council on the Arts.

C A R O L E L. G L I C K F E L D, born and raised in New York, has published in *William & Mary Review*, *Croton Review*, *Worcester Review*, *Crosscurrents*, *Madison Review*, and elsewhere. Her collection of short stories, *Useful Gifts*, was published in 1989 and won the Flannery O'Connor Award for Short Fiction.

B A R B A R A G O L D B E R G is the author of two books of poetry, most recently *Cautionary Tales* (Dryad Press, 1990), and co-editor of *The Stones Remember*, an anthology of contemporary Israeli poetry (winner of the Witter Bynner Poetry Award). She is currently director of editorial services for the American Speech-Language-Hearing Association.

J U D Y G O L D M A N has published two collections of poetry: *Holding Back Winter* and *Wanting to Know the End*. She writes and delivers commentaries for National Public Radio, reviews books for the *Charlotte Observer*, and teaches ongoing poetry workshops.

V I V I A N G O R N I C K's essays on literature and feminism have appeared in such places as the *Village Voice*, the *New York Times*, and the *Nation*. She is co-editor of *Woman in Sexist Society* and author of *Women in Science*, *In Search of Ali Mahmoud: An American Woman in Egypt*, and *Fierce Attachments*.

M A R I L Y N H A C K E R's publications in poetry include: *Going Back to the River* (Random House, 1990), *Love, Death, and the Changing of the Seasons* (Morrow, 1986), *Assumptions* (Knopf, 1985), *Taking Notice* (1980), *Separations* (1976), and *Presentation Piece* (1974). She received the National Book Award for Poetry in 1975.

J U D I T H H A R R I S is the author of *Poppies* (Washington Writers Publishing House) and a chapbook, *Song of the Moon*. Recent work appears in these magazines: *Antioch Review* (Nimrod Awards issue), *Helicon Nine*, *Hiram Poetry Review*, and *Midwest Quarterly*. She teaches at George Washington University.

M A R G A R E T K L E E's essays and articles have appeared in the *Nation*, the *New York Times Book Review*, *Ms.*, *Mademoiselle*, *Working Woman*, *Show*,

WomanSports, and *Crawdaddy*, among others. Her fiction has been published in *Mademoiselle* and her poetry in *Blackbird Circle*, *Epoch*, and *Anon*.

I R E N A K L E P F I S Z, a poet/activist in the lesbian and Jewish communities, is the author of *A Few Words in the Mother Tongue: Poems Selected and New* and *Dreams of an Insomniac: Jewish Feminist Essays, Speeches, and Diatribes* and co-editor of *The Tribe of Dina: A Jewish Women's Anthology*. A translator/critic of Yiddish women's writing, she is editorial consultant on Yiddish language and culture for the Jewish feminist magazine *Bridges*.

P H Y L L I S K O E S T E N B A U M was born in Brooklyn, New York, in 1930 and has a B.A. from Radcliffe College. She received a poetry fellowship from the National Endowment for the Arts and has been in residence at the MacDowell Colony and the Djerassi Foundation. Her work is included in *The Best American Poetry 1992*, edited by Charles Simic, and is forthcoming in *The Best American Poetry 1993*, edited by Louise Glück. She is an affiliated scholar at Stanford University's Institute for Research on Women and Gender.

M A X I N E K U M I N won the Pulitzer Prize for poetry in 1973 for *Up Country* and was consultant in poetry to the Library of Congress from 1981 to 1982. She is the author of four novels, eight volumes of poetry, a collection of short stories, and a collection of essays on country living.

S H I R L E Y L A T E S S A, a New Yorker, has had poems published in several literary magazines and a play performed off-off-Broadway. She is currently preparing a book of poems for publication and working on her fourth novel.

L Y N L I F S H I N, a poet, has authored numerous books and has edited three anthologies of women writers, including the much-praised *Tangled Vines*. Her awards include the Hart Crane Memorial Award, a New York State CAPS grant, and fellowships to Yaddo, Bread Loaf, Millay Colony, and MacDowell.

D E E N A L I N E T T, poet, fiction writer, and essayist, is the author of two novels, *The Translator's Wife* and *On Common Ground* (co-winner of the

1982 A.W.P. Award). She won a PEN Syndicated Fiction Award for her short story "The Visit."

ROSLYN LUND, author of the novel *The Sharing* and winner of a Friends of American Writers Award, is cited in *The Best American Short Stories* and *Pushcart Prize*. She is winner of two Illinois Arts Council Literature Awards.

YONA ZELDIS MCDONOUGH, born in Israel and raised in New York City, graduated from Vassar and Columbia University. Her fiction has appeared in *Family Circle* as well as in a number of literary magazines.

FAYE MOSKOWITZ is the author of *A Leak in the Heart*, *Whoever Finds This: I Love You*, and *And the Bridge Is Love*. She directs the creative writing program at George Washington University. She has been a commentator on National Public Radio and twice a winner of the PEN Syndicated Fiction Award.

LESLÉA NEWMAN's books of fiction and poetry include *Good Enough to Eat*, *Love Me Like You Mean It*, *A Letter to Harvey Milk*, and *Heather Has Two Mommies*. She has also edited a poetry anthology, *Bubbe Meisehs by Shayneh Maidelehs*.

JEAN NORDHAUS, a poet, is the author of *A Bracelet of Lies*, *A Language of Hands*, and, most recently, *My Life in Hiding*. For years she ran the poetry programs for the Folger Shakespeare Library, and presently she is president of Washington Writers Publishing House.

TILLIE OLSEN's books are *Tell Me a Riddle*, *Yonnondio: From the Thirties*, and *Mother to Daughter, Daughter to Mother: A Daybook and Reader*. She is also the author of *Silences*, essays on women's writing. Her many honors include an award for distinguished contribution to American literature from the American Academy and the National Institute of Arts and Letters.

ALICIA SUSKIN OSTRIKER, poet and critic, is the author of seven volumes of poetry, most recently *The Imaginary Lover* and *Green Age*. Her most recent book of criticism is *Feminist Revision and the Bible*. She is a professor of English at Rutgers University.

G R A C E   P A L E Y's short story collections include *The Little Disturbances of Man* (1959), *Enormous Changes at the Last Minute* (1974), and *Later the Same Day* (1985). Among her many awards are those from the National Institute of Arts and Letters, and Brandeis University. She has long been active in the peace movement.

L I N D A   P A S T A N is the author of eight books of poetry, most recently *Heroes in Disguise* (Norton, 1991). She has recently finished a term as Poet Laureate of Maryland. Her prizes include the Maurice English Award and the Virginia Faulkner Award from *Prairie Schooner*.

R A C H E L   P A S T A N, winner of a PEN Syndicated Fiction Award, has published stories in the *Georgia Review*, *Virginia Quarterly Review*, *Prairie Schooner*, and the *Mississippi Review*. She reviews books for *Isthmus*, a newspaper in Madison, Wisconsin.

L E T T Y   C O T T I N   P O G R E B I N is a founding editor of *Ms.* magazine and author of *Among Friends*, *Family Politics*, *Growing Up Free*, *Getting Yours*, and *How to Make It in a Man's World*. She is the editor of *Stories for Free Children* and co-developer with Marlo Thomas of *Free to Be You and Me* and *Free to Be a Family*.

M A X I N E   R O D B E R G, who teaches writing at Harvard, has had stories published in *Agni*, *Virginia Quarterly*, *Michigan Quarterly*, and other literary magazines. She won a PEN Syndicated Fiction Award in 1991.

A N N   R O I P H E is a novelist and journalist whose most recent books include *Lovingkindness* (1987), *A Season for Healing: Reflections of the Holocaust* (1988), *Generation Without Memory* (1990), *Pursuit of Happiness* (1991), and *If You Knew Me* (1993).

A D A   J I L L   S C H N E I D E R, a recipient of the Galway Kinnell Poetry Prize, is the author of *Fine Lines and Other Wrinkles*. She presents one-woman poetry programs and began writing at fifty-three.

L Y N N E   S H A R O N   S C H W A R T Z's most recent book is a collection of stories, essays, and poems, *A Lynne Sharon Schwartz Reader*. Her novels include *Leaving Brooklyn*, *Disturbances in the Field*, *Rough Strife*, and *Balanc-

ing Acts. Her story collections are *Acquainted With the Night* and *The Melting Pot and Other Subversive Stories.*

L O R E   S E G A L was born in Vienna, Austria, and came to the United States in 1951. Her books for adults include *Other People's Houses* (1964), *Lucinella* (1978), and *Her First American* (1985). A special favorite among her children's books is *Tell Me a Mitzi.* Segal teaches at Ohio State University.

P E G G Y   S H I N N E R lives in Chicago. Her fiction has appeared in *Other Voices, Central Park, Another Chicago Magazine, Sojourner,* and *Open Magazine.*

E N I D   S H O M E R's poems and stories have appeared in the *New Yorker,* the *Atlantic,* the *Paris Review,* and other periodicals. Recent books include *This Close to the Earth* and *Imaginary Men,* winner of the Iowa Short Fiction Award. In 1994 she will be writer-in-residence at The Thurber House.

J A N E   S H O R E's first book of poems, *Eye Level,* won the Juniper Prize, and her second book, *The Minute Hand,* won the Lamont Prize. She has received fellowships from the Guggenheim Foundation, the Bunting Institute, the Hodder Foundation, and the N.E.A. She is an associate professor at George Washington University.

J O A N   S E L I G E R   S I D N E Y, a poet, divides her time between Storrs, Connecticut, and Grenoble, France. Her two chapbooks are *Deep Between the Rocks* and *The Way the Past Comes Back.* She has published in *New York Quarterly, Massachusetts Review, Israel Horizon,* and *Yellow Silk,* among others.

The late K A T E   S I M O N is best known for her travel books, which include *New York: Places and Pleasures, Mexico: Places and Pleasures, Italy, Places Between,* and *Fifth Avenue: A Very Special History.* She also wrote *Bronx Primitive* and *A Wider World,* both memoirs.

M Y R A   S K L A R E W, winner of the 1993 Anna Rosenberg Award for Poems on the Jewish Experience, directs the M.F.A. program in creative writing at American University in Washington, D.C. She has seven books of poetry and is currently interested in cell biology.

JUDITH STEINBERGH writes and teaches in the Boston area. She has published four books of poetry, the most recent *A Living Anytime*, and she also performs and creates tapes for children and adults with Troubador.

MEREDITH TAX, active in the women's liberation movement since it began, is author of *The Rising of the Women*, a history book; *Families*, a children's book; and two novels, *Rivington Street* and *Union Square*. She is founder and chair of the Women Writers' Committee of PEN International.

HILARY THAM is a Chinese Malaysian who converted to Judaism. A vice president of her synagogue and past president of her synagogue sisterhood, she is the author of *No Gods Today*, *Paper Boats*, *Bad Names for Women*, *Tigerbone Wine*, and *Men & Other Strange Myths*.

JUDITH VIORST is the author of numerous books of poetry and prose, including bestsellers *It's Hard to Be Hip Over Thirty and Other Tragedies of Married Life* and *How Did I Get to Be Forty and Other Atrocities*, and, most recently, *Murdering Mr. Monti*. She is a graduate of the Washington Psychoanalytic Institute and lives in Washington, D.C.

PATRICIA VOLK is the author of the novel *White Light* and two collections of short stories, *The Yellow Banana* and *All It Takes*. Her work has been published in the *New York Times*, the *New Yorker*, *New York*, the *Atlantic*, *Playboy*, and other magazines.

RUTH WHITMAN's award-winning works include *Laughing Gas: Poems New and Selected 1963–1990*, *The Testing of Hanna Senesh*, *Tamsen Donner: A Woman's Journey*, *The Marriage Wig and Other Poems*, and *Hatshepsut Speak to Me*.

SUSAN P. WILLENS teaches English at George Washington University in Washington, D.C., where she directs reading groups, appears on radio talk shows, and lectures for the Smithsonian Institution. She is co-author of *Young Voices*, distributed worldwide by USIA.

LILA ZEIGER, author of *The Way to Castle Garden*, a collection of poems, teaches writing in the New York area and runs an innovative writing workshop in an AIDS day treatment program in Chelsea.

CREDITS

GOLDMAN "Pantoum for the Children, So They Will Know Yiddish" by Judy Goldman, copyright © 1992 by Kenyon College, first published in the *Kenyon Review*, new series, Fall 1992, vol. 14, no. 4. Reprinted by permission of the author.

GORNICK Excerpt from *Fierce Attachments* by Vivian Gornick, copyright © 1987 by Vivian Gornick, reprinted by permission of Farrar, Straus & Giroux, Inc.

HACKER "Autumn 1980," copyright © 1985 by Marilyn Hacker, from *Assumptions*, Alfred A. Knopf, 1985, reprinted here by permission of the author.

KLEE "The Different Landscape" by Margaret Klee, first published in *Ms.* magazine, November/December 1994, reprinted by permission of the author.

KLEPFISZ "Poland, 1944" by Irena Klepfisz, from "Bashert" in *A Few Words in the Mother Tongue: Poems Selected and New*, Eighth Mountain Press, 1990, reprinted by permission of Eighth Mountain Press.

KOESTENBAUM "Selfish" by Phyllis Koestenbaum, copyright © 1993, World's Best Short Short Story Contest, University of Florida, 1993, used by permission of the author.

KUMIN "The Chain," copyright © 1984 by Maxine Kumin, from *The Long Approach* by Maxine Kumin, reprinted by permission of Viking Penguin, a division of Penguin Books USA, Inc.

LINETT "Gifts" by Deena Linett, reprinted by permission of *Ms.* magazine, copyright © 1978.

MCDONOUGH "Second Person" by Yona Zeldis McDonough appeared in the *Cream City Review*, vol. 13, no. 1, Winter 1989. Reprinted by permission of the author.

MOSKOWITZ Excerpt from *A Leak in the Heart* by Faye Moskowitz, copyright © 1985 by Faye Moskowitz, reprinted by permission of David R. Godine, Publishers, Inc.

NEWMAN "Only a Phase" from *A Letter to Harvey Milk*, Firebrand Books, Ithaca, New York, copyright © 1987 by Lesléa Newman, reprinted by permission of the author.

NORDHAUS "On Rockawalkin Road" by Jean Nordhaus was featured in the *Quarterly Review of Poetry*, vol. 30, Fall 1991, reprinted by permission of the author.

OLSEN "Dream-Vision" by Tillie Olsen, copyright © 1985 by Tillie Olsen, reprinted by permission of the Elaine Markson Literary Agency.

OSTRIKER "Happy Birthday" and "Surviving" (part X) by Alicia Suskin Ostriker, reprinted by permission of the author.

PALEY Excerpt from *Later That Same Day* by Grace Paley, copyright © 1985 by Grace Paley, reprinted by permission of Farrar, Straus & Giroux, Inc.